JUDGMENT AND AGENCY

JUDGMENT
AND
AGENCY

ERNEST SOSA

OXFORD
UNIVERSITY PRESS

Great Clarendon Street, Oxford, OX2 6DP,
United Kingdom

Oxford University Press is a department of the University of Oxford.
It furthers the University's objective of excellence in research, scholarship,
and education by publishing worldwide. Oxford is a registered trade mark of
Oxford University Press in the UK and in certain other countries

© Ernest Sosa 2015

The moral rights of the author have been asserted

First Edition published in 2015

Impression: 1

All rights reserved. No part of this publication may be reproduced, stored in
a retrieval system, or transmitted, in any form or by any means, without the
prior permission in writing of Oxford University Press, or as expressly permitted
by law, by licence or under terms agreed with the appropriate reprographics
rights organization. Enquiries concerning reproduction outside the scope of the
above should be sent to the Rights Department, Oxford University Press, at the
address above

You must not circulate this work in any other form
and you must impose this same condition on any acquirer

Published in the United States of America by Oxford University Press
198 Madison Avenue, New York, NY 10016, United States of America

British Library Cataloguing in Publication Data
Data available

Library of Congress Control Number: 2014957468

ISBN 978-0-19-871969-4

Printed and bound by
CPI Group (UK) Ltd, Croydon, CR0 4YY

Links to third party websites are provided by Oxford in good faith and
for information only. Oxford disclaims any responsibility for the materials
contained in any third party website referenced in this work.

Acknowledgments

The book has benefited, at various stages and venues, from written or oral comments by Jason Baehr, Marina Bakalova, Heather Battaly, Bob Beddor, Matthew Benton, David Black, Paul Boghossian, Rodrigo Borges, Fernando Broncano, Fernando Broncano-Berrocal, Adam Carter, Andrew Chignell, Juan Comesaña, Kate Devitt, Zoe Drayson, Julien Dutant, Pascal Engel, Megan Feeney, Miguel Ángel Fernandez, Will Fleisher, Ángel García Rodriguez, Georgi Gardiner, Tamar Gendler, Hanjo Glock, Sandy Goldberg, Alvin Goldman, Simon Goldstein, Modesto Gómez Alonso, Peter Graham, Stephen Grimm, Thomas Grundmann, Frank Hofmann, Joachim Horvath, Paul Horwich, Dale Jacquette, Jesper Kallestrup, Christoph Kelp, Jens Kipper, Hilary Kornblith, Jon Kvanvig, Jennifer Lackey, Manuel Liz, Conor McHugh, Brian McLaughlin, Anne Meylan, Michael Mi, Alan Millar, Lisa Miracchi, Nenad Miscevic, Andrew Moon, Jesús Navarro, Ram Neta, Martine Nida-Rümelin, Kate Nolfi, Carlotta Pavese, David Perez Chico, Christian Piller, Duncan Pritchard, Jim Pryor, Baron Reed, Sebastian Rodl, Blake Roeber, David Rose, Andrew Rotondo, Daniel Rubio, Joao Carlos Salles, Josh Schechter, Susanna Schellenberg, Michael Slote, Jason Stanley, Josefa Toribio, Cheng-Hung Tsai, Jesús Vega, Tim Williamson, Stephen Woodside, and Crispin Wright.

These views have developed over many years with much helpful input from John Greco, Peter Klein, and John Turri. For such input and for detailed discussion of this manuscript in particular, I am especially indebted to David Sosa and Kurt Sylvan, each of whom provided excellent and detailed written commentary on the whole manuscript, which led to many improvements.

My warm thanks to Peter Momtchiloff for his editorial encouragement and support.

I am also grateful to Georgi Gardiner for preparing the index and for much editorial help.

I have drawn from previously published work as follows, with permission.

For part of Chapter 1, "The Unity of Action, Perception, and Knowledge," from "Mind–World Relations," *Episteme*, 12 (2015).

For part of Chapter 2, "Virtue Epistemology: Character versus Competence," from *Current Controversies in Virtue Theory*, ed. Mark Alfano (Routledge, 2015).

For Chapter 8, "Social Roots of Human Knowledge," from *Essays in Collective Epistemology*, ed. Jennifer Lackey (Oxford University Press, 2014).

For Chapter 9, "Epistemic Agency," from *Journal of Philosophy*, 90 (November 2013).

For Chapter 10, "Pyrrhonian Skepticism and Human Agency," from *Philosophical Issues*, 23 (October 2013).

For Chapter 11, "Descartes' Pyrrhonian Virtue Epistemology," from *Scepticism and Perceptual Justification*, ed. Dylan Dodd and Elia Zardini (Oxford University Press, 2014).

While my project was supported in part by a grant from the John Templeton Foundation, the opinions expressed in this resulting publication are my own, and do not necessarily reflect the views of the Foundation.

Contents

Introduction 1

PART I. VIRTUE EPISTEMOLOGY EXTENDED AND UNIFIED

1. The Unity of Action, Perception, and Knowledge 7
2. Virtue Epistemology: Character versus Competence 34

PART II. A BETTER VIRTUE EPISTEMOLOGY

3. Judgment and Agency 65
4. A Better Virtue Epistemology Further Developed 89
5. Objections and Replies, with a Methodological Afterthought . . . 107

PART III. KNOWLEDGE AND AGENCY

6. Knowledge and Action 133
7. Intentional Action and Judgment 154
8. Social Roots of Human Knowledge 168
9. Epistemic Agency 192

PART IV. MAIN HISTORICAL ANTECEDENTS

10. Pyrrhonian Skepticism and Human Agency 215
11. Descartes's Pyrrhonian Virtue Epistemology 233

Index 255

Introduction

The epistemology presented in what follows concerns knowledge of a basic "animal" form, along with higher levels of "reflective" knowledge, all within a framework of performance normativity encompassing, not only judgments and beliefs, but performances more generally, those constitutively aimed at a certain outcome. Such a performance might do well in one or more of three distinct ways. First, it might attain its aim; second, it might be an exercise of pertinent competence; third, its success might be attained through the competence exercised, not just by luck. An archer's shot might be accurate by hitting its target; it might be skillful or adroit; and, finally, it might be *apt*: accurate *because* adroit (in first approximation). When applied to epistemology in particular, this yields the triple-A normativity of accuracy, adroitness, and aptness of judgment or belief.

This book aims to develop that account of human knowledge further than before, by taking up issues of metaphysics and ethics (broadly conceived) that arise for it.

Part I: Virtue Epistemology Extended and Unified

The first chapter, "The Unity of Action, Perception, and Knowledge," places our approach within a broader project of metaphysical, semantic, and conceptual analysis that targets human attainments more generally, whether they take the form of action, perception, or knowledge. We consider problems—such as that of causal deviance—that arise for Donald Davidson's account of intentional action, for Paul Grice's causal analysis of perception, and for our own account of human knowledge. These can be viewed as metaphysical analyses of their respective targets. Thus viewed they are defensible against common objections—of either vicious circularity or insufficient content—that have been thought lethal.

Those accounts are also defensible, moreover, against critiques that have been thought to favor disjunctivist alternatives. Prominent such critiques apply only to a specific, and optional, form of analysis: namely, analysis into logically independent factors merely conjoined in the analysis. To the contrary, metaphysical analyses can be causal analyses that do not take that form. Action, perception, and knowledge are all forms of the manifestation of a competence. And a competence is in turn understood as a disposition to succeed in a given field of aimings, these being performances with an aim, whether the aim be intentional and even conscious, or teleological and functional.

The chapter's conclusion sketches a methodology appropriate for our inquiry.

Chapter 1 thus presents a form of virtue epistemology, a virtue reliabilism with epistemic competence at its core. This is united with virtue-theoretic treatments of perception and of intentional action.[1]

Chapter 2, "Virtue Epistemology: Character versus Competence," is a comparative study of the two sorts of virtue epistemology now widely recognized. It defends the following four claims:

> First, from its inception, virtue reliabilism has *always* included a responsibilist component within its focus.
>
> Second, responsibilists have advocated a *distinctive* conception of responsibilist, character-based intellectual virtue, but it is partial and insufficient.
>
> Third, and ironically, we should recognize a sort of active, volitional intellectual virtue that is a special case of reliable-competence intellectual virtue.
>
> Fourth and finally, we can best understand the responsibilist, character-based intellectual virtues (highlighted by responsibilists) as *auxiliary* to reliable-competence intellectual virtues.

A true epistemology will indeed assign to such responsibilist-cum-reliabilist intellectual virtue the *main* role in addressing concerns at the center of the tradition. To anticipate, that is so because of the *sort* of knowledge that lies at the center of traditional epistemology, from the Pyrrhonists through

---

1. If the account succeeds for these three, it shows promise for the analysis of reference as well, but we will not go into that here.

Descartes. (That it does so will be argued in Part IV, "Main Historical Antecedents.") This is a knowledge requiring free, volitional endorsement by the subject who judges, or at least the corresponding disposition to so endorse. Ironically, our reliabilist framework did always potentially, and does increasingly (actually and explicitly) give the place of honor to epistemic agency, a central place (in theory of knowledge) that responsibilists either emphatically deny to it (Baehr), or do not successfully provide for it (Zagzebski).[2]

According to this chapter, reliabilist, competence-based virtue epistemology must be understood broadly, in a more positively ecumenical way, with responsibilist, agential intellectual virtue at its core.

Part II: A Better Virtue Epistemology

Chapter 3, "Judgment and Agency," explicates a concept of the *fully apt* performance, which helps guide us beyond anything found in earlier virtue epistemology.

Chapter 4, "A Better Virtue Epistemology Further Developed," first integrates degrees of confidence with the foregoing account, and then considers two forms of representation, the functional and the judgmental. The last subsection, "A Theory of Competence," contains a theory of competence aimed to fit our AAA virtue epistemology, with two central notions: that of the apt belief, whose correctness manifests the pertinent *epistemic competence* of the believer, and that of the *fully* apt belief, one aptly guided to aptness.

Chapter 5, "Objections and Replies, with a Methodological Afterthought," is well described by its title.

Part III: Knowledge and Agency

Chapter 6, "Knowledge and Action," distinguishes a kind of knowledge generally involved even in simple, ordinary means–end human action, and

---

2. Or so the chapter will argue in detail, despite how implausible the thesis may seem to those familiar with the literature.

explores how Aristotelian virtue ethics fits within a framework of action that is often thus knowledge dependent.

Chapter 7, "Intentional Action and Judgment," returns to a topic broached in Chapter 1: the nature of intentional action and the conditions for its aptness. A notion of *simple intentional action* is defined and used to explicate judgment and its relation to action.

Chapter 8, "Social Roots of Human Knowledge," has recourse to social epistemology for an account of the "reliability enough" required for competence and for aptness.

Social factors affect epistemology in at least two ways. They bear on an important sort of belief—judgmental belief—and also on a corresponding sort of epistemic competence. This concerns both a kind of value that knowledge has, and also how the pragmatic can properly encroach on epistemology.

Chapter 9, "Epistemic Agency," is about varieties of epistemic agency, and about how such agency is related to normativity, freedom, reasons, competence, and skepticism.

Part IV: Main Historical Antecedents

Chapter 10, "Pyrrhonian Skepticism and Human Agency," offers a new interpretation of Pyrrhonian epistemology, one in line with the epistemology developed in the preceding three parts.

The concluding Chapter 11, "Descartes's Pyrrhonian Virtue Epistemology," argues that in his epistemology Descartes offers a virtue epistemological account of certainty, and by implication of knowledge more generally, and that in doing so he is focused on Pyrrhonian concerns, in line with the basic structure of Pyrrhonian epistemology.

PART I

Virtue Epistemology Extended and Unified

I

The Unity of Action, Perception, and Knowledge

Introduction: On Metaphysical Analysis

1. Three sorts of analysis can be distinguished: the linguistic, the conceptual, the metaphysical.

Take the familiar example of a cat's lying on a mat. Consider first the pragmatics and semantics of the corresponding sentence. For example, when exactly must the cat be on the mat in order for an utterance of that sentence, which takes time, to be true?

Consider next the analysis of the sentence's conceptual content. One sort of conceptual analysis would involve a bi-conditional claim of necessity, with the target content on one side and the explaining content on the other. On pain of vicious circularity, the explanation cannot contain the content to be explained. Grasp (understanding) of the target content would be explained through (prior) grasp of the explaining content.

The metaphysical analysis of *the cat's lying on the mat* is distinct from such linguistic or conceptual analysis. A metaphysical analysis, with respect to that cat and that mat, of the former's lying on the latter, would involve *the cat, the mat*, and a certain binary relation, that of *lying on*. But what is this relation? We might try this: it is a relation of being adjacent to and above. But that is problematic. Suppose the cat lies on a mat that is glued on the inside and bottom of a large wheel. And suppose the wheel starts to rotate with high acceleration so that the cat stays on the mat throughout the rotation, due to the forces involved. The cat continues to lie on the mat all through the rotation, but at the top is *below* the mat.

One reaction to the example would be to try to explain how the relation of *lying on* is a more complex relation than might have appeared. In doing this one might appeal to resultant forces, so that the actual relation involves previously unsuspected factors. Without the concept of force, one would not be able to entertain that proposal. Yet one could still gain a partial account of the relevant relation as follows: it is a relation of being adjacent in a certain way, *in the right way*. While unsure of what that way is, one might at least know that it is some way of being adjacent.

Such partial metaphysical analysis might or might not correlate with similar success involving linguistic or conceptual analysis. In any case, the subject matter is different. Our target concerns a state in the world of *the cat's lying on the mat*, or more generally a *sort* of state, instances of which we find in the world, of one thing's lying on another. And this is different from any words or any concepts.

Similar distinctions apply generally in philosophy. Thus consider the linguistic analysis of the terminology of "persons" and the conceptual analysis of a concept of a person, and how these differ from metaphysical inquiry into the nature of persons, such as the living human beings among us.

2. Metaphysical analysis goes beyond conceptual or semantic inquiry, and also beyond necessary bi-conditionals, which can fail to provide the metaphysical explanation of special interest to the philosopher.

Consider for example the metaphysics of persons. In the broad domain of persons, we find our threefold divide among: (a) words, such as the word "person," (b) concepts, such as the concept of a person, and (c) extra-linguistic, extra-conceptual entities, the living persons.[1] Concerning the latter, we find metaphysical options such as substance dualism, animalism, and so on. According to an Aristotelian view, a person is never *identical with*, but only *constituted by*, a body, which needs to be alive,

---

[1]. Objection: *"In addition to the living persons among us, which are particulars, there is the universal of personhood, which is also distinct from the concept of a person. Isn't it really the universal that interests the metaphysician, not particular living persons, as (c) and earlier formulations suggest?"* Reply: We can wonder how any arbitrary living person might be constituted ontologically. And this is of course different from how the property of being a person might be constituted. Any given person is arguably constituted by a living body, for example, unlike the property. The broader point is that issues of ontology such as that of the constitution of persons go beyond issues about the analysis of the words or concepts that pertain to that domain of entities. And the same goes, presumably, for instances of knowledge. Of course, the ontological analysis of persons may be closely related to the analysis of the property of being a person, if for example we countenance an "analysis" of the property that mirrors the ontological analysis of the persons themselves, so that to be a person (that property) might just be the property of being an entity grounded in a body with a certain psychological profile. But such a theory as to the identity of the property itself would go beyond any conceptual or semantic analysis.

and in possession of certain powers and abilities, in order to (thereby) constitute a person.

This Aristotelian view in the metaphysics of persons involves metaphysical dependence. One thing exists or is actual dependently on certain other things. The dependent thing then exists or is actual dependently on the other things and on how they are propertied or related.

3. Turning to epistemology, we can now discern three sets of issues that are quite distinct, however closely they may be interrelated. *First* are issues of the semantic or pragmatic analysis of epistemic expressions such as "S knows that p"? *Second* are issues of conceptual analysis of one or another sort. Here one might ask about how a certain concept is constituted, what it necessarily involves. Thus, is the concept of knowledge constituted partly by the concepts of belief, truth, etc., so that necessarily the former concept will apply to something only if the latter concepts do so as well? Alternatively, or additionally, with concepts understood as psychological entities, we might wonder what is involved in someone's possession and/or deployment of the concept(s) of knowledge? This problem thus concerns people's minds, their psychology. So much for our second set of issues, those of conceptual analysis. *Third* are issues of metaphysical analysis. Here we focus on an objective phenomenon that need be neither expression nor concept. Our focus is rather on a state that people host, or an act that they perform. This is the phenomenon whose ontology we now wish to understand. What is human knowledge? What is its nature? And how is it grounded? In virtue of what is it actual when it is actual? (And similar ontological questions arise about the *instances* of that state.) It is these metaphysical questions that determine our *third* set of issues.[2]

4. Performance whose success manifests the relevant competence of the performer avoids thereby a kind of luck. According to competence virtue epistemology, knowledge is a special case of that. Knowledge of a sort is belief whose correctness is attained *sufficiently* through the believer's epistemic competence, belief that is thus "apt."[3]

---

[2]. Here I have lumped together questions of grounding, questions concerning the *in virtue of* relation, and questions of *nature, essence, or constitution*, leaving it open whether these various ontological issues should be distinguished, and if so how. (These are issues taken up in my "Subjects among Other Things," *Philosophical Perspectives*, 1 (1987): 155–87.) Questions of grounding have recently attracted intense attention among metaphysicians such as Kit Fine, Gideon Rosen, Jonathan Schaffer, and others.

[3]. In my sense, my now owning two tennis rackets may derive *in part though not sufficiently* from my having got one as a gift. After all, the fuller source of my double-ownership will include

A serious problem affects the metaphysics and ideology of perception and action, however, and similarly affects the metaphysics and ideology of knowledge. This is the problem of *deviant causation*.

We shall consider a solution for the problem in its three varieties. To begin we examine Davidson on action, Grice on perception, and the account of knowledge as apt belief, as belief that gets it right through competence rather than luck. We take up the opposition between such traditional accounts and "disjunctivist" alternatives. And we explore how the point and substance of metaphysical analysis bears on the problem and on competing reactions to it.

What follows divides into four parts. In a *first* part, the main lines of the view are laid out, and it is shown how it applies with the same basic structure in all three domains. A *second* part then develops these ideas with finer grain and more detail. In a *third* part we consider how our account goes beyond Davidson and Grice. A final, *fourth* part, then presents a methodology that fits our approach.

First Part

Action, Perception, and Knowledge

A. Action

What is it to act intentionally? As a first approximation, you might think, to act intentionally is to succeed in a certain intentional aim, where the success is owed to the agent's intention.

But that has counterexamples, such as the following.

> A waiter intends to startle his boss by knocking over a stack of dishes right now, which makes him so nervous that he involuntarily staggers into the stack and knocks it over, thus startling the boss. But this is not something he does intentionally, even though the success here *is* owed to the agent's intention.[4]

---

also my having bought one earlier and kept it in my possession. (Compatibly with that, a sufficient explanation might still be improved so as to be not only *sufficient* but also *better* than the earlier sufficient one.)

4. Here is a terminological caveat not just for this passage but also for the remainder of this book. Theorizing about action can overlook an important distinction between what one does intentionally and what one does by design (on purpose, meaning to do *it* specifically). The sense of "intentionally" in what follows is restricted to that of "by design," although in ordinary language it stretches far beyond. Thus, one might wear down one's sneakers intentionally as one

So, we should require that the agent's intention must bring about the success in the right way, with "the right kind of causation." Or so Davidson advises repeatedly in his long struggle with the problem, and in his parting thoughts on the matter. Here is how he puts it (with minor variations): What is it for an agent to F intentionally on a particular occasion? There must be some G such that the agent's intending to G must cause ". . . in the right way, the agent's particular act of Fing."[5] The waiter's knocking over of the dishes is not caused in the right way by any such intention. But no account of "the right way" has won consensus.

B. Perception

1. What is it to perceive an entity? The account of perception defended in Paul Grice's "Causal Theory of Perception"[6] is an early, influential answer.[7] Grice begins with a view drawn from H. H. Price's *Perception*:

> X perceives M iff X has a sense experience that is causally dependent on some state of affairs involving M.

---

runs a marathon, without doing so by design (on purpose). In ordinary language, *intentionally* is compatible with mere knowledge aforethought, whereas *by design* goes with malice aforethought (or, more broadly, purpose aforethought). The issues that arise with this restriction are important for understanding the ontology of action, even if we do not tackle the broader subject of what one does "intentionally," whether it is done by design or not. (Compare Michael Bratman, *Intentions, Plans, and Practical Reason* (Stanford, CA: CSLI Publications, 1999), especially "Two Faces of Intention" and "Acting with an Intention.")

5. See p. 221 of his "Reply to Vermazen," in B. Vermazen and M. Hintikka, eds, *Essays on Davidson: Actions and Events* (Cambridge, MA: MIT Press, 1985). Davidson's thought evolved from "Actions, Reasons, and Causes," *Journal of Philosophy* (1963), through "Intending" in his *Essays on Actions and Events* (Oxford: Oxford University Press, 1980), and then to his replies in the Vermazen and Hintikka collection.
6. H. P. Grice, "The Causal Theory of Perception," *Proceedings of the Aristotelian Society Supplementary Volume* (1961): 121–53.
7. Grice does not distinguish clearly among our three sorts of analysis. Much of his discussion is clearly meant as linguistic analysis, as is his long discussion of a theory of implication. But he often moves swiftly from notions or concepts to words, and vice versa, and at times his focus switches without warning from analysis of words or concepts to analysis of the phenomena of perception in the world. See the top of p. 148, for example, where he reports the "contention of the CTP" (of the causal theory of perception) that perceiving is to be analyzed in causal terms. And the theory that he proposes in conclusion contains a claim equivalent to the following: that X perceives M if, and only if, M is causally responsible (in some way to be brought out through examples) for some sense experience of X's. His theory is in any case, as formulated, equivalent to a claim about perception and not just about a concept of perception or about a terminology of "perception."

This, he argues, is subject to counterexamples. Our visual sense experiences while in the sunlight, for example, are causally dependent on the sun even when we look away from it. Nor do we normally perceive our eyes even when our visual experiences are highly dependent on the state of our eyes.

2. The account is then revised to say that an object is perceived if and only if some condition involving it is a differential condition that affects some but not all of the perceiver's relevant sense experience at the time of perception. The sun is not seen when we look away from it; on the revised account, this is because no condition of it affects only some and not all of one's visual sense experience.

However, the revised account too has counterexamples. Torches can shine respectively on statues viewed concurrently, each torch thus affecting the perceiver's visual impressions differentially, though only the statues are seen, with the torches blocked from view.

3. Grice eventually arrives at approximately the following view:

> X perceives M if, and only if, X hosts a sensory experience for which M is causally responsible in the right way.

This is what Grice's view comes to, given how he thinks the "right" way is grasped, to be considered in section E.[8]

C. Knowledge

As a first approximation, propositional knowledge can be understood as belief that attains its aim (truth) and does so not merely by luck but through competence. Such knowledge is then a special case of performance that is not just lucky but apt: i.e., performance whose success is owed sufficiently to the performer's relevant competence. The aptness of a performance is thus supposed to block an important sort of luck, the sort that precludes Gettiered subjects from knowing what they believe both correctly and

---

[8]. In proposing this view, Grice hopes to deal not only with his examples cited in our text, but also with clear cases of causal deviance, such as those found on p. 142 of his paper.

competently. A belief falls short of knowledge when its truth is owed too much to luck and not sufficiently to the believer's competence.[9]

In a Gettier case, the believer's competence in one way makes some contribution to their getting it right in believing that p. We might conceive of "their getting it right" as a conjunctive state of affairs containing as conjuncts both P and the believer's believing P. The believer's exercise of epistemic competence does certainly make a contribution to their believing P, so it follows that it makes a contribution to the holding of the conjunctive state by making a contribution to the holding of one of its conjuncts. However, what is required for aptness of belief is not merely the holding of the conjunctive state that is sourced through those two separate channels: one for the holding of the belief, and the other for the truth of the proposition believed. This would leave it open that the combination of belief-plus-truth be entirely coincidental. Even if the believer's competence contributes heavily to their *believing* as they do, it may still contribute *not at all* to that coincidence's being more than a *mere* coincidence. So, in order for a belief to be apt, the coincidence of belief and truth must derive sufficiently through competence, so that it is not *merely* coincidental. And, more generally, in order for a performance to be apt, it must be sufficiently an exercise of competence that yields the coincidence of (a) the attempt and (b) the realization of the attempt's content.[10]

But this too has ostensible counterexamples. Take an archer's competent shot that (a) would hit the target absent intervening wind, and (b) does hit the target because, although a first gust diverts it, a second gust puts it back on track. Here the agent's competence yields the early orientation and speed of the arrow, and this combined orientation and speed, together with the two compensating gusts, results in the bull's-eye. So, why is this shot not apt after all? A performance is apt when it succeeds because of the agent's competence. But our archer's wind-aided shot *does* seem to succeed because of his competence! If the agent's competence had not resulted in

---

9. "We have reached the view that knowledge is true belief out of intellectual virtue, belief that turns out right by reason of the virtue and not just by coincidence" (E. Sosa, *Knowledge in Perspective* (Cambridge: Cambridge University Press, 1991), 277).
10. A recipient of testimony might contribute through his exercise of epistemic competence to the *existence* of his belief without contributing to its *success*, to its hitting the mark of truth. And the aptness of his belief requires that he make a contribution, which may be quite limited and small, to his belief's *correctness*, not just to its existence.

the right orientation and speed upon release from the bow, then the arrow would not have hit the target.

Taking a leaf from Davidson and Grice, we might judge success to be apt only if it derives causally from competence *in the right way*. Success essentially aided by lucky gusts of wind would not derive in the right way from the archer's competence.

D. Assessing the Three Accounts

1. All three accounts may be rejected as unsatisfactory until we are told what it is for success to derive "in the right way" from the relevant causal sources.

2. We are considering accounts of phenomena that are broadly "factive," such as perceiving x, killing x, perceiving that p, intentionally øing, and knowing that p. These involve relations spanning mind and world, relations between the subject/agent's mind and her environing world. Philosophical analyses proposed for these various relations then repeatedly appeal to some essential causal relation. And thus we reach the nub of the problem.

The problem is often posed by deviant causation, wayward causation that gives rise to counterexamples, whether the analysis targets action, perception, or knowledge. Time after time, a kind of "luck" or "mere coincidence" derives from the deviant character of the causation, incompatibly with appropriate success and relevantly creditable perception, action, or knowledge.

3. For all such "factive" phenomena, there is a good case and a bad case. In the good case the agent fully succeeds.[11] In the bad case she fails in some way or other.

Traditionalists take the good case to be constituted in part by what constitutes the bad case, plus something else that is missing in the bad case.

---

11. My "succeeding" is relative to the aim constitutive of the performance that succeeds. It means strictly just that the constitutive aim is attained by that performance. *Objection: It seems a bit strong to require that the agent must succeed "fully." An agent may come to know that p on the basis of good but imperfect evidence. Such an agent succeeds, but not as fully as an agent who comes to know that p on the basis of perfect evidence.* Reply: Yes, true. But in my sense you can succeed fully even if you might have succeeded even more fully. Compare Moore and Descartes on grades of certainty. (Ordinary speech is open to this, as when I say "My suitcase is full but I can still squeeze in this handkerchief.")

The phenomenon in the good case is constituted thereby so as to be metaphysically analyzable into factors. The good and bad cases share a highest common factor. What distinguishes them is that the good case combines that highest common factor with some other factor. In the bad case that further factor is missing.

Disjunctivists reject that traditionalist account. In their view there is no such common factor. Disjunctivism is familiar in accounts of perception, and in the knowledge-first theory of knowledge,[12] and is also applicable to action theory.

Disjunctivism provides an alternative to the three accounts recently viewed: Davidson's of intentional action, Grice's of perception, and the account of knowledge as apt belief. Each of these involves a distinguished factor shared by the good case and the bad case. Each of the three sorts of failure is said to involve a component that would also be present with success. For perception the component would be a sensation or sensory experience. For action it would be an intention or a trying. For knowledge it would be a belief or judgment. Traditionalists then propose that success differs from failure because a certain factor present in success is missing in failure. Otherwise the cases are the same. Causalist traditionalists argue that what is present in success and missing in failure is a certain causal connection relating, first, the factor shared in common by failures and successes—whether this be sensation, intention, or belief—and a relevant worldly item: that is to say, the item perceived, the doing intended, the fact believed.

Disjunctivists thus reject traditionalist analyses. Should traditionalists be worried?

4. According to one influential argument, there is no *conjunctive* analysis of the good case *with logically independent conjuncts*.[13]

---

12. Timothy Williamson, *Knowledge and Its Limits* (Oxford: Oxford University Press, 2000).
13. Section 1.3 of Williamson's book contains the following line of argument:
    1. Analyses of the concept *knows* of the standard kind always involve an irredundant non-mental component concept, namely truth.
    2. Any concept composed conjunctively of an irredundant non-mental concept would be bound to be a non-mental concept.
    3. The concept *knows* is a mental concept.
    4. The concept *knows* is distinct from (non-identical to) any conjunctive concept of the sort invoked by analyses of the standard kind.
    5. The concept *knows* is unanalyzable by any analysis of the standard kind, since a correct analysis would be a claim of concept identity.
    6. No standard analysis of the concept *knows* can be correct, which is also confirmed inductively by the Gettier literature.

In response it should be granted that there is no analysis of the good case in terms of independent factors conjoined in the analysis. This seems correct for all three phenomena: for perception, for action, and for knowledge. So "disjunctivism" is then right to claim that there is no analysis of the good case into independent conjunctive factors. From this it would follow, moreover, that there is no highest common factor, if this just means that no highest independent factor figures in an analysis of each case, the good and the bad, into independent conjunctive factors.

However, that leaves it open that the good case admit metaphysical analysis, if such analysis need not be a factorizing analysis that conjoins independent factors.

All three accounts—of action, of perception, and of knowledge—are analyses of the good case into factors, and in all three there would be a highest common factor shared by the good case and the bad case. But in none of them would this highest common factor figure as a conjunct in a conjunctive analysis of the good case into independent conjuncts. Why is there no such analysis? The reason is uniform across the three cases, as they all involve a causal connection said to be present in the good case and absent in the bad case. In no case is the causal connection *relevantly* detachable from other factors combined with it, and with each other, in the analysis.

No state of affairs that comprises relata related by causation will have a metaphysical analysis such that no two factors constitutive of the whole are necessarily related by logical or metaphysical necessity. *X's causing Y* thus comprises X and Y as relata related by causation, but the whole causal state of affairs is not fully resolvable by analysis into logically and metaphysically independent factors. Even if factors X and Y are logically and

---

7. That has implications not only for conceptual analysis but also for metaphysical analysis. Suppose, for example, that we grant that the concept *knows* is distinct from the concept *believes truly*. And suppose that, in spite of that, we insist that the metaphysical states of knowledge and true belief are identical, since knowledge, the state, just is true belief.
8. This would imply that the concepts are necessarily coextensive despite the diversity of the corresponding states. And that would be a bizarre (and presumably incredible) metaphysical coincidence.
    However, that line of reasoning applies only to a special set of traditional analyses. It does not apply to analyses that do not involve irredundant non-mental component concepts. So it does not apply to early Goldman (knowledge is belief caused by the fact believed), nor to Nozick (with his two conditionals: p → Bp *and* ~p → ~Bp). Nor does it apply to the account of (animal) knowledge as apt belief (as belief whose correctness manifests the believer's relevant competence).

metaphysically independent, there is no way of *conjoining* a further factor independent of these two that will secure the required causal connection crucially involved in X's causing Y.

5. The upshot is that if causal accounts of perception, action, and knowledge are to be rejected in favor of disjunctive or X-first views, the objection will need to go beyond any assumption that proper analyses must be conjunctive analyses into logically independent factors. In order to clinch their case, opponents of traditional analyses must argue more fully than has been done to date. They must show not only that there is no factorizing analysis of the relevant phenomena into independent conjunctive factors. They must show also that there is no acceptable causal analysis.

Suppose even that essential appeal to "the right way" spoils semantic and conceptual analysis. Suppose firsters are thus right in thinking that there is no such linguistic and conceptual analysis in any of our three domains: that of perception, that of action, and that of knowledge. Whether we are in a position to *give* it *in full detail* or not, however, there might still *be* a metaphysical analysis, even if the formulation of the analysis must make use of "in the right way." Any formulation we could give might then have to be partial, not complete. Recall in this connection our cat-on-mat example. And compare Leibniz on "infinite analysis."

Firsters thus owe further argument that there is no metaphysical analysis of perception, action, or knowledge into phenomena metaphysically more fundamental. Such metaphysical analysis is not precluded even if there is no interesting, non-circular, informative semantic or conceptual analysis of the words or concepts in the relevant domains (that of action, that of perception, and that of knowledge).[14]

---

14. *Objection*: "A central case for disjunctivism about objectual seeing is the argument that disjunctivism gets the phenomenology of perception right, which is a phenomenology that strongly recommends naive realism: it is the transparent phenomenology of acquaintance with objects in one's environment, where these objects seem to be constituents of the experience. Isn't this a further argument pressed by disjunctivists at least in the case of perception?" Reply: This argument too is inconclusive, however, since there is no such *sensory* phenomenology. There is only a "phenomenology" of seemings as inclinations to believe or the like. This is the sort of seeming in play, surely, when it "seems" to anyone that objects seen can be constituents of the corresponding visual experience. But such a prejudgment "seeming" has scant probative force to countervail how plausibly it also "seems" that the same sensory phenomenology can be shared by a hallucination and a veridical experience. In addition, the believer in subjective sensory experience need not deny that there is a sort of sensory objectual experience that is constituted by a seen physical object. For he can also insist that this sort of experience has a metaphysical analysis in terms of the subjective experience involved in such experience.

E. An Approach through Performance Theory

1. What follows aims to turn the tables on objections to traditionalist causal analyses. The use of a concept of "manifestation" will enable causal analyses in all three cases. Appeal to manifestation helps to develop a better solution to those problems. The notion of aptness (success that manifests competence) promises to be helpful not only in the theory of knowledge, but also in the theory of action, and in the philosophy of perception.

Both Davidson and Grice make a crucial move in defending their respective accounts. Even though their formulations are different, the move is essentially the same. They both in effect require *a particular sort* of causation, while ostensibly assuming that no verbal formula can non-trivially define it. Davidson then says that *no such formula is needed*, and Grice adds that *a grasp of the right sort of causation can be attained through examples*. Let us have a closer look.

2. Recall the waiter who intends to knock over a stack of dishes *right now*, but does so only through an attack of nerves caused by the nervy intention. Why is this *not* a way in which a doing can relate to an intention so as to constitute intentional action? What *is* the required causal relation? Can it be defined so as to reveal why the waiter's doing does not qualify? Davidson claims that we need *no armchair analysis of this matter*. In his view intentional actions are analyzable as doings caused by intentions *in the right way*, and no further analysis of *the right way* is possible or required. We might ask: "No further analysis is required *for what*?" And, in the light of our cat-on-mat example, here is one plausible response: We need not provide a further explication (of what that "right way" is) in order to make any progress. We can at least *partially* formulate an analysis of intentional action through appeal to *appropriate* causation "in the right way."

Still, it would be nice to be able to make further progress, by going beyond thus invoking "the right way."

Let us try an account in terms of *competences and their manifestations*. Consider:

Knowledge is *apt belief*.

Perception (propositional perception, perception that such and such) is *apt perceptual experience*, experience whose success manifests competence. A perceptual experience succeeds when it is *veridical* or accurate. An apt experience is one whose accuracy manifests the relevant competence of the subject's perceptual systems.

Action is *apt intention*.[15]

In all three cases, the following factors come to the fore:

Success, the attainment of the aim.
The competence of the performance.
The aptness of that performance: whether the success manifests competence.

And it is no accident that aptness—success that manifests competence—is the key to "the right way." Again, all three human phenomena involve *aimings*, performances with an aim. Perception involves functional, teleological aimings, through the teleology of our perceptual systems. Intentional action involves aimings that are full-fledged intentions. Knowledge divides into two sides: a functional perception-like side, and a judgmental action-like side.

The *sort* of causation essentially involved in all three phenomena is hence the causation of aptness. It is not enough that the success *derive causally* from competence, for it may so derive deviantly, by luck. Rather, the success must be *apt*. It must *manifest* sufficient competence on the part of the performer.

Second Part

The Approach through Manifestation Developed

A. Objectual Perception

How should we understand *objectual* perception specifically? Factive propositional perception does seem analogous to action and knowledge in the ways specified, since all three involve an aiming with propositional content, where it is clear how aimings lend themselves to AAA metaphysical analysis: in terms of success, competence, and success through competence. But how can we extend this approach to cover also the more specific topic of special interest to Grice?

---

15. This will be qualified below, starting with footnote 24 in this chapter, and further elaborated also in Part III of the book.

1. Grice on *objectual* perception.
    a. Grice defends his "causal theory of perception" with an essential appeal to examples, as follows:

    X perceives M if, and only if, some present-tense sense-datum statement is true of X which reports a state of affairs for which M, *in a way to be indicated by example*, is causally responsible.[16]

    b. Unfortunately, Grice's account is little more than a gesture at how an account might be obtained. Can we do better, even within the spirit of Grice's thought? Here follows an attempt to do so.

2. Perception as aptness of objectual image.

Our approach requires a finer grain than just the propositional content of experience. We must take note of the fact that experience is finer grained in containing images as well. We begin with visual images, aiming to provide an account of seeing things, individual things such as physical objects or events, or other objective individual entities.[17]

Some performances are not free or intentional and yet have aims nonetheless, such as the teleological or functional aims of a biological organism or its subsystems. Salient among the aims of our visual system is representing our environment appropriately. This our vision might do by representing proximate facts through the propositional content of experience, visual or otherwise. Images too can represent, however, through appropriate correspondence to individual worldly entities. In aiming to represent, an image will aim to correspond in some way.[18] Since an image can represent

---

16. Grice, "The Causal Theory of Perception," 151. My italics.
17. Eventually we would need to generalize beyond that so as to cover other sense modalities, if all goes well with our approach to vision. Admittedly, that would be no trivial exercise. We would need to do justice to the phenomenology of other senses, such as sound, smell, and touch. This may require appeal not only to direct perception by the naked eye, but also to indirect perception: through mirrors and television screens, for example, and even through photographs or films in a kind of delayed seeing. Similar ideas would then pertain to smell, as when we smell a skunk (with no conception that there is such an animal, never having encountered nor heard of any) by smelling its characteristic smell in the air. We might then smell a particular skunk thus indirectly.

    Some would banish any notion of directness from the philosophy of perception, but its prominence in the history of the subject makes that unwise. Better to try to *understand* the diversity of directness—cf. ch. 6 of my *Knowing Full Well* (Princeton: Princeton University Press, 2011).
18. More strictly, by hosting that image in visual experience, an animal's visual system, and in a way the animal too, aims to represent, through the operation of vision, and in so aiming they aim to correspond. But here I do not commit to a teleosemantic theory, especially not to one that restricts selection to natural selection over an evolutionary time span, nor even to a historical account, whether relative to species or to culture. Given how difficult and

despite massive illusion, the correspondence might be minimal. Macbeth might represent a walking stick as a sword, for example, in which case there will be some correct correspondence. The image and the stick will still share the property of being an elongated object.[19]

Thus we reach the following account.

3. An account of objectual visual representation

   a. First, two preliminaries:

Image Im corresponds to x IFF (a) Im aims to correspond to some worldly item: that is, aims for an outcome in which it shares content with some worldly item or other, and (b) there is some content of Im in respect of which it does correspond to x in particular, *through sharing of properties or conditions, including relational properties or conditions*.[20]

Image Im *aptly* corresponds to x IFF (a) Im attains its aim of thus corresponding to some worldly item or other, in virtue of its corresponding to x in particular, and (b) Im's thus corresponding to x manifests S's perceptual competence.

   b. And now the account of objectual visual representation:

S visually represents object x IFF a visual image hosted by S aptly corresponds to x.

According to one basic form of seeing, to see an individual "object" (in the broadest sense) is to visually represent that object.[21]

---

controversial these issues have proved to be, I stay at a high level of abstraction that leaves open just how in full philosophical detail we should understand these functional or teleological aims, and the "proper functions" involved.

19. Such sharing is of course not just co-exemplification. An image and an object can "share" properties in a different way, by the image's *containing* a property *exemplified* by the object. Images are here assumed to have a status like that of fictional characters. The character Hamlet for example *contains* the property of owning a sword, but *exemplifies* no such property, since characters have no legal standing to own swords. Images and characters are ontologically shallow, like shadows and surfaces, and are presumably grounded or supervenient on deeper, more substantial entities or phenomena. But one need not enter these metaphysical issues in order to grant ontological standing to such entities, while invoking them to elucidate other phenomena.

20. Here we may need to be flexible in allowing indexical conditions, as when my image contains the condition <is before me now> or even <causes *this* very image>. Even if we allow the latter self-referential content, we still need to block *deviant* causation, preferably without appeal to "the right way," since the point is to *improve* on Davidson and Grice.

21. *Objection:* "Sensations of secondary qualities do not share content with a worldly item—the object in the world does not have a property that corresponds to the sensation. (For example, our sensation of warmth does not seem to share content with the physical property of being warm.) Nevertheless, we perceive the object by means of having sensations of secondary qualities. More strongly, couldn't all of our sensations

4. It cannot be demonstrated that our account covers the defining examples envisaged by Grice, since he displays very few, nor does he take himself to have given a complete list, or even any list. He just issues the claim that examples could be used to convey what sort of causation it is that enables a causal account of perception.

We go beyond that by saying more about what sort of causation it is, even if in the end we too rely on showing rather than telling, as do Grice and Davidson. In order to convey how that is so, it helps to discuss an example.

Suppose Macbeth had suffered his dagger hallucination while at the same time there was a dagger at the relevant place and time, and indeed a dagger just like the one in his hallucination in every perceptual respect. We can surely understand the case even described so sparely. In doing so, I suggest, we rely on Macbeth's getting it right by accident, not competence.

And we can now explain why and how Macbeth fails visually to represent the real dagger before him: he lacks the representational relation to it defined in terms of competent and apt visual representing. No visual image hosted by Macbeth aptly represents that real dagger, since none *aptly* shares any content with it. Any sharing of content is only accidental and not through the competence of Macbeth's visual system as it interacts with the real dagger.

Moreover, the examples used by Grice to counter earlier theories, such as Price's, are also amenable to our competence-theoretic account. When we do not see the sun despite how it affects our visual experiences, it is because we do not "visually represent" it. And the same goes for our eyes. In neither case do we so much as host any relevant visual images, whereas according to our account we can visually represent only by hosting a visual image that aptly corresponds to the item represented.[22]

5. As we shall see presently, this approach also helps to solve problems faced similarly by Davidson's account of intentional action. What is "the right way" in which a doing can be caused by an intention? Here again,

---

be of secondary qualities? The world would be Kantian if that were so: the real properties of objects would be in a sense hidden from us. But we might still be perceiving them." Reply: We need to distinguish the property of being, say, blue, from the nature of that property. The property might have the nature of a secondary quality. And in that case the relevant image would "contain" that secondary quality, so that the image and the sky could "share" that property, in my sense.

22. Objection: "Suppose I see my eyes in a mirror and thereby host a visual image that aptly corresponds to my eyes. After I turn away from the mirror, my retina continues to be stimulated in exactly the same way (perhaps this is characteristic of how my retinal nerves work—they continue to provide the same signal for some time after the initial perceptual contact). My visual system continues to host an image that corresponds to my eyes, and it does so in virtue of its earlier competence. Is that enough for apt correspondence? It seems strange to say that I can still perceive my eyes even when I am no longer looking at them. On the

proper causation turns out to be causation through competence, be it perceptual competence or agential competence.[23]

B. A Defense of Manifestation in the Theory of Action

1. Recall the waiter's knocking over a stack of glasses (while intending to do so right then and there), but only through an attack of nerves caused by the nervy intention. Davidson claims that no armchair analysis of this matter is either possible or required. In his view intentional actions are analyzable as doings caused by intentions in the right way, with no need for any further analysis of what constitutes causation *in the right way*.[24]

2. Compare a wine glass that shatters upon hitting a hard floor, but only because it is zapped at the moment of impact by a hovering fiend who hates fragility meeting hardness, where the zapping ray would have shattered an iron dumbbell just as well.[25] Here the fragility is a source of the shattering, but not in the right way. Once again we appeal to the convenient "right way." We now say that in order for an ostensible "manifestation" of a disposition to be a real manifestation, it must derive from the disposition in the right way.

---

other hand, if it is not apt correspondence, why not?" Reply: I am encouraged by the fact that we continue to say that we see the stars at night, even once we understand what is really going on. In any case, the relevant competence would not be just the earlier competence. It must be the more encompassing competence whose exercise extends all the way to the present hosting of the relevant image, as with the seeing of the stars.

23. My earlier suggestion that reference might also yield to analysis through competence, manifestation, and aptness derives largely from the promise of a fruitful analogy between objectual perception and reference.

24. My approach to intentional action in terms of manifestation of competence is so far just a sketch. And the sketch is based on two restrictions of the subject matter. Here *intentions* are just *guiding aims*, and *intentionally øing* is just *øing by design*. My hope is thereby to skirt the broader territory covered by the "intentionally øing" of ordinary language.

   It is important to note, moreover, that an intention becomes an attempt when it is time for action. At that point the attempt might succeed or fail, and if it does succeed, it might do so aptly or inaptly. So, more strictly, action is apt attempt (intention that succeeds aptly right through the time of action).

   A fuller treatment of my more restricted topic would of course need to engage with a rich literature in action theory. But that is a project for another time. We proceed here at a higher level of abstraction by considering promising ways in which a virtue-theoretic approach may have something to contribute.

25. According to Merriam-Webster, 'to zap' is a transitive verb, defined as follows: "a: to get rid of, destroy, or kill especially with or as if with sudden force; b: to hit with or as if with a sudden concentrated application of force or energy."

3. Competences are a special case of dispositions, that in which the host is disposed to succeed when he tries, or that in which the host seats a relevant skill, and is in the proper shape and situation, such that he tries in close enough worlds, and in the close enough worlds where he tries, he reliably enough succeeds. But this must be so in the right way.[26]

C. A Defense of Manifestation in the Theory of Knowledge

We considered an account of propositional knowledge, in first approximation, as belief that attains its aim (truth) and does so not just by luck but through competence. Such knowledge is then a special case of performance that is not just lucky but apt: i.e., performance whose success is relevantly owed to the performer's competence. The aptness of a performance is thus supposed to block an important sort of luck or mere coincidence, the sort that precludes Gettiered subjects from knowing something even when they believe it both correctly and competently. A belief falls short of knowledge when its truth is owed too much to *such* luck and not properly to the believer's competence. In a word, the success of that belief, its truth, must be *apt*, must be appropriately due to competence. And this is where deviant causation impinges. Exactly how is it that success must derive causally from competence in order to be properly apt, in order to be apt in such a way that it does not derive excessively from (credit-denying) luck? Remember the archer's success when the two gusts intervene. In that case, the success is still owed causally to the archer's competence. Why then is it not apt? In what way is it due excessively to luck rather than competence? Here again success must do more than derive causally from sufficient competence in some way or other. It must do so by *manifesting* that competence.

Conclusion of the Second Part

We find unity across action, perception, and knowledge. All three are constituted by aimings, by performances with a constitutive aim. In perception the aim is functional, through the teleology of our perceptual systems. The aim of an intentional action is obvious in its constitutive intention.

---

26. It must not be so only with ad hoc intervention like that of our fragility-hating zapper. This is a first approximation, however, to be revisited in Chapter 4.

Knowledge comes in two sorts. One is functional, so that its aim can be teleological, like that of perception. By contrast, the aim of judgmental knowledge is like that of intentional action. This is because judgment *is* a kind of action, with judgmental belief the corresponding intention.[27]

When causation figures *in the right way* in all three of these phenomena, it is hence the causation of aptness. It is not enough that the success *derive causally* from competence, for it may be caused deviantly. Rather, the success must be *apt*. It must *manifest* the performer's sufficient competence.

Third Part

Are We beyond Grice and Davidson? What *Sort* of Account Is Ours?

A. Understanding and Ineffability

1. Our account goes beyond Grice and Davidson by specifying, in a performance-theoretic way, the "right way" in which causation must join together the relevant items: intentions with doings in intentional action, sense experiences with objects in perception, and beliefs with facts in knowledge.[28]

We would like to understand the metaphysics and epistemology of action, perception, and knowledge, which we must do through certain concepts,

---

27. This will be argued in Chapter 3.
28. We also go beyond Grice by placing perception—not only propositional perception, but also objectual perception—in the domain of biological and psychological competent functioning, and in the domain of biological and psychological performances that satisfy the AAA structure of accuracy, adroitness, and aptness.

    Note, however, that we *need not* agree with Grice or Davidson that either perception or action requires efficient causation "in the same way." Our progress beyond them might take the form of rejecting that idea altogether.

    It does seem plausible, however, that whenever a disposition is manifest in a certain outcome a causal relation holds between the triggering event and the relevant outcome. Such a causal relation is then *of a sort* involved in such manifestation. But we certainly do not need to assume that, in every case of manifestation, intrinsically the very same causal relation is involved. We need not even assume that, more specifically, in every case of *intentional action*, or of *perception*, the causal relation need be intrinsically the same. Neither Grice nor Davidson need assume anything that strong, in order to suppose that in every case of intentional action, or of perception, the causal relation is of "the same sort," or the relevant cause causes the relevant effect "in the same way." It can be left open that "sorts" and "ways" might be disjunctive or determinable, so that they are multiply realizable. And we can follow suit in that regard.

even when these are not helpfully expressible through verbal formulas. Nor need they be thus expressible even when widely shared among us.

Really? How do we understand those oracular claims?

2. Just compare how we manage to grasp what politeness is, what it requires. No verbal formula can fully convey or determine (by explicit convention) what is or is not polite conduct. Polite face-to-face conversation sets limits to the proper distance between the partners, and limits the volume of voice and the tone. How is any of this to be captured non-trivially through verbal formulas? It seems quite hopeless. Yet, somehow, antecedent community convention sets those limits. Such convention requires antecedent agreement, at least implicit agreement, which in turn requires content that is shared even without *explicit* conventional agreement.

Compare the "manifestations" of a competence. A community might similarly agree (however in the end we understand such implicit "agreement" and its content) on what are cases of "manifestation" of a given competence, even with no helpful verbal formula to cover all such cases. This is like "politeness," in both general and specific respects. Consider the SSS structure (skill, shape, situation) of complete competences, and our concepts of these, and the induced SS and S correlates. Take for example our complete driving competence on a certain occasion, including (a) our basic driving skill (retained even when we sleep), along with (b) the shape we are in at the time (awake, sober, etc.), and (c) our situation (seated at the wheel, on a dry road, etc.). Drop the situation and you still have an inner SS competence. Drop both shape and situation and you still have an innermost S competence: that is, the basic driving skill retained even when asleep (in unfortunate shape) in bed (inappropriately situated).

Such concepts are broadly shared with no benefit of linguistic formulation.

What counts as manifestation seems also graspable only in implicit ways, as with etiquette, and not through explicit (and nontrivial) verbal formulation.

B. Competences, Dispositions, and Their Manifestations

1. Driving competence comes in three varieties: Skill (basic driving competence), Skill + Shape (skill plus being awake, sober, etc.), and Skill +

Shape + Situation (skill plus shape plus being at the wheel of an operative car while the road is relevantly dry enough, etc.). Only with the relevant SSS competence are we fully competent to drive on a given road. What determines whether we have the innermost S competence? It is presumably a modal matter: that if we tried to drive safely we would reliably enough succeed. But in *any* conditions? Surely not. It is not at all likely that we would drive safely, even if we tried, when dead drunk, or on an oily road. But this may not bear on our competence to drive safely. There is an array of SSS conditions that *would* likely enough yield success for our attempts to drive safely. This involves certain ranges of the shape we need to be in, and certain ranges of how we must be related to the road, including the road conditions. Communities that use cars and roads are interested in certain particular combinations of Shapes and Situations, and we are pretty well implicitly agreed on what those are. Innermost driving Skill is then determined as the basis for our likely enough succeeding if we tried in *those* Shape + Situation combinations.

2. It is not immediately obvious that *dispositions* generally, as opposed to competences specifically, still have that triple structure. But with a bit of stretching they can be made to share it. Thus, we might consider complete fragility to require the fragile object not only to have a certain inner structure, but also to be within certain bounds of temperature, so that a piece of glass loses its fragility when heating makes it liquid (molten, flowing liquid). And one might even countenance that it loses its fragility once suspended in outer space. We do speak of our being *weightless* out there. Without much of a stretch, then, dispositions too can be viewed as coming in three varieties: first, Seat (or innermost basis); second, Seat + Shape, including temperature, etc.; and, third, Seat + Shape + Situation. Located in outer space we are weightless in a SeShSi way, while we might still retain our same exact weight, and still count as heavy, in a SeSh way, or in an innermost Se way.

There is an array of SSS conditions that *would* likely enough result in the breaking of an object when subjected to a certain sort of stress. This would involve certain ranges of the shape it needs to be in, and certain ranges of how it must be situated. We who use objects of that sort are interested in certain particular combinations of Shapes and Situations, and we are pretty well implicitly agreed on what those are. Innermost fragility—that is, Seat—is then determined as the basis for the likely enough breaking of the fragile object if it were subjected to the relevant triggers in *those* Shape + Situation combinations.

We have a large and varied array of commonsense dispositional concepts: fragility, flammability, malleability, etc. These can perhaps all be understood in terms of our SSS structures, along with relevant triggers and outcomes. An object's outcome behavior manifests a given disposition, then, provided it flows causally from that disposition's triggering event(s), when the object has the relevant Seat, and is in the relevant Shape and Situation. What are the relevant shape, situation, trigger, and outcome associated with a certain dispositional concept? This may simply not be formulable in full explicit detail by humans who nonetheless agree sufficiently in their grasp and deployment of the concept. A particular disposition, then, will have a *distinctive* SSS profile, with restricted Shape and Situation. Not all dispositions to shatter amount to fragility. Zapper-dependent dispositions, for example, do not count.

3. But why should we have all this implicit agreement on how to categorize dispositions, and their special cases, such as abilities, and in turn competences? Why do we agree so extensively on whether an entity's output is to be attributed to a certain, recognized disposition hosted by that entity, as its manifestation, and by extension attributed to the entity itself?

When the output is good, it is then generally to the entity's credit, when bad to its discredit. The entity might be an agent who manifests a competence, or it might be a lifeless patient manifesting a mere disposition. Why do we agree so extensively on these dispositions, abilities, competences, and on the credit and discredit that they determine (whether this be to the credit of a moral agent, or to the credit of a sharp knife), and on the sortals that they help to constitute?[29]

Is that not all just part of the instrumentally determined common sense that humans live by?

Such common sense helps us keep track of potential benefits and dangers and how the bearers of these are to be handled. As a special case of how to handle things and agents that manifest dispositions and competences, we have propriety of encouraging praise or approval, or discouraging blame

---

29. Objection: *"The cases you are interested in here (cases of deviant causation, Gettier cases) are intermediate between the good and the bad cases. And it is interesting that our intuitions about credit tend not to be as clear in these cases. Take the case of the nervous waiter. When he succeeds in startling his boss, but succeeds because his nerves led him to drop the plates, is he blameworthy for this happening? I think many people will say yes, at least to some extent."* Reply: Perhaps. In any case, if my analogy with etiquette is apt, then competences will be subject to twilight zones, as is etiquette. Moreover, a subculture might recognize competences different to some extent from those recognized by the majority. Of course, this goes beyond the relativity of recognized competences to well-defined domains, such as those of particular sports, or of particular professions, or even scientific disciplines. We may not be interested in the knowledges that are specific to such domains. In general epistemology, we may focus rather on structural features of knowledge in general, and study these in connection with commonsense, general "knowledge."

or disapproval, which in turn helps to fix the relevant dispositions, abilities, and competences in ourselves and in our fellows.

Such an instrumentally determined common sense must of course be structured against background implicit assumptions about what is normal or standard, either in general or with respect to the specific domain of performance that may be contextually relevant. Many are the domains of human performance that allow and often require degrees of expertise beyond the ordinary: athletic, artistic, medical, academic, legal, etc., etc. Expert perception, agency, and knowledge would be determined proportionally to the respective levels of competence set for the specific domain. This is often set largely by convention, or, for more basic competences and dispositions, by the requirements of success in our evolutionary niche. After all, how we credit, discredit, trust, and distrust, has a large bearing on human flourishing, individually and collectively.

Manifestation determines credit and discredit, and is attributable causally to the host of the manifest disposition in a way that is projectible, though this is no more amenable to formulation than seems the projectibility of greenness (or "green") by contrast with grueness (or "grue"). When something shows its true colors through manifestation, we can take notice and revise our view of what to expect from the host of the manifest disposition. This is in contrast to when the disposition is only mimicked, so that the correlated trigger prompts the correlated ostensible manifestation, but only through the trumping action of the mimic. Such fake manifestation is not to the relevant credit, causal or otherwise, of the disposition. And the host in turn acquires no credit or discredit thereby.

4. Recall the mimicking of fragility when a fine wine glass is zapped upon hitting the hard floor. By hypothesis the causal action of our zapper trumps the inner structure of the glass, whereby it normally shatters on impact. Still that inner structure can be causally operative, as it is through the agency of the zapper (who hates the impact on the hard floor of the fragility that he spots in the fragile glass). Despite being causally operative in that way, through the knowledge of the zapper, that inner structure is not causally operative in the right way. And this is why the fragility that we normally attribute to the glass is not really manifest on that occasion.[30]

---

30. We might of course understand a broader, more determinable sort of "fragility" that generalizes from the situations we require for our ordinary fragility. This more determinable fragility would allow that an object acquires a temporary fragility in the presence of the hateful zapper. *This* sort of fragility the glass might even share temporarily with an iron dumbbell (so long as the zapper hovers and extends his hatred beyond fine glass hitting hardness to iron meeting hardness). However, that would be an extension of proper English; and of

When does the relevant belief, experience, or intention yield success in such a way that it is, respectively, knowledge, perception, or intentional action? That requires an SSS-joining of seated Skill, Shape, and Situation, so as to cause the manifestation upon the onset of the trigger. And this must occur appropriately. Consider for example what is required for a true manifestation of fragility as a fine wine glass shatters upon hitting the hard floor. The shattering of that glass does not manifest its fragility if it shatters because it is zapped by someone who hates fragility-meeting-hardness, if it is zapped with enough power to shatter an iron dumbbell. This despite the fact that, through the zapper's knowledge and action, he *does* manage to link causally the fragile structure of the glass with the shattering upon impact.

The example of fragility zapped suggests that a disposition can be manifest in a certain outcome only if it accounts *appropriately* for that outcome.[31] This requires a joining of seated skill, shape, and situation, so as to cause the manifestation, upon the onset of the trigger. And this must take place in the normal way, which by common consent excludes the action of our zapper, even when he does deviantly manage to link the trigger with the ostensible manifestation.

C. How We Go beyond Appeal to "The Right Way"

1. That is to present our account with a certain modesty, by relying explicitly on a requirement of "appropriateness." More boldly we might claim

---

proper cross-linguistic ideology, since the same surely goes linguistically for other natural languages. Our discussion in the main text suggests reasons why it might or might not be advisable to so extend our language and ideology. This would probably depend on how likely it is for the relevant community to encounter such zappers. Thus, recall the suggestion in the text: "Such an instrumentally determined common sense must of course be structured against background implicit assumptions about what is normal or standard, either in general or with respect to the specific domain of performance that may be contextually relevant."

Chapter 4 will develop a fuller account of competence, an account that recognizes the distinction between distal and proximal competences. Strictly, a fragile glass *can* manifest its fragility by shattering under weak enough zapping. And indeed fragility seems a proximal disposition involving the degree of (proximal) stress that will cause (relevant) disintegration. Epistemic competences are often enough importantly distal, however, since they include the empirical competences required for knowledge of the external world.

31. However surprising it may be to the verbally accomplished, much of our useful conceptual repertoire is not given substance, nor even so much as adequately described, through linguistic formulation. Our shared conceptual scheme of dispositions, abilities, competences, and their manifestations is plausibly a special case, where our agreement lacks explicitly

that when the power zapper shatters the glass because he knows it to be fragile, the shattering simply does not intuitively *manifest* the glass's fragility, and that there is no *need* to rely on any such requirement of appropriateness. Anyone who joins me in finding that plausible enough can make the following bold claim:

> Manifestation enables us to go beyond the need to rely on "the right way," or on "an appropriate way," or any such phrase. The manifestation of competences and other dispositions then provides a solution to the problem of specifying "the right or appropriate way" as it pertains to action, perception, and knowledge.[32]

That includes the problem of causal deviance. But it also includes a problem faced by Grice in his analysis of causation, not exactly a problem of deviance, but one that is closely related nonetheless. The causal bearing of our eyes on our visual experience is not really deviant, nor is that of the sun even when our eyes are open to the daylight with the sun out of view. However, Grice too must rely on an assumption that the causation linking an object and one's sensory experiences must be causation in a particular way to be brought out through examples.

Both problems of specifying the right, appropriate way are solved through a primitive relation of manifestation that has outcome manifestations (successful performances) on one side, and competences (perceptual, agential, epistemic) on the other. We can fail to see our eyes, as well as the sun, despite the heavy dependence of our visual experience on both, as we

---

formulable content. Coordinately, we also lack any non-trivial way of *securing* it through explicit convention. All of this is in line with how etiquette is constituted, learned, and invoked.

32. *Objection:* "*One pitfall of this approach is that it depends on there being widespread agreement, even if inarticulable, regarding instances of the right kind of causation or of manifestation. But there is disagreement over Gettier cases—some people think barn façade cases count, others do not.*" Reply: Yes, there is this dependence, but is it really a pitfall? Consider the growing sense among X-Phi researchers that, for the folk, Barney *does* know. Still, the clear majority opinion among philosophers who write on this topic is that he does not really "know." We can deal with this if the folk have implicitly in mind, for perceptual sorting competence, a situational condition wherein appearance (I mean *objective* appearance) goes with reality. And it is enough that, for the barn that Barney happens to see, that condition be met. Philosophers tend on the contrary to extend the situational condition further across modal space, so that the appearance/reality connection could not too easily fail or have failed for that subject at that time. According to common sense, given how Barney is propertied and related to his environment, too easily might he have faced a juncture with a failure of that sort, where the objective appearance set by a façade is *unaccompanied* by the reality of a real full barn. Here, I suggest, we might do well to recognize not just one but two "competences." Philosophers impose the more demanding of the two situational conditions. The folk are more easygoing.

view a sunlit scene. Our account would explain that failure by noting that we would have no corresponding images.

2. Some may well remain skeptical of the powers alleged for our primitive concept of "manifestation." To such skeptics we can offer, as a fallback, a more modest option whereby, perhaps through examples, we can still explain what is required for proper *manifestation*. And we could even disown any ambition to rely exclusively on explicit verbal formulation (as by invoking "manifestation").[33]

Even on this more modest option, we will have made progress. We will have specified more fully the *sort* of causation involved. And we will have seen that it is the *same* sort of causation in all three of our cases: in perception, in action, and in knowledge.

Fourth Part

Methodological Context for our Inquiry

In philosophy we often appeal to what we would ordinarily say, or think, in the exercise of generally shared concepts. But our main interest is not restricted to semantic or conceptual analysis. When we wonder about personal identity, freedom and responsibility, the mind and its states and contents, justice, rightness of action, happiness, and so on, our main focus is not, or not just, the words or the concepts. There are things beyond words and concepts whose nature we wish to understand. The metaphysics of persons goes beyond the semantics of the word "person" and its cognates, and even beyond the correlated conceptual analysis.

The same goes for epistemic concerns such as the nature of knowledge and other epistemic phenomena. Consider the semantics of epistemic vocabulary, and even the conceptual structure of epistemology and its normativity. It seems an open possibility that our words and concepts are not in the best shape, just as they stand, for grasping and understanding the relevant domain of objective phenomena. Why not leave open the possibility of terminological

---

33. We might even grant that we *cannot* rely exclusively on explicit verbal formulation. Analysts who live by the word might fail by the word. In analysis, whereof we cannot tell, thereof we might still show.

and conceptual improvement in epistemology in a way analogous to what is familiar in science when we reconfigure terminology? This often happens even with terms and concepts firmly entrenched in common sense, as with the ideology of fish, or of vegetables, fruits, and much else. If so, semantic and conceptual analysis might still remain an excellent start in epistemology. Such analysis would remain important in various ways to the epistemologist, and to the philosopher generally. But we might also be able to delineate phenomena whose importance is obscured by ordinary speech and thought.

If so, that might also, as a bonus, help throw light on pervasive and persistent disagreements so common in philosophy. Some of us may just be trying too hard for the exact, fully general semantic or conceptual analysis, one that will apply smoothly and directly to all thought experiments. And those of us impressed by a simple and illuminating take on some range of phenomena may just be right to "bite certain bullets," if by so doing we can distinguish a type of phenomenon that seems plainly important in the domain of interest, whose relations to other such phenomena should also be of interest. We may then reject an ostensible counterexample, while allowing that the example points to some further phenomena interestingly related to those of more direct and central interest to us in our specific inquiry.

Philosophical progress might then take a form *similar* to the kind of scientific progress that involves conceptual innovation. We may find in the phenomena themselves differences that seem important even if there are no proprietary terms or concepts that correspond to them neatly and without exception. If so, it may behoove us to stretch close terms or concepts so that they will help us to mark the relevant phenomena, and to cut the domain more closely at the joints.

Finally, once our objective is analysis that is metaphysical, rather than linguistic or conceptual, bullet-biting does *not* amount to giving up on intuitions. The metaphysical project is driven crucially by intuitions concerning the phenomena themselves, and not just by intuitions about the (proper use of) the language used to describe them, nor about the content of the related concepts. After all, to bite the bullet, on the proposal floated, is precisely not just to describe or understand but to *change* our given language or concepts, at least by addition, but perhaps also by subtraction, or by modification. True, the relevant metaphysical intuitions will need conceptual content, but our focus on the phenomena may lead to concepts that are modified, or even quite new. We need not be restricted to concepts used when we *begin* our inquiry. On the contrary, our inquiry may properly lead to revision.

2

Virtue Epistemology: Character versus Competence

Introduction

It has long been received wisdom that there are two quite distinct forms of virtue epistemology. One of these finds in epistemology important correlates of Aristotle's moral virtues. Such responsibilist character epistemology builds its account of epistemic normativity on the subject's responsible manifestation of epistemic character. The other form of virtue epistemology cleaves closer to Aristotelian intellectual virtues, while recognizing a broader set of competences still restricted to basic faculties of perception, introspection, and the like. This orthodox dichotomy of our field is deeply misleading, and will be challenged in this chapter.

1. In his book, *The Inquiring Mind*,[1] Jason Baehr argues for a distinctive approach, while presupposing the dichotomy and offering detailed critiques of rival approaches. Against my own virtue reliabilism, he charges that it deplorably neglects responsibilist, agential intellectual virtues. Against other responsibilists, he argues that character epistemology can have only very limited success with the issues of traditional epistemology, such as skepticism and the nature of knowledge. Given that there is more to epistemology than those perennial issues, he proposes a focus on his preferred character, responsibilist, agential virtue epistemology. This in his view is how we can best locate epistemological character traits within epistemology, thus bringing epistemology and ethics closer together than in the past.

---

1. Oxford: Oxford University Press, 2011. An outstanding contribution to virtue theory, the book is in large part a treatise on the relation between the two forms of virtue epistemology.

What is more, not only have virtue reliabilists neglected responsibilist, agential intellectual virtues, which are so important for issues beyond those of traditional epistemology. They have even overlooked how important responsibilist virtues are in dealing with those traditional issues once we consider levels of human knowledge more sophisticated than those attainable through simple mechanisms such as sensory perception.

Given how thoroughly and how well Baehr has discussed those issues in his book, that is an excellent place to start our own discussion. In particular, I will discuss his critique of my own alternative approach, and offer a defense. In its discussion of my views the book misfires, or so I will argue. But I aim to rise above polemics to an overview of virtue epistemology, one that reveals more fully the current state of the field, and options now available at its cutting edge.

2. Baehr contends "... that the concept of intellectual virtue does merit a secondary or supporting role" in traditional epistemological inquiry into the nature, conditions, and extent of human knowledge. By intellectual virtues, moreover, he means *responsibilist*, agential, character intellectual virtues, not reliabilist faculties. He concludes his fourth chapter as follows:

> We have seen that virtue reliabilists ... must expand their focus to include, not just the more mechanical or faculty-based dimension of human cognition, but also the more active, volitional, or character-based dimension.... The cost of *not* doing so, we have seen, is that reliabilists are unable to account for the sort of reliability involved with ... much of the knowledge that we as humans care most about.

3. I will defend four claims in response.

First, from its inception, virtue reliabilism has *always* had that expanded focus.

Second, responsibilists *have* advocated a *distinctive* conception of responsibilist, character-based intellectual virtue, but it is partial and inadequate.[2]

Third, and ironically, we should recognize a sort of active, volitional intellectual virtue that will be a special case of reliable-competence intellectual virtue.

---

2. On this, as we shall see, there is dissension in the ranks of responsibilists. Linda Zagzebski hopes and believes that responsibilist virtue theory can solve traditional problems of epistemology, whereas Baehr declares defeat, at least in crucial part. Here I side with Zagzebski's aspirations, but agree with Baehr that they have not yet been attained. Rather than conceding defeat, however, I will offer a better responsibilist account, one that welcomes responsibilism at the core of virtue reliabilism.

Fourth and finally, we can best understand the responsibilist, character-based intellectual virtues highlighted by responsibilists as *auxiliary* to the virtues that are a special case of reliable-competence intellectual virtue.

A true epistemology will indeed assign to such responsibilist-cum-reliabilist intellectual virtue the *main* role in addressing concerns at the center of the tradition. To anticipate, here is why that is so: because the *sort* of knowledge at the center of traditional epistemology, from the Pyrrhonists through Descartes, is high-level *reflective* knowledge.[3] This is a knowledge requiring free, volitional endorsement by the subject who judges, or the corresponding disposition. Ironically, our reliabilist framework did always potentially, and does increasingly (actually and explicitly) give the place of honor to the agential, volitional approach, a central place that responsibilists either emphatically deny to it (Baehr), or do not successfully provide for it (Zagzebski).

So, my main thesis will be that reliabilist, competence-based virtue epistemology must be understood broadly, in a more positively ecumenical way, with responsibilist agential intellectual virtues at its core.[4]

Before we turn to that, however, here follows a defense against the specific critique offered by Baehr in his book.

A. Character Theory versus Competence Theory

We begin with quotations showing responsibilist competences to have been present in virtue reliabilism from its inception. Here are two relevant passages (from among many).

1. First an early passage:[5]

   Note that no human blessed with reason has merely animal knowledge of the sort attainable by beasts. For even when perceptual belief derives as directly as it ever does from sensory stimuli, it is still relevant that one has *not* perceived the signs of contrary testimony.... [E]ven when response to stimuli is most

---

3. Part IV will make a detailed case for this: in Chapter 10 re. Pyrrhonism, and in Chapter 11 re. Descartes.
4. In what follows I will characterize my view indifferently as "reliabilist" or "competence" virtue epistemology (CVE).
5. Ernest Sosa, *Knowledge in Perspective* (Cambridge: Cambridge University Press, 1991), 240.

direct, *if* one were also to hear or see the signs of credible contrary testimony, that would change one's response. The beliefs of a *rational* animal hence would seem never to issue from *unaided* introspection, memory, or perception. For reason is always at least a silent partner on the watch for other relevant data, a silent partner whose very *silence* is a contributing cause of the belief outcome.

That same view stays in place over the many succeeding years until we reach the following:

> I speak of "mechanisms" or processes of belief formation, and sometimes of "input/output mechanisms," but I want to disavow explicitly any implication that these are simple or modular. . . .[A] mechanism can be something close to a reflex, or it can be a very high-level, central-processing ability of the sort that enables a sensitive critic to "decide" how to assess a work, based on complex and able pondering.[6]

Of course the intention was always to explain knowledge of all sorts, including sorts where the competences involved are those of a skilled art critic, scientist, mathematician, or detective, and not just the sorting competence of a chicken sexer.[7]

2. Those quoted passages should already lay to rest the notion that virtue reliabilism is *restricted* to peripheral or modular or automatic mechanisms of belief formation. What then can possibly have suggested that virtue reliabilism *does* exclude the more sophisticated, actively volitional dimensions of our cognitive lives? Consider this from Baehr's book:

> The tight logical connection between character virtues and faculty virtues is also evident in the fact that when epistemologists offer detailed characterizations of the latter, they have a hard time avoiding talk of the former. Sosa, for instance, in a discussion regarding the fallibility of faculty virtues, notes that the reliability of one's cognitive faculties can be affected by one's intellectual *conduct*. Interestingly, the conduct he proceeds to describe is precisely that of certain intellectual character virtues and vices. . . .
>
> . . . Again, an exercise of character virtues is often manifested in and partly constituted by the operation of certain faculty virtues. Moreover, as the passages from Sosa indicate, the reliability of faculty virtues often implicates one or more character virtues. Therefore the attempt to make a principled

---

6. Note 9 of ch. 4, "Epistemic Normativity," of my *A Virtue Epistemology* (Oxford: Oxford University Press, 2007)
7. And, besides, dictionaries reveal that a "mechanism" need not reside in a machine. A google search will turn up "trading mechanisms," "defense mechanisms," "mechanisms for dealing with stress," etc.

exclusion of character virtues from the reliabilist repertoire of intellectual virtues on the grounds that faculty virtues but not character virtues are "sources" of belief seems bound to fail.[8]

The *restrictive* view attributed to me may well need correction, but it never has been my view. The attribution is based on no supportive reference, but only on what is "suggested" by the simplicity of the examples that I use as clear cases of simple knowledge to be explained. It is assumed that the view is *restricted* to the sorts of competences in examples of simple perceptual, introspective, or mnemonic knowledge. But no such explicit restriction can be found in my published work. Passages *are* cited (as Baehr indicates above) where I show clear signs of making *no such restriction*, but those passages are used (surprisingly) to demonstrate the *inadequacy* of my view, for imposing such a restriction. Nevertheless, what has never been *excluded* from my virtue reliabilism is *agential competences*.

On the contrary, the right conclusion is that the restrictive view is *not* my view. I restrict not the competences but only the examples. I focus on those simple enough to reveal more starkly certain basic problems that any theory of knowledge must solve. Further problems may of course arise when less simple instances of knowledge are highlighted. But first things first, and frankly it has been challenging enough to try to deal with the simpler examples first.[9] Although I have always recognized *both* an animal and a reflective level of knowledge, as it happens my current project is to develop the more agential and reflective side of my virtue epistemology.[10]

3. What could have led to the misunderstanding of my position? *In part*, the reason may perhaps emerge in the following note of Baehr's:

> As I note below, an additional requirement for what Sosa calls "reflective" or "human" knowledge is that the person in question have an "epistemic perspective" on the known belief, which consists of an additional set of coherent beliefs about the source and reliability of the original belief (see 1991: ch. 11). *Our concern here, however, lies with the virtue component of Sosa's analysis.*[11]

---

8. These passages are from the concluding paragraphs of section 4.2 of Baehr's book.
9. What follows will take up problems of epistemic agency as its main focus, and will exploit distinctions that deal directly with additional problems that arise once virtue epistemology becomes more explicitly and voluntaristically agential.
10. And I am now fully engaged in the project; witness the present text.
11. This is note 4 of chapter 4 of Baehr's book. Italics added. The reference is to my *Knowledge in Perspective*.

Here Baehr restricts his discussion of my views to their *animal* component, leaving aside the *reflective* component. Is it any wonder that virtue reliabilism is thought to neglect the active, agential, responsibilist side of epistemology, *when its main attempt to do so is left out of account*?

Does virtue reliabilism leave out agency? Does it at least leave out the conscious, intentional, volitional agency that is involved in deliberation and in conscious pondering, or weighing of reasons? Not at all; *at most*, the animal side of virtue reliabilism would be guilty of such negligence if it aspired to be an account of *all* human knowledge.[12] But it has no such ambition. Rather, it has always been joined to an account of the more distinctively human sort of knowledge, the *reflective* sort.

4. Baehr lays out what he takes to be the formal conditions that must be satisfied by any intellectual virtue, *according to Competence Virtue Epistemology*:

> IV-CVE *What Intellectual Virtues Are According to Competence Virtue Epistemology* (according to Baehr)
>
> [Intellectual virtues are] personal qualities that, under certain conditions and with respect to certain propositions, are reliable means to reaching the truth and avoiding error.

And he attributes to John Greco the idea that intellectual virtues would need to play a critical or salient role in explaining why a person reaches the truth.

Baehr focuses on agential virtues. These virtues have, in his view, certain distinctive features:

a. They are virtues exercised in intentional agency.
b. They are developed through repeated agency.
c. They bear on the personal worth of the possessor.
d. They aid agential success.
e. In epistemology, they concern intentionally conducted inquiry.[13]

Because of its focus on traditional faculties such as perception, memory, and inference, virtue reliabilism is said to *overlook character traits*, such as open-mindedness and intellectual courage. These traits are said to possess the five features of agential virtues listed, and to satisfy the formal

---

12. In fact, not even animal knowledge is necessarily so exclusive, as should have been clear already in the main text, and will be emphasized in section D3.
13. Baehr, *passim*; e.g., section 2.2.1, pp. 22–5.

conditions accepted by competence virtue epistemology (spelled out in *IV-CVE* above). Such overlooked character traits are indeed, under certain conditions and with respect to certain propositions, a reliable means to reaching the truth and avoiding error, and their exercise can most saliently explain why the subject gets it right in believing as they do.

Does competence virtue epistemology (virtue reliabilism) plead guilty?

5. Reliabilist intellectual virtues, according to Baehr's *IV-CVE*, are to be understood *simply*, by definition, as traits (a) whose manifestations reliably yield true belief, and (b) that *play a salient role* in explaining why one reaches the truth in cases where one does so. That is indeed an account in the literature, an account of epistemically relevant belief-yielding sources. And there are early passages of mine, such as the following, which might misleadingly suggest that I subscribe to that account:

> We have reached the view that knowledge is true belief out of intellectual virtue, belief that turns out right by reason of the virtue and not just by coincidence.[14]

Although I later retain that view of knowledge,[15] my account of intellectual virtues still differs from *IV-CVE* in a way that matters for how we should understand virtue reliabilism, or so I will now argue.

6. Competence virtue epistemology aims to solve two Platonic problems: the *Theaetetus* problem as to the nature of knowledge, and the *Meno* problem as to its distinctive value. Knowledge is analyzed as belief whose correctness manifests the believer's pertinent competence. So, the pertinent competence (the pertinent reliabilist intellectual virtue) must be one whose exercise can *constitute* knowledge. That is what I claim knowledge *to be*: belief that is correct, that thus succeeds, through the exercise of competence. At least, that is what an important, basic sort of knowledge amounts to.[16] However, the

---

14. *Knowledge in Perspective*, 277. This, by the way, is the earliest statement of the *knowledge as apt belief* view of knowledge, so in advocating it I do not follow suit, contrary to Baehr's footnote 8, on p. 37.
15. This is emphasized in footnote 2 of ch. 2 of Sosa, *A Virtue Epistemology*. That footnote makes it explicit that the view developed in that later book is essentially that same view, now better formulated, based on an improved conception of aptness, with its scope explicitly amplified to cover performances generally. And the conception of intellectual virtues required for this view differs importantly from the *IV-CVE* that Baehr attributes to virtue reliabilists.
16. Here I have in mind *credal* (belief-constituted) animal knowledge. We shall find in due course that there is a *sub*credal sort of animal knowledge.

"through" must be restricted. A belief might attain correctness "through" competence only because the exercise of competence puts one *in a position to know*. And that will not suffice to make that correct belief an instance of knowledge. For, that exercise of competence may not immediately take the form of the correctness of a belief. It may rather take the form of putting one in a position to exercise a competence, such as *sorting by eyesight*, whose exercise *does* amount to a correct belief, a correct sorting.

It may be thought that a virtue such as open-mindedness or intellectual courage could be a directly knowledge-constitutive virtue. Accordingly, Baehr alleges, the reliabilist, competence-based view neglects responsibilist virtues that it should welcome within its fold, since they too can be important in explaining how a subject gets it right. And it must indeed be granted that, in certain instances, a responsibilist virtue can provide the salient explanation, especially where the truth must be won through complex and competent effort. Courageous and open-minded pursuit of truth—by a scientist, or journalist, or detective—might well enable someone to uncover a truth that escapes all others. Baehr has a telling objection to any form of reliabilist virtue epistemology that requires for knowledge only that the correctness of the knowing subject's belief must derive somehow, perhaps at a great remove, from the exercise of a certain intellectual virtue that is normally a reliable aid to reaching the truth. Such a form of virtue epistemology *would* be negligent if it ignored, or declared irrelevant, any responsibilist virtues that did help one attain truth, including open-mindedness and intellectual courage.

However, Baehr's objection is not relevant to a virtue reliabilism for which the virtues or competences that matter are not simply those whose exercise through inquiry can reliably help one reach the truth. In my view, for example, there are distinctive competences whose exercise can *constitute* knowledge. And a competence whose exercise reliably aids our search for truth—*even* so as to be the salient explanation of why truth is then attained—might easily be one whose exercise would *not* constitute knowledge. It may just fail to be of the right sort to be thus constitutive.

For example, a scientist may follow a healthy regimen with strict discipline, and her good health may help explain why she makes her discoveries, by contrast with her wan, depressed rivals; and may even be the salient explanation.

Or, it might work the other way around. It might be that someone's obsessive pursuit of truth, even at the cost of malnourishment and depression, puts them in a position to attain truths that are denied to their healthy rivals.

Even if such obsession to the point of ill health does reliably lead to truth on certain matters inaccessible otherwise (even *if*, I say), the exercise of such personal qualities (obsessiveness) would hardly *constitute* knowledge. The long hours, the intense concentration, the single-minded avoidance of distractions, may put the inquirer in a situation, or enable her to attain a frame of mind, or certain skills, through all of which she can have and exercise the competences more directly relevant to the attainment of knowledge. She might acquire important data through a perilous voyage to distant lands, or through extensive observation of the night sky, none of which she could have done without persistent dedication over many years with enormous care.

7. But the point does not require reference to the heroics of a Darwin or a Brahe. A simple example from everyday life should suffice. Suppose a mysterious box lies closed before us, and we wonder what it contains. How can we find out? We might of course just open the lid. In pursuit of this objective we will then exercise certain competences, perhaps even character traits (if the box is locked, or the lid stuck), such as persistence and resourcefulness. And perhaps these qualities (in certain contexts, and in certain combinations) do lead us reliably to the truth. Nevertheless, the exercise of *such* intellectual virtues need not and normally will not *constitute* knowledge, not even when that exercise does indirectly lead us to the truth.

Contrast what happens when we manage to open the lid and look inside. Now we may immediately know the answer to our question, with a perceptual belief—say, *that there is a necklace in the box*—which manifests certain cognitive competences for gaining visual experience and belief. Perhaps this complex, knowledge-constitutive competence first leads to things seeming perceptually a certain way, and eventually to the belief that things are indeed that way, absent contrary indications. A belief manifesting *such* a competence, and, crucially, one whose *correctness* manifests such a competence, *does* constitute knowledge, at a minimum animal knowledge, perhaps even full-fledged knowledge (including a reflective component).

It is such knowledge-constitutive competences that are of main interest to a Competence Virtue Epistemology aiming to explain human knowledge. Other epistemically important traits—such as open-mindedness, intellectual courage, persistence, and even single-minded obsessiveness—are indeed of interest to a broader epistemology. They are of course worthy of serious study. But they are not in the charmed inner circle for traditional epistemology. They are only "auxiliary" intellectual virtues, by contrast with the "constitutive" intellectual virtues of central interest to virtue reliabilism.

My distinction has on one side intellectual virtues whose manifestation *helps to put you in a position to know,* and on the other intellectual virtues whose manifestation in the *correctness* of a belief thereby *constitutes a bit of knowledge.*[17] In my view, a competence can *constitute* (credal) knowledge only if it is a disposition that can be manifest in the correctness of the constitutive belief. A competence in general is a disposition to succeed with a certain aim, and a competence to believe correctly is a special case of that.

The crucial point is that a competence whose exercise can aid one's attaining a correct and even an apt belief is not necessarily one that is *manifest* in any such attainments. For it *need not* be a competence *to attain* any such things as correctness or aptness, despite being a competence whose exercise *furthers* such attainments. The competences of focal interest to competence virtue epistemology are those whose manifestations in such attainments *constitute* knowledge. These are the competences whose manifestations constitute apt belief.

8. Granted, the avoidance of negligence can be constitutive of a full competence whose manifestations might constitute knowledge. And character traits such as open-mindedness and intellectual courage might help us avoid such epistemic negligence. But their role would be epistemically tangential. What really matters here for epistemology is the *epistemically* auxiliary virtue of avoiding negligence. This might in a particular case be aided by an ethical virtue of intellectual courage (proper assessment of whether a certain degree of personal risk is worth taking for the sake of a bit of knowledge on a certain question whose answer would be personally valuable). But the role of such courage is ethical and only accidentally epistemic. Thus, consider readily available evidence whose lack would block the agent from knowledge on the question at hand. Obtaining such *epistemically* needed evidence might require a crazy degree of personal foolhardiness rather than any ethically proper intellectual courage.

Accordingly, we should distinguish between an intellectual ethics that is purely epistemic, and an intellectual ethics that is properly a part of ethics. Suppose what makes "open-mindedness" a virtue is (even just partly) that it is required for the proper respect due our fellow rational creatures, simply because other members of a kingdom of ends are *deserving* of such

---

17. To be "in a position to know" that p is in my view to possess the complete competence whose manifestation in a true belief that p (or, better, in a true *and apt* belief that p) would constitute one's knowledge that p (or one's knowledge *full well* that p). This idea will be developed more fully below, as in Chapter 4, with an account of competence (the "SSS" account).

treatment. Or suppose "intellectual courage" is thought to be a virtue in a certain instance because it helps us properly to assess how much personal risk to take for an answer to a certain question. This would presumably involve estimating the proper value of having that answer and comparing this with the risk to one's personal welfare. Such open-mindedness and such intellectual courage would then be properly *ethical* competences, part of corresponding *ethical* virtue (where the full virtue would include not only intellectual assessment, as above, but also an executive competence to act on that assessment, thus avoiding *akrasia*, for one thing).

The study of such ethical intellectual competences and virtues would be a part of applied ethics. Biomedical ethics is a branch of ethics that studies ethical issues concerning the practice of medicine, or of biomedical research, *in particular*. Business ethics is a branch of ethics that studies ethical issues concerning the practice of business in particular. A correlate intellectual ethics is thus a branch of ethics that studies ethical issues concerning scientific or other research, and concerning the value of various sorts of knowledge for human flourishing, and concerning issues of the acquisition and retention and sharing of such knowledge. Et cetera.

What then is the implied contrast? What would be the purely epistemic correlates of such ethical competences or virtues of open-mindedness or intellectual courage? For the purely epistemic correlates we would bracket any *specific* evaluative or ethical values or desiderata. In determining how we ought to proceed, individually or collectively, we would take a question as given. By contrast, the assessment of what questions are properly pursued does seem straightforwardly a question of ethics. Once a question is given, however, there arises the familiar threefold issue: affirmation, denial, suspension. If, for simplicity, we restrict ourselves to cases of conscious judgment, then our threefold issue is a matter of choice. The epistemic agent faces a choice among three intentional actions. In making that choice, one might take certain preliminary steps (such as opening the lid of a mysterious box, in order to find out what it contains, or such as seeking evidence, which is readily available, and which it would be *epistemically* negligent to disregard). In determining one's answer—once having gathered enough evidence to avoid negligence—one can now make one's choice, in doing which one should exercise proper *care* and *attentiveness*, which will enhance the reliability of one's choice procedure.

I hope our example will have suggested traits of *purely epistemic intellectual character* that can bear on one's epistemic threefold choice. Some of these are competences and virtues of inquiry, of how to put oneself *in a position to know* (often in an *evidential* position to know). But others are competences and virtues of *judgment* proper, as with proper care and attentiveness. The latter can be manifestations, in a particular case, of stable character traits of an epistemic agent. As such, they will help constitute the complete intellectual competences or virtues that the agent exercises and manifests in particular judgments, and in the correctness of these judgments. So, these traits will be implicated in competences whose manifestations might constitute the agent's knowledge.

Other such traits—intellectual perseverance, for example—will be virtues of inquiry. These will not be part of the competences whose manifestation might constitute the agent's knowledge. Someone lazy could have as much knowledge in a given domain as would someone industrious. The lazy knower could just by luck be placed in the position to know, a position that the industrious knower would need to win with much effort and persistence. The lid that someone industrious would have to pry open laboriously might just open of its own accord for someone lazy. And so on.

So, intellectual virtues of both sorts can be stable traits of character, and some are indeed constitutive of the competences whose manifestation in true belief (and in true and apt belief) amount to human knowledge. But these are all *purely intellectual* virtues, with no admixture of practical assessment. The factors involved in their exercise are only the purely epistemic factors of truth and aptness. So these are not matters of the applied intellectual ethics sketched above. They are rather integral to a *purely epistemic* intellectual ethics.

B. Responsibilist Virtue Epistemology: Baehr versus Zagzebski

Here is the internecine disagreement in brief.

1. Baehr and Zagzebski share a high-minded conception of intellectual virtues. For them these are character traits that bear on the personal worth of the *person*. They are inherently motivational. Such virtuous character traits are manifest in actions that must be motivated by a virtuous pursuit of the truth. In their view, a belief that derives (at least in important part) from such a virtue must derive from actions that express the subject's love of truth.

2. Zagzebski believes that such character-based responsibilist epistemology can help with the traditional problematic of epistemology, at the core of which is the project of defining knowledge. Indeed, for Zagzebski it is emphatically *this* motivational component that explains the distinctive value of knowledge, the value that knowledge has beyond whatever value might be found in the corresponding merely true belief. So, she proposes that knowledge is best understood as belief that gets it right through such responsibilist intellectual virtue.[18]

3. For Baehr, however, that approach is blocked by simple counterexamples, such as a pang of pain, or a strike of lightning out of the blue, which one knowingly discerns with no delay. These one *can't help knowing*, sans deliberation and *unmotivated* by love of truth.

4. Zagzebski responds:

> [My definition] . . . does not rule out easy knowledge by sense perception. A person who believes that she sees an easily identifiable object typically knows that she sees the object, provided that there are no indications in her environment that she should not trust her visual sense or understanding of the concept under which the object falls.[19]

And she extends the point to testimony, and presumably would go further.[20]

---

18. Occasionally, and more recently, she takes the somewhat different view that it is the knowledge that *does* manifest such high-ranking virtues that has relevant distinctive value, even if there is a lower order of knowledge that lacks it. But this will not help with the Meno problem, which is not really solved through appeal to such worthy belief motivated by the love of truth. What makes knowledge of the right way to Larissa better than mere true belief need not depend on its being an achievement that deserves admiration, nor on its being pregnant with pragmatic value. This is increasingly clear if we switch the example to one of knowing which is the *shortest* road to Larissa. Of the two obvious roads, the shortest may be just infinitesimally shorter, so that its increment of pragmatic value is negligible, nor is one motivated by love of truth, by contrast with desire for instrumental means. Moreover, one's knowledge may have been attained through the most ordinary testimony, by asking a passer-by, which would merit little personal credit or admiration. And yet knowing what one believes is in that case still better than merely getting it right by luck. The sense in which it is still better comports with the fact that epistemology is not a department of ethics. Epistemic attainments, like good shots, are not quite generally and inherently valuable in any objective sense. In spite of that, the good ones are still "better" than alternatives even so. Knowledge is in that way a better attainment than belief that does not succeed or does so just by luck. But this *general* superiority is not a quasi-ethical matter of motivation. It is rather a matter of competence, which is often and importantly enough a matter of intentional agency, but can also be just a matter of functional, biological, or psychological teleology.
19. Linda Zagzebski, *On Epistemology* (Belmont, CA: Wadsworth, 2008), ch. 5, p. 128.
20. Compare Sosa, *Knowledge in Perspective*, 240: "The beliefs of a *rational* animal hence would seem never to issue from *unaided* introspection, memory, or perception. For reason is always

5. But Baehr insists as follows:[21]

> [If as I work late at night there is a power outage] ... I am, as it were, *overcome* by knowledge that the lighting in the room has changed. ... Nor is it plausible to think that I am "trusting my senses" in the relevant, motivational sense. ... Again, knowledge of this sort seems not to involve or implicate the knower's agency at all.

And this line of criticism seems right at least to the following extent. We cannot explain the appropriateness of the belief that the room has gone dark as a matter of *non-negligent agency*, if that belief is *not at all* a product of intentional agency, which is the sort of agency important to character epistemology. Surely *motivation* relates to agency, not to passive reactions that approximate or constitute mere reflexes.

It might be replied that one can take a kind of agential credit for a locomotive's staying on a certain track, despite one's having actively intervened *not at all*. One might still deserve credit even so, *if* there have been junctures where as conductor one could have intervened, where one was free to intervene and, without negligence, freely opted not to do so. Unfortunately, this will not do. The problem is that in the cases urged by the critics, there is no freedom to intervene in what seems clearly to be a belief, and even an instance of knowledge, as with the knowledge that the room has gone dark.

6. Here is the upshot. If we restrict responsibilist virtues to those that are *both* agential *and* bear on the personal worth of the agent, in virtue of their motivational component, then Baehr is right to think that we cannot build a traditional epistemology on such virtues, and Zagzebski wrong to think otherwise. Not even knowledge can be accounted for in those terms. However, in my view Zagzebski is right to think that a traditional epistemology *can* be built on responsibilist virtues, and Baehr wrong to think otherwise. Where they both go wrong is in supposing that responsibilist virtues must involve the personal worth of the agent, must be virtues of *that* sort, involving motivation that passes muster.

Moreover, my point here cannot be dismissed as *merely* terminological. Understood in a metaphysically interesting way, my claim is that the relevant kinds for building a responsibilist virtue epistemology are not just the

---

at least a silent partner on the watch for other relevant data, a silent partner whose very *silence* is a contributing cause of the belief outcome."

21. *The Inquiring Mind*, 44.

following two: (a) non-agential faculties, and (b) personal-worth-involving, motivationally appropriate agential virtuous competences. We may or may not consider the latter to be a category or kind worth emphasizing. We may or may not consider it worth emphasizing in a responsibilism that aspires to solve traditional epistemological problems. Regardless of all that, there is at a minimum *also or instead* the following epistemic kind: (c) agential virtues. *These obviously go beyond non-agential faculties. So, they go beyond a reliabilism restricted to such faculties.* And so I submit that they can reasonably be considered "responsibilist" intellectual virtues, in the sense that agents would be epistemically, agentially responsible in exercising them, and irresponsible through their neglect, and even vicious through exercise of conflicting dispositions. In other words, they are traits or competences of agents as agents. And among these are the traits or competences of conscious, intentional agents as such.

C. Virtue Epistemology: Responsibilism as a Kind of Reliabilism

1. In order to circumvent the impasse within responsibilism, we must first be clear that epistemology is not a department of ethics. An extremely high epistemic status, certain knowledge, can be attained with a deplorable state that represents a sad waste of time, as when someone spends a morning determining with certitude how many beans are left in their coffee bag.

Moreover, that is quite compatible with there being special instances of knowledge that *are* outstanding accomplishments, which require an admirable love of truth (on a certain matter) and willingness to pursue it with persistent toil and sacrifice. And it is also compatible with the fact that *possessing knowledge of certain sorts*, for various sorts, is an indispensable part of any flourishing life. Moreover, having sufficient knowledge of a certain sort may be indispensable without *any* particular bits of knowledge of that sort being indispensable, or even much desirable.

Independently of all that, it remains that there is a distinctive dimension of epistemic assessment isolated from all such broadly ethical (or prudential) concerns. Moreover, within this epistemic dimension, love of truth plays a negligible role *at most*, if any at all. Hedge fund managers, waste disposal engineers, dentists, and their receptionists, can all attain much knowledge in the course of an ordinary workday despite the fact that they seek the truths relevant to their work only for their instrumental value. That is why they want them, not because they *love* truth. That seems indeed to be true of service professionals generally, including medical doctors and lawyers. It is not love of truth that routinely drives their professional activities, by contrast with desire for professional standing, wanting to help someone, or trying to make a living.

Disinterested, high-minded motivation must be distinguished from intentional, volitional agency, as must even any sort of positive motivation, except the *purely* instrumental. Dispositions to succeed when one tries need not be closely allied with, and much less do they need to be constituted by, a high-minded motivation, one that can bear on the personal worth of the agent, on how fine a person they are. Professionals *are* indeed routinely engaged in intentional, volitional truth-seeking in their work lives, even when they do not disinterestedly, lovingly seek the truth. Nor need they evince any "respect" for the truth, properly so-called. An assassin may even have *no desire whatever* for the truth on the location of his victim *except only* for the fact that it will make his crime possible. Indeed, if he thought a false belief would at that juncture get him more efficiently to his objective he might heartily approve of his so believing, and be glad he did so, with no regrets whatever. His search for truth, since agential, is subject to the full range of responsibilist assessment nonetheless. And his knowing the location of the victim in believing as he does about that location, is still better *epistemically* than his *merely* believing correctly, and of course better epistemically than his believing incorrectly. Similarly, his shot may be an excellently apt shot, and thereby better than an inapt shot (whether successful or not), despite the murderous motivating intention. (That is to say, it is better *as a shot*; it is *a better shot*. It need not be a better entity, or a better thing to happen, nonetheless.)

In conclusion, once we distinguish the *sort* of comparative evaluation (epistemic *performance* evaluation) that is involved in our taking knowledge to surpass merely true belief in (the relevant sort of) value, this removes any temptation to take personally laudable motivation to be the key, even if *in a broad sense* one's cognitive prowess may be a component of one's personal worth, as might be the shooting prowess of our assassin. *Broad* "personal worth" is not what responsibilist, character epistemologists have in mind, at least not Baehr. The assassin is not a better person for being such a good shot. A more accomplished person, yes, but not a better person, in any sense closely related to ethical assessment.

2. Someone might believe in knowledge only as power and in accuracy only as instrument. So, he neither endorses nor does he adhere in general to any truth-centric norm such as: *It is correct to believe P only if P is true.* Rather, what he endorses and adheres to is this: *It is correct to believe P only if so believing will help me gain fame, wealth, and power.* (Notoriously, such people abound, and some even become famous, wealthy, and powerful.)

Someone like that can still attain vast stores of useful knowledge, however, so long as they keep track of the areas of life where they need to supplement their deep indifference to objective value (to what is true, good, beautiful, just, honest, etc.). They do not care one bit about any such value, nor even, truth be told, about their own happiness or pleasure, except only insofar as their favoring and pursuing any such normal values will gain them fame, wealth, or power. Such monstrosity is quite compatible with the acquisition of vast stores of knowledge useful to the monster, well beyond the normal allotment enjoyed by a more normal human being. How so? Because the monster can be super-intelligent, and can discern when he had better ensure that his beliefs are true, but only because access to the truth is required if he is at all likely to attain his deepest objectives, which are restricted to self-aggrandizement. So, he does follow the norm of believing only what is true in those instances, but he does so exclusively for his own twisted ends.

Might such considerations apply to epistemic cases like that of some schoolchild learning his tables, or some accountant doing his thing, or a dental assistant using her records? Someone might after many years of rote labor still attain knowledge and well-justified belief despite how much they despise having to go through their motions in order to attain the knowledge that they need instrumentally for the attainment of their non-epistemic objectives.[22]

Let us next turn to a second distinction that will help accommodate responsibilism properly in epistemology.

---

22. Properly understood, might some subjects like this be epistemically irrational even if perfectly knowledgeable? Kurt Sylvan takes up related issues concerning rationality, rather than knowledge, in "Truth Monism without Teleology" in *Thought*, 1.3 (2012): 161–9; and in *On the Normativity of Epistemic Rationality* (Ph.D. Thesis, Rutgers University, 2013). And he continues to develop that view in papers under preparation.

3. At a certain level of abstraction, we can distinguish two sorts of "belief," one implicit and *merely* functional, the other not merely functional but intentional, perhaps even consciously intentional. It is the latter that needs our attention in giving *responsibilism* its proper place in epistemology. This is because our rational nature is most fully manifest in such reasoned choice and judgment. Accordingly, it is consciously, rationally endorsed judgment that is at the focus of the epistemological tradition from the Pyrrhonists through Descartes. It is not only the *act* of conscious, intentional judgment that is of interest, however, since by extension there is also the correlated *disposition* to judge upon consideration.

Still, although we do not here focus on functional, implicit belief, what we learn about intentional belief—even conscious, intentional belief—should carry over to belief generally, whether intentional or merely functional. The key to the carryover would be a conception of functional belief as still aimed at truth, or at representing accurately and reliably enough. Functional belief might aim at truth only functionally: for example, through psychological or biological teleology. This would enable thinking of functional belief also as a kind of action, even when it is only implicit, and neither *conscious* nor *intentional*. Anyhow, I distinguish such functional belief only to put it aside, so as to focus on the sort of belief that does turn out to be a form of intentional action.

What is intentional belief? How is it structured? We focus on affirmation, and the corresponding disposition to affirm, in the endeavor to answer a given question correctly.[23] Consider the great importance of these for a collaborative social species. Affirmation seems essentially required for collaborative deliberation and for information sharing. Take *collaborative deliberation*, right up to the most complex, as in a nation's governance; also, *information sharing*, crucial as it is in a great many contexts, prominently in scientific inquiry.

Such affirmation can be conscious and intentional. If you add a column of figures in your head, for example, you may seemingly obtain a certain result. But if the problem is complex enough, you may still hesitate to affirm accordingly. You may first take out pencil and paper, or a calculator. Eventually, coincidence of results may provide strong enough evidence,

---

23. In what follows, nearly always "affirmation" will be short for "*alethic* affirmation" (where what makes it "alethic" is that it is aimed at truth).

which leads you to assent (properly so). You *decide* when to assent; you wait until the evidence is strong enough.[24]

We need not assume, however, that affirmation *must* be conscious. Even when a chain of reasoning takes place *silently*, with no conscious inner speech, there must be *steps* of reasoning sequentially involved. And these steps are presumably occurrent events rather than pure dispositions. Such steps are then taken intentionally, in pursuit of truth on the question addressed. They are hence acts of "affirmation," even if they are relevantly silent and subconscious.[25]

We focus on such intentional, judgmental belief. How is it structured? Judgmental belief is definable as a certain sort of disposition to affirm. What sort of disposition? For a start let us take *judgment* that p to be a certain sort of *alethic* affirmation, *in the endeavor to get it right on whether p*. Judgmental *belief* can then be understood as a certain sort of *disposition to judge* in the endeavor to get it right on whether p, if one so endeavors.

Compare pragmatic affirmation, whether as a means *to reduce cognitive/affective dissonance*, or *to instill confidence that will enhance performance*, or the like. On our conception the latter is not proper belief. It is rather a sort of "make-belief" or mock belief.[26]

---

24. This is both how it seems (at least to me) and, in the absence of any ostensible defeating reason, this is (I say) how it is. I find that claim no less proper than the following: that sometimes I *decide* to raise my right hand, and that sometimes I *know* that I see my right hand (and see it go up); that these things seem to me to be so, and that, in the absence of ostensible defeating reasons, they really are so.
25. The implicit *reasoning* that we often postulate would seem to be a sequential causal process that is episodic, whereby there are immediate inferences at various junctures and preservation of lemmas in memory. And the drawing of the immediate inference, even when subconscious, will be episodic. So, our postulation requires episodic *acts*. If there is subconscious *conditional* reasoning, then some such acts will be suppositional, and will not plausibly count as affirmations. But not *all* subconscious reasoning that we have reason to postulate will be just conditional reasoning. And when reasoning is *not* conditional, then it will be affirmational, and steps of *such* reasoning would seem to count as acts, not just dispositions. These then are the acts that I am viewing as subconscious affirmations.
26. It might be wondered whether this cuts psychological reality at the joints. Although I am not entirely sure what is at issue in this question, I do think there is such a thing as the act of affirming, and that it can take the form of public assertion or that of private affirmation to oneself. I think that this is an act of crucial importance for a social species that depends as heavily as we do on collective deliberation and on the sharing of information. Moreover, it also seems crucial to distinguish various importantly different objectives that one might have in performing that act. And, for epistemology, there is a particularly important intention that one might have in performing it, namely that of getting it right *thereby* on the relevant whether question: the act of *alethic* affirmation. And, I submit, we do well to recognize a further particular act for special attention: the act of affirming in the endeavor *thereby* to

4. What distinguishes true belief from make-belief? The difference involves the subject's intentions. In make-belief one affirms in pursuit of some non-epistemic, practical aim. By contrast, in judgment and judgmental belief one constitutively aims at *getting it right* on the question addressed. Perhaps that is all there is to the difference?

Before us so far is a partial account of judgment as *a certain sort* of affirmation *in the endeavor to get it right on whether p*.[27] Judgmental belief could then be understood as a corresponding disposition: to judge in the endeavor *thus* to get it right on whether p, if one so endeavors.

5. *Suppose* that reflective knowledge is knowledge properly so-called, and that the highest level of reflective knowledge, of distinctive interest to the philosopher, is the knowledge that gains conscious, agential, judgmental endorsement. This then is *more plausibly* the knowledge at the center of the epistemological tradition from the Pyrrhonists to Descartes and beyond. It is not just the knowledge that is acquired implicitly, with normal automatic processing, in the course of an ordinary day. Rather, it is the knowledge that does or at least can stand up to conscious reflective scrutiny, no holds barred. The knowledge that falls short includes not only the merely implicit belief acquired automatically. Also lacking and inferior is the explicit and conscious judgment that reflects what is absorbed uncritically through the culture's hidden persuaders. These judgments can be willingly rendered, explicitly and consciously, while still falling short because unendorsed *and not properly endorsable* by that subject, who lacks the rational wherewithal even dispositionally.

D. Responsibilist Virtue Theory in the Tradition

1. The Pyrrhonists stop short of *endorsed beliefs*. If we define *reflective knowledge* as animal knowledge properly endorsed, then the Pyrrhonists fall short of

---

get it right *reliably enough and indeed aptly*: the act of *judgment*. Closely related to that is of course the corresponding disposition, which one might then label "judgmental belief."

27. Judgment is, I suggest in first approximation, "a certain sort" of (alethic) affirmation, of affirmation aimed at correctness. But, again, and as will be argued below in greater detail, one can thus affirm (alethically, in pursuit of truth) without judging.

that, and settle into a state of judgmental suspension, even while continuing inquiry. Moreover, they allow their *functional* seemings to have sway over their lives: they opt to live by appearances. Resultant functional seemings result from competing vectorial seemings, as when one resolves conflicting testimony from two friends in favor of the one trusted more. The testimony of one friend makes it seem that p, that of the other makes it seem that not-p, and the clash may be resolved in favor of the friend trusted more. The Pyrrhonists seem to guide their quotidian conduct on the basis of such resultant seemings. That is the regimen they seem to advocate explicitly. But they will not *judgmentally* endorse any such seemings. They are impressed by the fact that resultant vectors rarely or never warrant endorsement. So, they prefer to suspend conscious endorsement. This is why they remain skeptics (in a state of continuing *skepsis*, or inquiry, with little or no settled judgment or judgmental belief).[28]

2. The endorsement of Pyrrhonian interest is agential. Crucial agential performance and competence thus attend even the most basic perceptual knowledge. Functional, perceptual seemings are passive states that we cannot help entering. But *endorsement of them* remains volitional, agential.[29] And such endorsement is *required* for those functional states to ascend to the level of fully reflective, judgmental knowledge, the level to which the Pyrrhonists aspire, in which they are followed by Descartes.[30]

3. Conscious epistemic agency can be found *not only* in the second-order endorsing judgments, moreover, but *also* in corresponding first-order judgments themselves: not in the *merely functional* introspective or perceptual beliefs, but in correlated judgments and judgmental beliefs. This point can be developed through the following items and distinctions.

   a. Affirmation pure and simple, as a means to whatever objective, if any. (This is normally a free act, whether it is affirmation to oneself or to others.)

---

28. My account of Pyrrhonian epistemology is in Chapter 10, "Pyrrhonian Skepticism and Human Agency."
29. I see no sufficient reason to accuse the Pyrrhonists or Descartes of lying or self-deception when they claim to withhold endorsement; not when we can understand such endorsement as a matter of the willful act of affirmation. Skeptics generally through the ages often refuse to flat-out affirm things that the rest of us do affirm flat out. At least they refuse to do so publicly. But once we recognize a private correlate, that of affirming to oneself, I see no reason to deny that one can refuse to affirm even privately, as a skeptic, especially when our quotidian lives can go on with minimal if any disruption, since they can proceed on the basis of credences understood more functionally in terms of degrees of confidence. (But we return to this issue in section 11.)
30. See Part IV.

b. Affirmation in the endeavor to answer a whether-question correctly.

c. Affirmation in the endeavor to answer correctly *and also competently, reliably enough, even aptly.*

Consider *such* affirmation to oneself, or to others when this is called for. This is an act of crucial importance to a species as heavily dependent as is ours on collaboration, intellectual and deliberative. And it is thus an act that one would expect to be subject to social norms.

4. Consider, more specifically, item 3b above. Such alethic affirmation is compatible with guessing: game show contestants do affirm, even to themselves, and do so in the endeavor to answer correctly, since only thus will they win the prize. Only with 3c do we have *judgment*. And judgmental belief is the disposition to judge when one faces a question *honestly*, with intellectual honesty, which does *not* mean *purely disinterestedly*, and this for more than one reason. Thus, one may be looking for financial reward, or professional recognition, or even to reduce cognitive/affective dissonance.

5. For the Pyrrhonists, proper endorsement requires the ability to answer the skeptic satisfactorily. So, there is a kind of knowledge of special value (reflective knowledge) that does require agency even when we most simply and passively take the given. Even when one (Müller-Lyer) line seems to us (passively) longer than the other, the question of endorsement is in place, and can be pursued with inquiry (as it is pursued by the Pyrrhonian skeptics). And the endorsement is also paired with the questions consciously addressed even on the first order, where again intentional agency is required. Ironically, reliabilist, competence epistemology is a more radical responsibilist epistemology. It considers responsibilist, agential competences to be crucial for a proper treatment of the most central, most traditional issues of pure epistemology.

6. It might be objected as follows:

> Do you really think that Pyrrho or Descartes or any other normal human withholds endorsement on, say, questions of causation in billiards or whether a crying child is distressed? I don't buy it for a second. Sure, they might say "I don't agree with that," but I think those are just empty words.

To my critic, I reply that it is not plausible to accuse philosophers of lying or of self-deception, or of carelessness, or of empty talk, when we are assessing their ostensibly considered stances. They are surely able to withhold public endorsement, public affirmation. Consider next what happens when you turn something over in your head. Don't you sometimes hold off when you ask yourself a question, and sometimes eventually get to the point where you *are* finally willing to say *yes* flat out? This is affirmation (of at least one sort). I see no reason to deny that the Pyrrhonists or Descartes are honestly holding off where we are willing to say yes flat out. That's what they suggest they are doing, and I cannot see why they must be lying or self-deceived. Perhaps they do so because they have unrealistically high standards, or perhaps they share approximately our same standards, yet think we are not giving proper weight to skeptical arguments in being willing to affirm. So, what they do in serious philosophical dialectic when they refuse to affirm publicly, they also do in auto-dialectic, in the privacy of their own thought.

7. But the critic has a further objection:

> If our practical lives really can be basically insulated from the effects of withholding, doesn't that call into doubt the value or interest of knowledge associated with the affirmation? It just makes it seem idle and, in turn, makes me wonder whether the philosophical tradition really could have been concerned with this.

Reply: Myself, I am convinced that there is a separable act that humans and perhaps other species can perform, which is (in first approximation) the act of serious public affirmation in the endeavor to truth-tell. And this has special importance for linguistic species. (Compare how Descartes takes language to distinguish the human species so significantly from the lower orders.) Again, we need such affirmations for activities of the greatest import for human life in society: for collective deliberation and coordination, and for the sharing of information. We need people to be willing to affirm things publicly. And we need them to be sincere (by and large) in doing so, where sincerity involves essentially the alignment of public affirmation with private judgment. After all, we do want to coordinate in terms of our real wants, and we do want to share information that is reliably enough known, and conveyed through the informant's desire to join properly in the community.[31] So, *private* affirmation also acquires crucial importance on the present approach. And this extends naturally to the dispositions corresponding to these acts of judgment, the public and the private. Suppose that such judgment and judgmental belief can then be seen to be detachable from functional belief (which is just a matter of

---

31. Even if there may be other ways, this is a big part of a natural human way to attain the socially necessary collaboration and coordination.

degrees of confidence, and can be implicit and functionally understood, in a way that connects it with behavior). Does that make judgment idle and of doubtful concern to the philosophical tradition? I cannot see why that would be so, given the specified respects in which judgment and judgmental belief are of such crucial importance to a social (and especially to a linguistic) species.

8. Here is how Hume joins the critic encountered in 6 and 7 above:

> A Stoic or Epicurean displays principles, which may not only be durable, but which have an effect on conduct and behaviour. But a Pyrrhonian cannot expect that his philosophy will have any constant influence on the mind: or if it had, that its influence would be beneficial to society. On the contrary, he must acknowledge, if he will acknowledge anything, that all human life must perish, were his principles universally and steadily to prevail. All discourse, all action, would immediately cease, and men remain in a total lethargy, till the necessities of nature, unsatisfied, put an end to their miserable existence. It is true; so fatal an event is very little to be dreaded. Nature is always too strong for principle. And though a Pyrrhonian may throw himself or others into a momentary amazement and confusion by his profound reasonings; the first and most trivial event in life will put to flight all his doubts and scruples and leave him the same, in every point of action and speculation, with the philosophers of every other sect, or with those who never concerned themselves in any philosophical researches. When he awakes from his dream, he will be the first to join in the laugh against himself, and to confess, that all his objections are mere amusement, and can have no other tendency than to show the whimsical condition of mankind, who must act and reason and believe; though they are not able, by their most diligent enquiry, to satisfy themselves concerning the foundation of these operations, or to remove the objections, which may be raised against them.[32]

Granted, the Pyrrhonian regimen is subject to a weighty objection if it requires suspension of private and public affirmation in the whirl of everyday life. How can we suspend so radically without enormous harm to our welfare as a social species, given the importance of collective deliberation and the sharing of information? The answer requires a proper interpretation of the regimen. There is at least one reasonable interpretation that escapes the dire Humean consequences. On this interpretation, in moving from serious philosophical dialectic or meditation, Pyrrhonists can lower their standards for "competent and reliable enough judgment."[33] Thus, they can distinguish

---

32. David Hume, *An Enquiry Concerning Human Understanding* (1748), section XII.
33. Recall the three sorts of affirmation distinguished in section 3 above, and note what is required for the third sort, 3c, affirmative judgment.

everyday judgment from (intellectually) serious judgment. And they can now continue to affirm judgmentally and to assert publicly, in ordinary contexts, a world of things on which they would still suspend serious judgment.[34]

To object that suspending thus is silly or empty is to court antiphilosophical philistinism. We who are serious about philosophy should not be quick to dismiss the love of truth in favor of what suffices for the hurly-burly of the everyday. Even *le bon David seems* implicated in passages where he *ostensibly* approves of dismissal rather than solution of deep skeptical ponderings.[35] I am not sure how best to explain that ostensibly philistine reaction but is it not obvious that it should be a last resort? Comfortably settling into a shallow common sense should hold little attraction to a lover of wisdom (which says nothing about the common sense of a Reid or a Moore).

9. A further defense of the Pyrrhonian regimen would, *alternatively or in addition*, distinguish qualified affirmation from affirmation flat out. Even in philosophical contexts we very plausibly have need of qualified affirmation, as we engage in dialectic, with others or with ourselves, as we tentatively work out a view. Similarly, then, we may in everyday exchanges engage in such qualified affirmation. We do not commit flat out to what we say, while still willing to convey it as probable enough for purposes of everyday deliberation and sharing of information.

Accordingly, even when we enter a context of serious dialectic or meditation, we can distinguish two different acts: that of qualified affirmation and that of affirmation flat out. The former we can still perform even in that

---

34. Compare Descartes's method in his philosophical meditations by contrast with his approach to daily life: "As far as the conduct of life is concerned, I am very far from thinking that one should assent only to what is clearly perceived. On the contrary, I do not think that we should always wait even for probable truths; from time to time we will have to choose one of many alternatives about which we have no knowledge." *The Philosophical Writings of Descartes Volume II*, trans. J. Cottingham, R. Stoothoff, and D. Murdoch (Cambridge: Cambridge University Press, 1984), 106. Whether here (in the Second Set of Replies) he is opting for the option that I see for the Pyrrhonists is not entirely clear, but in any case his stance seems closely related.
35. "This skeptical doubt, both with respect to reason and the senses, is a malady, which can never be radically cur'd, but must return upon us every moment, however we may chase it away, and sometimes may seem entirely free from it. 'Tis impossible upon any system to defend either our understanding or our senses; and we but expose them farther when we endeavor to justify them in that manner. As the skeptical doubt arises naturally from a profound and intense reflection on those subjects, it always increases, the farther we carry our reflections, whether in opposition or conformity to it. Carelessness and inattention alone afford us any remedy. For this reason I rely entirely upon them..." (*Treatise of Human Nature*, ed. L. A. Selby-Bigge (Oxford: Clarendon Press, 1968), 218).

context as we explore a view. At an extreme it can even merge into mere supposition, as we then draw out consequences. But it can be something more substantial than that, if we become convinced that what we affirm has a lot to be said for it, though still unready to affirm it flat out.

10. Cartesian epistemology, too, just like the Pyrrhonian, concerns pondering with a view to judgmental endorsement. It too involves agential, volitional assent, as Descartes recognizes in distinguishing the volitional faculty of judgment from the faculty of passive understanding. But Descartes had clear and distinct awareness that judgment without competence and reliability would not be epistemically adequate. When he finally attains what he considers true certainty (*cognitio* certainty) at the start of Meditation III, therefore, he asks himself what gives him such certainty, and finds no plausible answer beyond "*clear and distinct perception.*" And he then declares flatly, with no need of argument, that clarity and distinctness could never give him the certainty that he has finally found, *unless nothing could ever be so clear and distinct without being true.* No more ringing endorsement of reliabilism could be uttered.

11. For that reason, among many others, Descartes was a virtue reliabilist, a complete virtue *reliabilist* for whom aptness of belief is at the core, and for whom reflective knowledge (*scientia*) is also crucial. Notably, Descartes was also the greatest and most explicit virtue *responsibilist*, for whom the volitional faculty of judgment is of supreme importance, front and center.

Aligning structurally with Descartes's epistemology, my own AAA, animal/reflective virtue reliabilism also recognizes the importance of agential, volitional, responsibilist epistemic virtues at its core.[36]

12. Of course, we must recognize a distinction between *expert* knowledge and *ordinary* knowledge. Standards rise for expert judgment. Similarly, we can distinguish radical from moderate skepticism.

The radical skeptic applies standards for ordinary affirmation that go beyond ordinary social epistemic norms. If he then conducts his everyday life in accordance with his high standards, he is in effect a social rebel. He violates the norms that enable humans to collaborate socially. So, we can properly disapprove and condemn his intellectual conduct.

---

36. I defend this interpretation of Descartes in several recent publications, and in Chapter 11, "Descartes's Pyrrhonian Virtue Epistemology."

The moderate skeptic, by contrast, applies his higher standards only to expert affirmation, in the context of serious philosophical dialectic or meditation. He will continue to speak *and think* with the crowd when in quotidian contexts. This can even take the form of flat-out affirmation, but it can alternatively or in addition take the form of qualified affirmation. And the difference will reside in what is "reliable *enough*." Just as standards for this do rise with perfectly familiar shifts from ordinary contexts to professional contexts, so do they with a shift from ordinary contexts to serious philosophy. The philosopher will properly require the ability to respond to a great variety of skeptical concerns that need not, and should not trouble us in ordinary life.

13. Thus do we admit a sort of pragmatic encroachment. The relevant difference between the study or seminar room and the market place is constituted by practical concerns. Practical concerns do bear on whether we affirm reliably *enough*. However, our grade of encroachment need *not* go all the way to the *particular* practical context of the believer whose belief is up for epistemic assessment. Social epistemic norms can abstract from such specific contexts.[37] And yet the approach is nonetheless receptive to a high grade of pragmatic encroachment that would make room for varieties of knowledgeable expertise, and also for the difference between a Cartesian assent that is properly meditative versus one that must suffice in the everyday.

14. In conclusion, I submit that important virtues of inquiry are auxiliary to the attainment and exercise of knowledge-constitutive competences.

However, we should also recognize that an auxiliary epistemic virtue might still be an overall personal vice. The example of obsessiveness to the point of ill health is already suggestive.

Compare the example of Gauguin as he abandons his family for the sake of his art. Gauguin may have exercised artistic auxiliary virtue in his escape to Tahiti, and it is conceivable that his art was great enough to justify his action all things considered. And epistemic accomplishment might then be analogous, and assessable analogously.

In any case, there is another respect in which aesthetics and epistemology enjoy autonomy. Artistic and epistemic performances are properly assessable

---

37. That they not only can but do abstract that way is argued in Chapter 8.

within domains unto themselves, the artistic or epistemic domains relevant to such performances. And such assessment is autonomous from the values pertinent to other domains, *as well as* from overall value or moral standards. When we say that knowledge is better than mere true belief, the alleged superiority is epistemic. This superiority must be understood autonomously, so that it does not derive from any moral or personal worth that may attach to the believer's motivation, if any. And this is so *even if* some particular epistemic and artistic accomplishments can withstand conflicting extraneous values, as conceivably in the case of Gauguin.

15. Finally, an irenic parting. Again, we should gladly recognize the many important intellectual virtues beyond the knowledge-constitutive. And we should welcome the philosophical study of such virtues.[38]

Still, the virtue of some *auxiliary* virtues must be understood within the framework of virtue reliabilism. The reason for this is that what makes them auxiliary virtues is their enabling us to acquire or sustain the *complete* competence—the Skill, Shape, and Situation, SSS complete knowledge-constitutive competence—in virtue of whose manifestations we know answers to questions in a given domain. (Compare how the competence to drive safely on a certain road would be constituted by the innermost Skill that the driver retains even asleep, by the Shape that requires his being awake and sober, and by the Situation involving a road that is dry enough, not covered by a thick layer of oil.) We are helped to understand why some auxiliary competences count as auxiliary *epistemic* virtues (and not just as general moral or other practical virtues), then, if we understand the structure of knowledge-*constitutive* competences, and can better see how auxiliary virtues might enable us to attain and exercise our knowledge-constitutive virtues.

---

38. And celebrate their insightful study, as in the books of Zagzebski (*Virtues of the Mind*, Cambridge: Cambridge University Press, 1996); and Baehr (*The Inquiring Mind*).

PART II

A Better Virtue Epistemology

3
Judgment and Agency

> Let us imagine that some people are looking for gold in a dark room full of treasures . . . [None] of them will be persuaded that he has hit upon the gold even if he has in fact hit upon it. In the same way, the crowd of philosophers has come into the world, as into a vast house, in search of truth. But it is reasonable that the man who grasps the truth should doubt whether he has been successful.
>
> Sextus Empiricus[1]

Our lodestar concept, that of the *fully apt* performance, will guide us in what follows beyond anything to be found in earlier virtue epistemology.

A. What Is a Fully Apt Performance?

1. *Practical performances*. In order to introduce the concept we turn first to practical performances, to how they are constituted and to a special normativity that pertains to them. Two examples yield initial insight, whereupon we turn to performances that are epistemic rather than practical, on which

---

[1] *Against the Logicians*, 27 (M vii, 52). Translated by Jonathan Barnes, in *Toils of Scepticism* (Cambridge: Cambridge University Press, 1990), 138–9. Compare *Against the Logicians*, 2.325, on p. 153 of the translation by Richard Bett (Cambridge: Cambridge University Press, 2005): "[The] . . . skeptics very aptly compare those who are investigating unclear things with people shooting at some target in the dark. For just as it is likely that one of these people hits the target and another misses it, but who has hit it and who has missed it are unknown, so, as the truth is hidden away in pretty deep darkness, many arguments are launched at it, but which of them is in agreement with it and which in disagreement is not possible to know, since what is being investigated is removed from plain experience."

a further example will also shine its light. Those examples show the way to a better view of human knowledge, which is our main objective.

As a preliminary, let us first bring into focus our distinction between two varieties of knowledge: the judgmental and the functional.

At the core of judgmental knowledge is the act of judgment, a certain sort of affirmation.[2] Affirmation can be either public, through assertion, or private, to oneself. Either sort can have pragmatic ends: impressing others, for example, instilling confidence, reducing dissonance, etc.[3] An affirmation whose ends are only thus pragmatic is a pretend judgment, however, of a piece with make-belief. Genuine judgment is affirmation in the endeavor to affirm with apt correctness. To judge is to affirm with that intention, and judgmental belief is the disposition to so judge. Such conscious judgments and the corresponding beliefs are important to a social species for which information sharing and collective deliberation are essential, as is cooperation more generally. This largely accounts for the great value of the judgmental knowledge constituted by such acts or dispositions. Affirmation and judgment (as defined) are crucial to the various forms of human cooperation.[4]

---

2. By affirming that p you say that p (at least to yourself), but you also do more. Not every saying is an affirmation: not, for example, when you premise something for *reductio*, nor when your speech is in a play, or when you tell a story.
3. When we postulate implicit *reasoning*, this would seem to be a sequential causal process that is episodic, whereby there are immediate inferences at various junctures and preservation of lemmas in memory. And the drawing of such an immediate inference, even when subconscious, will be episodic. But in that case we need episodic *acts* as part of such reasoning. If there is subconscious *conditional* reasoning, then some such acts will be suppositional, and will not plausibly count as affirmations. But surely not all subconscious reasoning that we have reason to postulate will be just conditional reasoning (even if, implausibly, some is). And when reasoning is *not* conditional, then it will be affirmational, and steps of *such* reasoning would seem to count as acts, not just dispositions. These then are the acts that I am viewing as subconscious affirmations.

    Such intentional representations, whether conscious or subconscious, are worth distinguishing from their merely functional counterparts. Even when subconscious, the intentional tends to be pliable through dialogue with others or within oneself. It can be brought up to the surface for such molding, and for use in conscious deliberation or pondering, and for sharing with others. This distinguishes it from the merely functional, which resists exposure, molding, expounding, and sharing.
4. It might be thought that in addition to judgmental beliefs there are the quasi-judgmental credences that we might express with language like 'Probably p', 'Maybe p', and so on, just as we can express our judgmental beliefs with just 'p' or '<p> is true'. And no doubt we *can* express lower credential states that way, and higher ones by 'Certainly p' or the like. That much seems quite right. And we could *also* correctly recognize respective dispositions to make those qualified affirmations. In doing so, however, we need not go beyond dispositional beliefs, since we can just recognize a subset of judgmental beliefs with a certain sort of subject matter. (And if the qualified "affirmations" are distinctive speech acts other than true affirmations, then we can recognize dispositions to perform such alternative acts, whose relation to true affirmations, and whose relevance to epistemology, would remain to be explored and delineated. More on

Not all beliefs are judgmental, however. For example, some guide everyday action entirely below the surface of consciousness. Unlike *judgmental* beliefs, these are not accessed through a simple conscious response to the relevant "whether" question. On the contrary, it can take thought and analysis to pull them up. These and other *functional* beliefs we mostly set aside, for simplicity, but they too can be understood through an extension of the account of judgmental belief to be proposed below.[5] We might recognize parallel states of intention and belief and then define choice and judgment as the events of entering those states, where the entry might or might not be volitional. We might then also recognize a kind of judgment that is not the event of entering a state of belief, but is rather the episodic expression of that state. It would then be natural to allow also events of "voliting" that are not really decisions, since they need not be events of *entering* a state of intention, but can rather be events of expressing one.

Here however we take a different view. Our emphasis is on humans as social animals who reason, often consciously, who do so individually and collectively, both practically and theoretically. So, we focus on the practical and theoretical acts by means of which humans accomplish all of that.

---

this can be found in Chapter 10, on Pyrrhonian epistemology, where we consider how the Pyrrhonian skeptic might reason without recourse to judgments or judgmental beliefs.)

5. The key to the extension is that beliefs of both sorts are performances, doings, aimed at certain objectives. It's just that the aiming can be of *at least* the following two sorts: (a) conscious (at least dispositionally so), or at least intentional, sometimes even deliberate, as with pondered judgment; or (b) deeply subconscious and unintentional, perhaps teleological, biologically or psychologically. Here I do not go into the nature of such functional beliefs, beyond noting that the relevant category includes states with *aims*, even if these remain below the surface of consciousness.

   It may be thought that stable, functional beliefs are states and that no state could be a performance with an aim. (Compare Matthew Chrisman's "The Normative Evaluation of Belief and the Aspectual Classification of Belief and Knowledge attributions," *Journal of Philosophy*, 109 (2012): 588–612.) But this is implausible if we are clear that in our sense a "performance" is just any state or action or process that has a constitutive aim. Take a disposition to affirm that p if one endeavors to get it right on whether p. This disposition is a state, then, but it too is then plausibly aimed at getting it right on the question whether p, an aim that it shares with the affirmations in which it is manifest.

   Similarly, functional states can have teleological aims. Thus a state of alertness in a crouching cat may be aimed at detecting vulnerable prey. Whether as a state it can count as a "performance" in any ordinary sense is hence irrelevant to our focus on "performances" that have an aim and to which we may then apply our AAA aim-involving normative account. All that really matters for this latter is that the entity have a constitutive aim, whatever may be its ontological status or the label appropriately applicable to it in ordinary parlance.

   Any performance with an aim will be subject to the categories, distinctions, and normativity of the theory to be proposed, even if the intentional and the functional varieties must be distinguished variously.

These acts come in two important varieties, both affirmations, some praxical, some alethic. An alethic affirmation can be public, through a natural language, as an assertion. Praxical first-person affirmations take various forms whereby you commit to a certain course of action. These acts enter conscious reasoning constitutively, along with judgments, to the effect of practical conclusions. It is such acts that most directly matter for immediate practical conclusions and for the ensuing actions, *since one can change one's intentions right up to the last minute.* So, if our interest is rational actions or beliefs that are outcomes of reasoning—practical or theoretical, individual or collective—then acts are where the action is. Of course dispositions to perform such acts are also important in obvious ways.

On this view, acts are basic and the most relevant states are dispositions to so act. But this is not incompatible with the importance of credences, which differ from acts or dispositions to act. Credences are rather resultant seemings, and these are very often passive states different from any acts or dispositions to act.

In any case, here we focus on the act of conscious, or at least *intentional* judgment, and the disposition to so judge when one attempts to answer aptly the relevant "whether" question. (And this account will retain its own interest regardless of whether we can extend it to cover also beliefs that are not judgmental but functional.)

We begin with the promised practical examples.

2. *First example*: Diana's performances. The competitor archer does not have much choice. Once up to the line, he must shoot, without discretion. By contrast, shot selection is integral to the competence of a good huntress. Diana thus needs the second-order competence to assess her first-order competence and its required conditions. Since hunting is in part an exercise in shot selection, she must gauge her level of skill as well as her shape and situation, so as to assess risk properly.

Diana's shot is apt if and only if its accuracy manifests its adroitness. It is reflectively competent if and only if it corresponds to a competent second-order awareness that the shot would be apt. Either of these—aptness and reflective competence—can be present without the other.

Suppose Diana sees a distant rabbit scurry in twilight fog, when she has drunk much wine. She might think there's little chance of success, *underestimating* her prowess. She shoots anyway and hits her target aptly. But the shot then fails to be reflectively competent. Its accuracy does not fit any competent second-order awareness on her part.

It can also turn out the other way. Seeing a still deer in the middle of a sunny field well within her range, she might competently judge that her shot would be apt and safe enough to be worth taking. Yet it might be one of those times when she misses anyhow, so that the shot is reflectively competent without being apt.

A shot falls short if it is inapt, of course, but a shot that is apt, and known to be apt, might *still* fall short. Diana, for example, might consider whether to take a shot that she knows would be apt. What if she now decides by tossing a coin? Her shot then still falls short. It is not properly guided to aptness. Diana selects her shot *in the light of* her apt belief that it would be apt, but fails to be *guided* by that belief. So, there is still credit-reducing luck in her success.

Finally, let us say that a performance is *fully* apt if and only if it is guided to aptness through the agent's reflectively apt risk assessment. The agent must perform not only *in the light of* her apt belief that she would perform aptly, but also *guided* by that belief.

That is the account of the fully apt belief in my *Knowing Full Well*.[6] It illuminates a path to a better account of human knowledge, which we enter only now.

3. *Second example*: A basketball shooter's animal, reflective, and full aptness.

   a. Consider next basketball shots. Even a player who overconfidently takes low-percentage shots too frequently may retain an excellent ability to sink his shots close enough to the basket. Success even in his low-percentage attempts may still be creditable to his competence, moreover, and properly so. This need not be affected by his lowered reliability when he tries too often beyond his safe zone, *not if he is well aware*

---

6. Princeton: Princeton University Press, 2011. I often encounter reluctance to admit that there is any such substantively distinct epistemic *kind* as reflective knowledge or knowledge full well. But my view makes no such commitment. Ontologically, it can rest with affirmations and dispositions to affirm, whether public, or private, in inner speech, or even subconsciously silent, as suggested earlier. The hierarchy that begins with the mere telling or affirmation and rises to the fully apt affirmation need not be viewed as a hierarchy of ontologically distinct entities. The rising statuses can rise in tandem with more and more demanding properties of the qualifying entities, all of which entities remain *ontologically* the same, while qualifying for the higher statuses through difference in properties only, not in ontological nature. Optionally, however, it is also plausible to admit an ontologically different entity, the judgment, constituted by alethic affirmation in the endeavor to affirm aptly, and to admit correlatively a corresponding disposition. Here I will take the latter option, with no deep commitment.

Each of the foregoing options is compatible, moreover, with there being an ontological difference between functional knowledge and judgmental knowledge. We here repeatedly take note of *this* difference, from various angles.

of his limits while taking deliberate risk. What is more, his success *within his limits* still seems creditable even if, *while unaware of those limits*, he continues to shoot confidently beyond them.

Before us then are two interestingly different cases:

In one case, the player is unaware of the limits of his competence, and shoots indiscriminately at distances too near his threshold of sufficient reliability.

In a second case, the player still shoots at distances beyond his limits of competence, below his threshold of reliability, but now well aware that he is so doing, as he willingly runs the risk involved.

Here is a notable difference between those two cases. In the latter, the player can still perform with full aptness, when he knowingly performs within his limits. In the former, the player no longer performs with full aptness, not when so near his threshold of reliable enough performance. In that zone—*barely above the threshold*—he *is* still likely enough to succeed, even without knowing that he is. So, even in his ignorance he can still perform with *animal* aptness, but full aptness is now beyond him.

    b. Does a basketball player normally aim merely to get the ball in the hoop? *That* aim *can* be attained creditably (somewhat), even with the shooter too far away from the basket, below the relevant threshold of reliability. This is so especially if the success attained even that far away is due to a level of competence well above the average.[7] However, basketball players aim not *just* to succeed no matter how aptly. Normally they aim *to succeed aptly enough* (through competence), *while avoiding too much risk of failure*. Their shots are assessed negatively when they take too much risk.

    A shot that makes a goal in the closing minutes of a game may be welcome in *one* respect: it does score a needed goal! But it is extremely unwise, poorly selected, if the shot crosses the whole court, when there was plenty of time to dribble safely to a much better range. So it is a successful shot, provided the player's aim was just to score a goal. However, no good player will normally have only that aim in the thick of a game. Relative to a more ambitious aim to shoot aptly, that shot is deplorable. In

---

7. Even when we put it aside for simplicity, how he does *as a team player* is relevant to this assessment. For example, should he pass rather than shoot? This too can affect the quality of his action as he intentionally shoots by choice.

that situation, moreover, the player is negligent even if he does not flout, but only disregards this fuller aim. The coach may well deplore the shot and scold the player for ignoring the importance of shot selection. Due to the player's negligence, the shot is poorly selected, and thus inferior.

What *more specifically* is the required, more ambitious aim? What is reliability *enough*? This obviously varies from domain to domain. In basketball we know at least roughly where it lies, with due allowance for the position of the player and his teammates, the time remaining on the clock, whether the shot to be taken is a three-point shot, etc. Many factors thus bear in diverse ways, and good players will take them into account, aiming not *just* to sink a basket, but to manifest in so doing the full competence required.[8]

c. Consider now a shooter as she approaches a distance to the basket near her relevant threshold of reliability. And suppose her to be above the threshold, but *indiscernibly so to her.* A statistician-coach-observer might know perfectly well that the player is now barely above the threshold. Suppose he has studied her success rate extensively, aided by a device that measures with exactitude her distance from the basket. That way he can tell that she *is* reliable enough at that distance (given the circumstances noted above). But she herself is very far from knowing any such thing.

The player may still attain her basic aim: namely, to sink that shot in the basket. In that respect her shot may also be apt. Its success may manifest the competence that the statistician knows her to possess even at that distance.

What then is she missing? Anything? Well, although her first-order animal aim *is* attained aptly, not so the *reflective* aim of succeeding thus aptly, an aim that she should also have, whether or not she has it. She does aptly score her goal, but she fails to attain aptly the aim of *aptly* scoring it. Unlike the statistician, she is unable to tell that her shot is still reliable enough at that distance. If she shoots anyhow, and her shot turns out to be reliable enough, she may *aptly* reach her aim of scoring that goal. What

---

8. Granted, it seems initially implausible that any significant difference in credit could derive from just barely surpassing a sharp threshold of reliability. Shots taken from just below that line would seem about as creditable as those taken just above it. But this problem is a figment of our simplifying assumption that what separates competence from incompetence is a thin line. Even once we recognize that competence is a vague concept, it will still be plausible enough that a player could fail to recognize the fact that she is competent to shoot reliably enough from where she stands (when she is barely so competent).

she does *not* aptly reach, however, is the aim of *aptly* scoring. And the success of her shot is hence not *fully* creditable to her, given this important element of luck. Even if her first-order success *is* apt, it is not guided to aptness through apt meta-awareness that the shot would be apt; and hence it is not a *fully* apt shot.

4. Our basketball example suggests a distinction between first-order safety and second-order safety. The player's shot will be safe when she is (even barely) above her threshold of sufficient reliability. So situated, not too easily would she then fail in her attempt to make that goal. Unlike that first-order performance, however, her second-order performance may still be unsafe. Unaware of her threshold's location, she might too easily have shot inaptly, below that threshold. Properly situated as she is *in fact* (though barely), she *is* thereby disposed to shoot *successfully* and *aptly*. Because she is unaware of her threshold, however, she might too easily have shot inaptly. She might so easily have been *improperly* situated and still have shot just the same.

Suppose moreover that the lights might easily have dimmed just as she was taking her shot. Because of this, she might easily have shot inaptly, in a way that did not manifest complete SSS competence. Even if the lights *might* then easily have dimmed, however, so long as in fact they *did not*, her shot could still be apt. Two things are here plausibly compatible: first, she might too easily have shot inaptly (since the lights might so easily have dimmed); but, second, she in fact shot aptly, with a shot whose success manifested her relevant complete shooting competence, which *in fact* was present in its entirety.

When our subject is disposed to succeed reliably enough with her shots, this may be because she satisfies the SSS (seat/shape/situation) conditions of a relevant first-order competence. These are conditions that determine whether one is disposed to shoot *accurately*, and reliably enough. But the SSS conditions of the competence to shoot *aptly* are not the same. For basketball shots on goal, the competences are different: the SSS conditions are different. A shot aimed at hitting a target is apt if its *success* manifests first-order competence. For a shot to be *fully* apt it must succeed aptly, and, in addition, it must *aptly* succeed aptly. It must be aptly apt, with its *aptness* manifesting second-order competence.

5. Take any domain of human intentional performance, of intentional action, whether of athletic performance, of the performance arts, of service-professional performance, as in medicine or the law, and so on. In any such domain, achievement is creditable to the extent that it is through competence rather than luck. Whenever an aim is attained there will be a dimension with pure luck at one

end and pure competence at the other. And there will be a threshold below which the aim is attained too much by luck, too little by competence. This is the threshold below which the agent's attempt, given their SSS situation, would be *too risky*. This means "too risky relative to the aim, internal and proper to the domain, at which the agent's performance should aim on that occasion." This is a notion familiar to spectators and assessors of athletic performance. Thus, a swing by a batter is too risky if the pitch is way out of the strike zone, a basketball shot too risky if taken beyond safe range, a serve too risky if hit too hard and too flat for the occasion, and a hunter-archer's shot too risky if the conditions are too unfavorable, in respect of lighting, wind, distance, etc.[9]

What sets such a threshold? This will vary from domain to domain. It may be conventional and formalized, as in some professional contexts, or it may be less formal, more intuitive, as in the domain of a hunt. In each case, the threshold will be set by considerations distinctive of the domain and the proper basic aims of performances in it, and not by external pragmatic aims that the performer might *also* have for their performance.

Aims external to the domain might of course properly motivate a performer to take outrageous risk. Even so, from a domain-internal perspective the performance can still be too risky, and the performer negligent in deliberately taking such risk, or even in being too insensitive to the risk taken. Thus, a basketball player might be offered a vast sum for taking a shot from across the full length of the court, and *might* thus act quite rationally and appropriately in taking that shot, all things considered, especially if the offer is innocent and not a bribe. But the shot is then still bad as a basketball shot, because of how poorly selected or negligent it is *as a basketball shot taken in a game*, if there is plenty of time to dribble safely to within a safer range.

6. Performing with *full* aptness would normally require knowing that one *would* then perform aptly. This is the knowledge that must *guide one's performance* if it is to be fully apt.[10] This will be seen to play a role in epistemology.[11]

---

9. Compare J. Adam Carter's "Robust Virtue Epistemology as Anti luck Epistemology: A New Solution," *Pacific Philosophical Quarterly* (2014).
10. Here I do not take up the question of how one attains one's knowledge of subjunctive conditionals. One interesting proposal is in Timothy Williamson's *Philosophy of Philosophy* (Oxford: Blackwell, 2007), ch. 5. Without necessarily endorsing that proposal, I do share the emphatic assumption (p. 141) that we regularly know the truth of such conditionals, knowledge that we put to much important action-guiding use. (But I do not attribute to Williamson any agreement that subjunctive conditionals help guide our actions in the specific way that I suggest: that is, by enabling their full aptness.)
11. But we should take note of a qualification. Many performances cannot aspire to success that is fully apt in the demanding way specified. Athletic performances, for example, nearly

B. The Place of Full Aptness in Epistemology

1. In earlier work I distinguish two varieties of knowledge, the animal and the reflective, and argue that the reflective variety fits better both with common sense and with the epistemological tradition stretching back through Descartes to the Pyrrhonists.[12]

Now I would like to present a more explanatory account. The distinction between animal and reflective knowledge follows from a deeper distinction, between animal knowledge and knowing full well. It is mainly because knowing full well *entails* reflective knowledge that the latter gains its special interest. The more important concept, it now seems clear, is that of knowing full well. It is *this* variety of knowledge that enables a better treatment of the full array of epistemic examples gathered over recent decades. And *knowing full well* also illuminates the skeptical problematic, from the Pyrrhonists through Descartes.

That, in any case, is what I propose to argue.

2. Consider first an example in which a *guess*, surprisingly enough, might still qualify as a case of "knowledge." Please recall your yearly eye exam.

> When I go for my exam, I am asked to read the lines of a chart with letters that shrink line by line from a huge single letter at the top, to those barely visible at the bottom. At some point I start to lose confidence that I am getting the letters right, but I keep going until the technician tells me to stop and then records some result. At that point there are many cases where I am quite unsure as to whether it is an "E" or an "F," say, or a "P" rather than an "F," etc. Suppose, however, it turns out that (unbeknownst to me) I am in fact unfailingly right year after year at a line where I am thus unsure. At that point I am in effect "guessing." I do affirm, to myself in private and to the technician in public, and I do so in the endeavor to get it right. That is after all what the test requires: that I *try* to answer correctly. And we can surely stipulate that I thereby manifest a competence, one
>
> always aspire not to antecedently *assured* success, but only to success that is likely enough. But what needs to be assured is that the success *would* be likely enough. This is not quite like assurance, based on a fair sample, about the percentage breakdown of an urn's contents.
>
> In what follows we will mostly focus on cases of assured success and the corresponding full aptness. This is for simplicity, though a complete account needs to cover the more general phenomenon of performance that is apt "fully" *to the extent possible without flaw*. Thus, the complete account will need to cover also performance guided by prior knowledge that it would *likely enough* be apt.

12. Section D displays some of this reasoning.

I do not recognize as reliable enough. *This latter* is why I resort to guessing, when I continue to affirm as I undergo the test. Unbeknownst to me, however, my affirmations turn out to be surprisingly reliable.

How then do we assess my performances? We are here conflicted. *Somehow* I *do* know what letters I see, as shown by my impressive reliability. But there is also a pull to say that I do not *really* know. What accounts for this?[13]

3. First we need a distinction. We still affirm at the lower rows, while aiming *to get it right*. We give it our best shot, since only thus will we undergo the vision test properly. But do we aim to get it right *aptly, reliably enough*? No, by that point it matters little whether we do get it right *reliably at all*. We just make our best guess, aiming to undergo the test successfully, so as to get the right eye-glass prescription. Whether at that row we are still reliable does not matter much, since the letters are there tiny and our vision will be fine either way. Accordingly, we make our guess without *endeavoring* to get it right *aptly*.[14] Still it turns out that we are nearly flawless at that row; that is how it turns out *by hypothesis*.

Many will insist that *somehow* our vision-test subject does know, even without knowing that he does. All who attribute knowledge to the blindsighters and chicken sexers of Gettier lore will agree. Moreover, the vision-test example is easily conceivable, with no need to indulge in science fiction.[15]

---

13. And it would be easy to construct a similar example concerning one's memory. With ageing comes the need for assurance that ostensible memories are still reliable enough.

14. However, even if we normally do *not* aim to get it right *aptly*, we still might so aim, and we might *still* be guessing. In order to go beyond guessing, we must affirm confidently enough *both* on the first *and* on the second order. If we confidently enough affirm on the first order but remain too unsure on the second order, then we are still *in that way* guessing. Chapter 4 tries to take better account of the place of confidence in epistemology, and particularly in judgment.

   An eye-exam subject will normally guess both on the first and on the second order when viewing a row far enough down the chart. Take subjects who feel confident on the first order. They may still feel unsure on the second order, as to how or even whether they have a competence that reliably delivers that first-order assurance. This stance seems possible even if not perfectly coherent.

15. By contrast, some of the earlier cases are hard to imagine for an actual human, since the attribution of knowledge clashes so radically with our background knowledge. That applies both to Norman the clairvoyant and to Truetemp, who can tell ambient temperature directly, and does so (unbeknownst to him) through a thermometer implanted in his brain. For all I really know, however, I myself in fact qualify as the vision-test subject (without the confidence or confirmation, but with extremely reliable guesses) at some row where I can no longer reasonably take myself to be reliable. The vision-test subject fits better with our background beliefs, as do blindsighters and chicken sexers, by contrast with clairvoyants or truetemps.

4. Again, as the letters get smaller, even as we start guessing, we might still know in some very basic way, with a subcredal "animal knowledge" *below* even the animal knowledge that requires belief. What are we missing, as we descend to that lower level of knowledge? What distinguishes the higher knowledge that we enjoy at the rows with bigger letters?

Perhaps what makes the difference is just more confidence? In order to know when the letters get smaller, do we just need to be more assertive? Given how reliable we are by hypothesis, is that all we need at that point: just more confidence? Is that the difference that gives us knowledge of the bigger letters?

Some of us are constitutionally assertive risk takers; others can acquire confidence through therapy. Suppose we gain our confidence only through therapy, with no other change. That would not give us the sort of knowledge we enjoy with the larger letters. Indeed such artificial increase of confidence can *worsen* the subject's epistemic position.

Compare someone who gains not just confidence but also *confirmation* that he remains reliably right even when the letters shrink. *This* is perhaps the gain that raises him to a higher epistemic level. Now he might attain the knowledge requiring judgment, not just a guess. *His* knowledge would then comprise not only more confidence but *also* the proper *meta*-assurance that, even for those very small letters, his level of competence limits epistemic risk within proper bounds.

Absent such additional confirmation, the vision-test subject lacks well-founded confidence *on the second order* that his first-order affirmations are more than sheer guesses. Even if by hypothesis his guesses are *not* right just by luck, he cannot be sure of that, not competently.

By contrast, when the letters near the top are clearly and distinctly discernible, we do not just guess, which comports with our knowledge *that we can identify those letters for what they are,* that our affirmations at those rows would be apt.

Perhaps what is missing at the lower rows is our taking our "guesses" to be reliable enough? As our confidence wanes, we still affirm, even once we start to guess. What then is missing? Reflective competence is missing, as is reflective aptness, and also aptness full well.[16]

---

[16]. And we take up a further lack in Chapter 4, in a discussion of how confidence bears on knowledge.

5. Again, epistemic agents do not aim just for correctness of affirmation. They also *judge*, aiming for *aptness* of affirmation. So, even a properly confident subject who affirms aptly might fail with his judgment. Why so? Because even while affirming aptly in the endeavor *to affirm correctly*, he might fail to *judge* aptly. While affirming in the endeavor *to affirm aptly*, he might fail to affirm *aptly* in *that* endeavor. In other words, his *alethic* affirmation, aimed at truth, might be apt without being fully apt, in which case his *judgment* would not be apt.

We rely here on two facts: (a) that one may do something as a means to more than one end; and (b) that aptness pertains not just to the means but to the whole structure of the form: *taking means M to end E*. Thus, one might flip a switch aptly in the endeavor to illuminate a room without doing so aptly in the endeavor to alert someone, even if by flipping the switch one aimed concurrently to attain each of those two aims. That is to say, the first aim might be attained aptly thereby, without the second aim being attained aptly, or at all.

Similarly, one might affirm aptly in the endeavor to affirm correctly (an aim required if the affirmation is to be alethic and not just pragmatic). Compatibly, one still may *not* affirm aptly in the endeavor to (alethically) affirm aptly, not even if one does then endeavor to affirm not just correctly, with truth, but also (thereby) aptly. Only with apt success in this second endeavor does epistemic affirmation count as fully apt. And only thus is *judgment* also apt, beyond the aptness of one's affirmation.

Equipped with our distinctions, we next consider some problematic issues of epistemology.

C. The Gettier Tradition

1. Consider the examples that have proved important in the Gettier tradition:[17]

   (a) *Inferential cases.* Gettier's own examples are inferential. And compare the Havit/Nogot example due to Keith Lehrer: S believes on excellent

---

17. Here I understand the tradition *broadly*, to include not just the original Gettier examples, but the whole tradition meant to understand what *propositional knowledge* is in the light of examples that bear on whether it is *justified true belief.*

evidence that Nogot here has a Ford. Nogot has no Ford, however, unlike Havit, who is also here and does have a Ford, quite unbeknownst to S, who concludes that someone here has a Ford only from his premise that Nogot does. This conclusion belief is thus justified, and also true. Yet S does not thereby *know*, since that belief is true only because of Havit, not Nogot. It is conventional wisdom among epistemologists that in these cases the protagonist fails to know.

(b) *The barns example.* Barney sees a barn and believes accordingly, although he might as easily be viewing a mere barn façade, of the many to be found nearby. Most epistemologists deny that this subject knows, but there is a substantial minority who are not so sure.[18]

Compare Simone, who nears the end of her pilot training and each morning might to all appearances, from her viewpoint, as easily be piloting in a simulator as in a real plane. When she happens to be really flying a plane, can she then know that she is doing so?

(c) *Norman the clairvoyant, Truetemp, the chicken sexer, the blindsighter.* These subjects finds themselves believing something, quite reliably in fact, but with no idea how they are doing so, nor even *that* they are doing so. These cases divide epistemologists more evenly. Some take such subjects to know; others think the opposite. And many can feel the pull of the opposing view, but decide to "bite the bullet."

2. Subjects of sort 1(b), such as Barney and Simone, seem to fall short because of their poor situation. What deprives them of knowledge is the danger posed by nearby possibilities, because of the nearby façades or the simulation cockpit. But just where is the *unsafety* located? This question

---

18. However, X-phi survey results imply that, on intuitions about Barney, the folk are in sharp disagreement with the philosophers. See D. Colaco, W. Buckwalter, S. Stich, and E. Machery, "Epistemic Intuitions in Fake-Barn Thought Experiments," *Episteme*, 11 (2014): 199–212. This paper tests versions of the original fake barn case. "Knowledge" attributions are high. Josh Knobe and John Turri have both independently replicated those findings (the "knowledge" attribution findings, though not the age effects) with very large sample sizes. Overall, on a 0–6 scale, mean response is about 4.75. See also J. Turri, W. Buckwalter, and P. Blouw, "Knowledge and Luck," *Psychonomic Bulletin & Review*, doi:10.3758/s13423-014-0683-5. This paper tests a more general category of cases, "failed threat" cases, to which fake barn cases belong. "Knowledge" attributions are high (sometimes topping 80%) and do not differ from ordinary examples of perceptual knowledge. Finally, there is also a paper by Turri (under review), "Knowledge and Assertion in 'Gettier' Cases," which tests a version of the original fake barn case. The result here is that attributions of "knowledge" and "assertability" are high (> 80%) and do not differ from ordinary examples of perceptual knowledge.

arises once two orders of safety emerge, as in our basketball example. Where and how do Barney and Simone perform unsafely? Is it on the first order, or is it on the second?

3. Plausibly, Barney falls short of knowledge because he affirms *somehow* unsafely. Too easily might Barney have affirmed that he then faced a barn when he faced only a barn façade. However, that would not explain why it is so intuitively attractive that Norman and Truetemp likewise fail to know. The alethic *affirmations* of Norman and Truetemp might be confidently safe!

By contrast, if knowledge requires aptness of *judgment*, this explains why Norman and Truetemp fall short and *also* why Barney's affirmation needs to be safe. Aptness of judgment *entails* safety of affirmation.[19] In *judging* as he does, Barney must on some level be aware of the following, by taking it for granted, perhaps, or presupposing it: *that not too easily might he affirm incorrectly on the matter of a facing barn, if he affirmed at all*. For, in so judging, Barney aims to affirm aptly that he does face a barn. So, his *judgment* will be apt only if he aptly attains *this* aim: that of affirming aptly. And this will happen only if he is guided to the aptness of his affirmation (that he does face a barn) by his second-order awareness that if he then affirmed (that he faced a barn) he *would* (likely enough) be right.[20] And from this it follows that if his judgment is apt then his affirmation is safe. We thus co-opt *this* safety requirement, and agree that Barney and his like fail to judge aptly, and *thus* fail to know (fail to know full well).

Again, in order to know full well, Barney must know that if in his conditions he affirmed that he faces a barn, not easily would he be wrong. He needs knowledge of this conditional in order to guide himself to apt affirmation in the way required for *full* aptness of affirmation, which is what apt judgment requires. So, his judgment can then be apt only if safe. Accordingly, Barney knows full well only if his constitutive judgment is safe. But it is implausible that his belief is safe, given the nearby fakes, and hence implausible that he knows full well. Thus we can understand the attraction to think that Barney does not know, if the knowledge of interest to us is judgmental knowledge full well.

We are focused on apt judgment (and judgmental belief), and on the corresponding knowledge, which lies above merely subcredal animal

---

19. This will be developed in this same section.
20. Again, this awareness need be neither conscious nor temporally prior.

knowledge (as in the eye-exam case). Judgment is *affirmation* in the endeavor *to affirm aptly*. In judgment one aims *to alethically affirm aptly*. Judgmental affirmation that p must hence manifest competence not only to get it right on the question whether p, *but also* to do so aptly. In order for a *judgment* to be apt, the subject must *aptly* attain aptness of affirmation.

Accordingly, Barney's *judgment* succeeds if and only if it attains not just correctness but also aptness. And *this* aim is aptly attained, finally, if, and only if, the *aptness* of Barney's affirmation manifests his competence for success *in affirming aptly*.

That being so, in order to be apt Barney's judgment must be safe. Since it is constitutively an affirmation aimed at getting it right *aptly*, a judgment will succeed only if it meets two requirements: (1) the embedded affirmation must of course be apt. And (2) the embedded affirmation must be one that *would* be apt, in the following way: The subject must possess a complete competence in virtue of which he *would* then reliably enough affirm correctly *and aptly* on that question, if he affirmed through exercise of that competence.

In the best-case scenario the agent who *judges* aptly knows that they would affirm correctly if they affirmed as they intend. The agent *affirms* fully aptly only if guided to a correct *and apt* affirmation by second-order awareness of their competence to so affirm. It follows that if a *judgment* is apt, the embedded *affirmation* is then *fully apt*, and must hence be safe, so that the judgment must be one that *would* be true, and must itself in that way be safe. The affirmation must be safe because the agent must know that they *would* then succeed aptly if they tried, so that *if they affirmed they would do so correctly*, which is tantamount to safety of affirmation, and, in turn, to safety of judgment.

By contrast, an affirmation can be apt without being safe, without being one that *would* be true if made.[21] This is because an apt affirmation can be *unsafely* apt, unlike a *fully* apt affirmation.

What is more, if knowledge full well does require *full* aptness of affirmation, that *also* explains the pull to think that Norman and Truetemp do not really know. Supposing they do not *guess*, but *judge*, this judgment of theirs will *not* be apt. Even if the embedded affirmation *is* apt, as stipulated, these subjects still do *not* succeed *aptly* in thus *affirming aptly*. They affirm aptly

---

21. Note the specific sort of safety involved here: a performance constitutively aimed at X is "safe" iff it *would* then attain X if made.

through luck, not competence. Although Norman and Truetemp have animal knowledge, as do our eye-exam subjects, they still lack knowledge full well. And the same goes for blindsighters, chicken sexers, etc.[22]

Consider the intuition that our eye-exam guessers do not *really* know (even if somehow they do "know"). That intuition plausibly flows from their failure to affirm fully aptly, and hence from their failure to know *full well*. They lack the required apt awareness that they are so conditioned (SSS well conditioned) that if they affirmed on the first order they would (likely enough) do so correctly and aptly. Of course what they are missing is not just full meditative conscious awareness. *Rather* do they fall short through lack *even* of an apt presupposition—an apt *implicit* awareness—that their relevant first-order affirmations are and would be apt.[23]

We can thus explain our divided intuitions in the 1(b) and 1(c) cases. The subjects in those cases do enjoy the sort of animal knowledge that comes with apt affirmation. But they do not know full well. As for the inferential 1(a) cases, these subjects clearly have no knowledge of any sort: not of the animal sort, and even less of the reflective sort. Nor of course do they know full well.

The requirement of full aptness accounts for all three sorts of examples. The fact that knowledge has varieties accommodates the apparent conflict of intuitions. Some intuitions are sensitive to the lower and some to the higher varieties, even if no such sensitivity need be conscious or explicit in order to have its effect.

---

22. We are helped to see more clearly into this nest of issues if we distinguish (a) S's aptly affirming, or judging, that he would affirm aptly if he answered the question whether p, from (b) S's aptly attaining his objective of aptly answering the question whether p. Only the latter requires that S's affirming, in answer to the question whether p, be *guided* by his apt second-order awareness that his answer to the question whether p would be an apt answer. And for *this* to be so, it does not suffice that one enjoy second-order awareness that one's first-order affirmation would be apt. This second-order awareness must also *guide one* to the relevant aptness on the first order. Our attainment of aptness on the first order must *manifest* one's pertinent second-order competence.
23. Some features of a situation might of course rationally sustain our implicit assumption that the light is good for color judgments. For example, we might rely on the fact that the light is natural, which we know based on various factors, such as the open window, the sunny scene, the light bulb off, etc. When we judge that the surface seen is red, we may thus rely not only on its red look but also on those other factors. That is indeed so if specific reasons are needed for taking the lighting conditions to be appropriate for color judgments. And this is not to suppose that one *always* needs such specific positive evidence for the appropriateness of one's first-order SSS conditions. On the contrary, in other cases one might have default trust in such appropriateness absent specific signs to the contrary. (Of course, we could rather say that the very absence of such signs is then an implicit factor to which one responds rationally in making one's first-order judgment. But this would seem just a notational variant.)

D. On the Epistemology of the Reflective

1. Independently of the importance of knowing full well, human knowledge intimately involves higher-order phenomena. Allow me to sketch some reasons why that is plausibly so—a, b, c, and d below—even without a full display of the supporting arguments.

   a. Judgment is affirmation with the intention to *thereby* affirm competently (period) and indeed aptly. That distinguishes judgments from mere guesses. The game show contestant affirms in the endeavor to thereby affirm correctly (and thus win the prize), while taking his affirmation to be a sheer guess, far from apt epistemic performance.[24]

Judgment thus involves a second-order stance regarding one's own affirming. When one judges, one affirms with the aim to get it right aptly by so affirming (where aiming is more than just wishing or hoping).

   b. Suspension of judgment is an intentional double-omission, whereby one omits affirmation, whether positive or negative. Inherent to rational suspension is the assessment that affirmation is then too risky, which implies that, whether positive or negative, it would not then be apt, or at least the *absence* of assessment that it *would* be apt.

Suspension thus understood involves a second-order intention to double-omit (an intention that need not be conscious or temporally prior). Judgment, whether positive or negative, is on a level with suspension, as part of a threefold choice: affirming, denying, suspending. Judgment too thus involves a second-order intention to affirm in the endeavor to affirm aptly, whereas intentional suspension involves intentional double-omission (of affirmation, both the positive and the negative) in the endeavor to affirm *only* aptly. So, an aim that might be shared by epistemic affirmation and suspension is the aim *to affirm aptly and only aptly*.

   c. For competence of judgment on a first-order question, epistemic negligence must be avoided, through responsiveness to reasons that a fully proper judgment must weigh. Reasons of what sort?

---

24. "But a guesser might try not just to get it right but to get it right aptly, while recognizing that the chance of his getting it right aptly is very low." Still, the two actions are quite distinct: aiming to get it right is still different from aiming to get it right aptly. Thus, we can distinguish the guess from a judgment made through the same act of affirming. (But a more fully satisfactory reply awaits Chapter 4.)

Reasons against judging that p can be *counter-weighing* reasons, reasons for the *opposite* judgment, the judgment that *not*-p.

By contrast, *undermining* reasons work against the judgment that p without favoring the opposite judgment. These might be reasons, first, for thinking that no good reasons are available. Second, they might be reasons for thinking that one is not then in good *shape* to render a judgment. Third, they might be reasons for thinking that one's *skill* for rendering a judgment is degraded or altogether absent. (Skill is an innermost competence that one might keep even when in bad shape or poorly situated.)

These three at least are reasons to which one must be sensitive so as to avoid epistemic negligence in first-order judgment. And note what is true about them all: one's sensitivity is on the second order, involving second-order competence.

Since first-order judgment must be responsive to such factors, which one must not neglect, one's first-order judgment must be aided by second-order competence. Consider a belief that remains in place because no second-order defeaters emerge, *where, being unresponsive* to their presence or absence, the agent would have believed the same *even if defeaters had emerged*. Here again is a kind of luck that reduces or removes any credit that might otherwise be due.

> d. Finally, consider that historical paradigm of the highest form of certain knowledge: the Cartesian *cogito,* the thought *that I now think*. What accounts for its particularly high status? Our approach offers a distinctive way to illuminate that status. Consider my judgment *that I now think*, and suppose this to be my affirmation of the indexical content <I now think>, an affirmation made in the endeavor to affirm aptly (indeed with utmost, infallible aptness). If so, my judgment will attain its objective if and only if my affirmation attains aptness *and does so aptly*. This means that my aptness in so affirming must itself be secured aptly. So, I must then enjoy a second order competence to secure aptness in my first-order affirmation. It is not enough that my first-order affirmation attain correctness, nor even that it do so aptly (with enough reliability). It is required *in addition* that *this* aptness of one's affirmation be *itself* attained aptly. And this is precisely what the *cogito* does, paradigmatically so.

In a way it does so already once we arrive at the *cogito* passage at the beginning of Meditation III. By then Descartes has satisfied himself that in affirming the indexical content <I now think>, and in the correlative judgment, he is right, *and he is bound to be right*. Having attained and defended this insight, aided by his skeptical scenarios, he is now aware that if he ever affirmed <I now think> he would affirm correctly. So, as he now ponders whether he thinks, he is aware that if he were to affirm positively he would affirm correctly. Suppose this insight guides him to affirm positively, which he would then do aptly. In that case, the *aptness* of that affirmation (of <I now think>) is attained under the guidance of his apt belief that this *would* be an apt affirmation, which makes his knowledge that he then thinks a case of knowing full well.

2. The foregoing considerations—in a, b, c, and d of the preceding section—suggest why *reflective* competence is epistemically significant.

It might be replied that such second-order competence is *not* necessarily competence to form a *judgment* that one's first-order judgment would be apt. And of course no such conscious judgment is *required*, even if in certain cases it is importantly present, as in the case of the *cogito*, and even if it *is* required for a certain special level of meditative ascent of special interest to the thoughtful. But the second-order stance required need not *in general* take the form of a conscious judgment. It might just be a presupposition, an implicit awareness that all's well enough for first-order judgment. And in certain basic cases this might even be a default stance properly sustained absent defeaters. No special rational basing is required, since it suffices that one be sensitively ready to detect defeaters.

So much for the earlier distinction, of animal versus reflective knowledge, and for reasons in favor of its deployment. What speaks in favor of going beyond that, to a more developed virtue epistemology?

E. The Reflective: Important but Subsidiary

1. Why is the new theory more explanatory than the earlier account? In animal/reflective virtue epistemology, the reflective component is said to import a notable epistemic dimension already, as argued through considerations a, b, c, and d in the section just above. But why should that second-order dimension matter for our first-order knowledge? Why does it matter whether one has merely animal knowledge or "ascends" rather to the more reflective levels? Why isn't reflective knowledge just *more* knowledge, animal knowledge on top of animal knowledge? And why should the

second-order animal knowledge *improve* the knowledge on the first order, raising *it* to a *better* level of knowledge?

Reflective quality is important for human knowledge *largely* for the reasons already suggested: (a) because of the nature of judgment and how it differs from guessing; (b) because of the nature of suspension; and (c) because of how competence must avoid negligence and insensitivity to defeaters. All of these—a, b, and c—involve ascent to a second order, in the ways noted. And, as a bonus, (d) we also gain insight into the special status of the Cartesian *cogito*.

But let us now consider whether and how we should go further.

The importance of the reflective is not explained *fully* until we see what really matters: namely, that the aptness on the first order be attained *under the guidance* of the second-order awareness. The performance on the first level must be guided to aptness through the apt second-order awareness (explicit or implicit) that the subject is *in that instance* competent to avoid excessive risk of failure. This would comport with the subject's apt awareness that if they performed on the first level, they *would* (likely enough) do so aptly.

Requiring *full* aptness provides a more satisfactory treatment of the complete array of data. The account of human knowledge as requiring knowledge full well attains that further success. We have seen how much better it fares in guiding us through the Gettier problematic. But it is not just its explaining Gettier data that matters. The account of a desirable level of human knowledge as knowing full well is in fact a special case of something much more general.

The fully desirable status *for performances in general* is full aptness: it is aptness on the first order guided by apt awareness on the second order that the first order performance would be apt (likely enough). A first-order performance will aim to attain a certain basic objective: hitting a target, as it might be. This will induce the correlated aim to succeed *aptly* in that basic aim. Attaining the basic success aptly is better than attaining it inaptly.

Moreover, attaining aptly the aptness of one's success is also better than attaining *this* inaptly. That is a lesson drawn from our basketball player near her threshold of competence, and especially from the amazing shot that spans the full length of the court to score a goal. This success suffers by comparison with that of a shot aimed not just at scoring but at doing so competently enough, and even aptly. A shot suffers if it falls short of *full* aptness: that is, if the player fails to guide herself to aptness through knowledge that her shot *would* then be apt. What is needed for these further levels of success is what is still lacked by our player when she stands too near her threshold of reliable enough competence. She fails to know that she is above the threshold (even if she now is, barely so).

The amazing shot that suffers because it is not fully apt is of course still admirable in many ways. It scores the winning points for the player's team, for one thing, and it is quite creditable if it manifests competence high above the ordinary. But the coach is still right in scolding the player for having taken such a risky shot when she need not have done so. So, the shot still falls short in being very poorly selected. Moreover, it is not just the temporally prior selection that is deplorable. The more importantly deplorable aspect of the shot is that the decision to so shoot *is carried through intentionally*. After all, the player could have reconsidered right up to the point where the ball is released. What matters most is the player's intentionally shooting in disregard of whether the shot would be likely enough apt.

That respect of evaluation is important for performances generally. A performance is poorly selected if it falls below the threshold of reliable enough competence operative in its domain. Hence, even while succeeding in its basic aim, a performance falls short if it neglects attaining that aim *aptly*. This latter is an aim also required for full credit in the domain of that performance. What is yet more, full credit requires that *this* aim too be attained *aptly*. The performance will still suffer if it attains aptness only by luck.

That is so for all first-order performances, in whatever domain, whether cognitive or not.[25] The case of cognitive performance is a special case, where the aptness of *epistemic affirmation* on the first order is attained *through the guidance* of apt second-order awareness that such affirmation *would* then be apt. *This* case of fully apt performance is just that of *knowing full well*.[26]

---

25. Although the emphasis on full aptness seems to institute a potential regress, I can't see that it is vicious. True, as we ascend to the second order we get a boost of epistemic standing (as does a basketball player through enhanced risk assessment based on knowledge of their own competence in the situation wherein they now perform). Arguably, you might then get a further boost if your competence assessment is *itself* not just apt but fully apt. But this need not keep going forever. Returns may in fact diminish quickly to the effect of asymptotic approach to a limit near where you reach already with ascent to the second order. And this is plausibly because we soon hit a limit where human competence gives out as we ascend through the higher orders. Beyond that limit, creatures better endowed might attain incremental enhancement not attainable by limited humans. Since *ought implies can*, however, failure to surpass that limit is no human flaw.
26. Granted, animal-level attainments are importantly different from the lucky grasp of gold in the dark (as in our opening analogy from Sextus). The latter is more like a gambler's lucky guess. But this just reveals how epistemic luck can be found at different levels and in different ways. Suppose our seeker of gold *unknowingly* enters a dark room that contains only gold

2. We advance over earlier versions of virtue epistemology in two steps. First we highlight that full aptness of performance requires guidance through the agent's knowledge that their performance would be apt. Through that fact we then explain why knowing full well is not just animal knowledge on top of animal knowledge, which explains also our spread of intuitions in the full array of Gettier cases. It is crucial to this further explanatory benefit that in order to know full well the subject must be aptly aware that their affirmation would be apt.[27] Barney fails to know—*fails to know full well*—because his judgment, his affirmation *in the endeavor to affirm aptly*, might so easily have failed.

In falling thus short of knowing full well, does Barney fall short of something epistemically significant? In assenting here, I am guided by a more general, intuitively plausible principle: namely, that *any* performance suffers if it is not fully apt.[28] That is the lesson of our basketball shot across the full length of the court, and even of the mid-court shot taken in ignorance that it lies just above the threshold of reliability.

Fully apt performance goes beyond the merely successful, the competent, and even the reflectively apt. And it is the human, rational animal that can most deeply and extensively guide his performances based on the risk involved, in the light of the competence at his disposal. That is why reason must lord it over the passions, both the appetitive and the emotional.[29]

Opting for such rational guidance does involve judgment and risk in any given case, and a faith in reason as our best guide. When research reveals the hidden influences that move us, moreover, that may just help us to enhance the competence of our management. Those revelations may lead us to avoid certain situations, competently, *virtuously* so, and to undergo relevant therapy over time, thus counteracting inappropriate influences. The evidential basis for situationism may hence aid virtue, without refuting virtue theory.

---

objects. In one way, then, it is no accident that what he pockets is gold, but in another way it surely is. Thus tweaked, the Pyrrhonian gold-in-the-dark example still helps to show why and how one needs a reflective perspective aiding the apt correctness of one's belief while avoiding an important element of *blind* luck.

27. And, more generally, that their *representation* would be apt, if we include cases of functional belief, including belief owed to psychological or biological teleology.
28. Or so does any potential performance beyond the limit of human competence, where *oughts* lapse for lack of *cans*.
29. Thus concludes the footnote to Plato that is this chapter.

The dimension of cognition is moreover just the special case where our modularly competent seemings must be subject to a rational competence that assigns them proper weights. It is such rational competence that determines the proper balance required for the wise, fully apt choice, which for cognition is the choice of whether to affirm, positively or negatively, or whether to suspend.[30]

---

30. And, again, the case of functional belief and knowledge would require an analogical extension of this framework, based on the shared focus on performances with an *aim*.

4

A Better Virtue Epistemology Further Developed

A. The Place of Confidence

1. A certain level of confidence comports with the level of reliability required for storage of a belief so that it will *properly* stay in place even after its initial basis has lapsed. We need to rely on sincere affirmations, private and public, to oneself and to others. That is why a certain minimum level of reliability is required for proper storage, so that the information will be properly available even when the initial rationale is gone beyond recall. A certain level of confidence is presumably required for that content to be properly affirmed and retained in memory. Moreover, that degree of confidence must line up with the degree of reliability given to that representation (to that instance of representing) by the competence through which it is acquired and sustained. However, that degree of confidence, along with its perfect reliability, can still fall short epistemically. This we have found by supposing that the level of confidence is artificially induced through mere therapy.

2. Take, however, confidence that derives instead from epistemic competence. Suppose it is acquired through a disposition that systematically aligns degrees of confidence with corresponding degrees of reliability, and does so sufficiently well. And suppose one's degree of confidence to be aligned with a degree of reliability above the threshold required for storage of a belief even after one forgets the basis on which it was acquired.

Some level of knowledge is plausibly attained thereby. One has at least animal knowledge. This is a level attainable by blindsighters, chicken sexers, and their ilk. In order to attain that level, one's belief must derive from an epistemic competence to fix confidence to a degree commensurate with its level of reliability. Such competence would deliver a degree of confidence aligned with how reliably true are such deliverances. And the competence exercised must be more than just competence to some degree or other. It must rather be competence *period*. It must be reliable *enough*. And this reliability "enough" is reliability above a threshold for proper storage, one set by either social or biological norms, depending on the sort of belief involved.

3. How does such animal, functional knowledge relate to the corresponding judgmental knowledge, which requires one to affirm with the aim to affirm aptly? In order to rise *fully* above guessing, that is how one must affirm. One must not affirm merely in the endeavor to affirm correctly. After all, the game-show guesser does affirm in the endeavor to affirm correctly.

Is it enough that one affirm in the endeavor to affirm correctly, when one affirms in line with high confidence that comports competently with a high enough degree of reliability? One is then confident to a degree competently in accord with the reliability of the operative competence, a degree high enough to support one's storing that belief even after one forgets its basis. Would this still fall short? What more could be desired?

4. Consider the following competence: While able to tell when one is confident enough, one affirms based properly on one's confidence to at least that degree. Consider further the broader competence that includes *also* one's ability to thus acquire and sustain that degree of confidence. So, the broader competence will include (a) the policy of affirming only based on sufficient confidence, and also (b) the sufficiently able acquisition and sustainment, when in that shape and situation, of that degree of confidence. Take now affirmations that derive from the exercise of such two-ply competence. In what way might these still fall short?[1] Suppose they are *alethic*

---

1. The "basing" in (a) is *not* the basing on a factive reason to which one adverts, awareness of which then motivates one to proceed in a certain way. It is rather the transregional basing that will be introduced and defended below, whereby one can base an act, or a propositional attitude, *statively* on certain other *mental states*. Thus, it might seem that one line is longer than another, and this conceptual seeming might be based on a visual experience (not a seeming). Or one might base one's judgment that p on a certain degree of confidence that p. Or one might base a judgmental belief that p on a functional degree of confidence that p, where the basing here is not of a sort where one adverts to the fact that one is confident to that degree, and then reasons from *that* perceived fact as a premise to the conclusion that p. Our sort of basing requires the causal influence of the basis itself on the based, but the influence need not route via some intermediate awareness of the basis. For more on this form of basing, see Section D of Chapter 9.

affirmations: affirmations in the endeavor to affirm correctly, with truth. Are they not what we ordinarily recognize as knowledge?

As earlier observed, we do seem to recognize as knowledge *even* a subcredal affirmation that the subject takes to be a *sheer* guess. Thus our eye-exam subject is flawlessly right unaided by much if any confidence at all. Our subject still tries to affirm correctly, as he must for a proper eye exam. And he turns out to know the letters even far down the chart, given his spotless performance.

5. So, take again the subject who is confident enough, and who *competently* acquires and sustains that degree of confidence. Suppose he affirms based on that degree of confidence, and that his affirmation too is competent in the following way: it is properly based on that adequate degree of confidence. If the subcredal guesser does know the letters at the bottom rows, our competently confident subject cannot plausibly be denied an even higher epistemic status.

B. Credence and Judgment

1. We may thus recognize a familiar state of being confident to some degree or other, a *resultant* state of alethic seeming, aimed at truth. If the subject is functioning properly in epistemic respects, then that degree of confidence will comport with the degree of reliability provided by the competence that yields the degree of confidence. If all goes well, the degree of confidence will be proportional to that degree of reliability.

2. That degree of confidence will lie somewhere in the unit interval. Associated with the unit interval will be a belief threshold C+ somewhere between 0.5 (exclusive) and 1 (inclusive), and a disbelief threshold C− between 0 (inclusive) and 0.5 (exclusive). Functional suspension is then confidence between C− and C+. (This is often a passive, merely functional state, which might be more or less stable.)

3. What determines those thresholds? The options here correspond to various sorts of belief or belief-like states. For purely functional belief the thresholds might be set by what conduct the belief would prompt given suitable desires. For linguistic, rational creatures, however, there will be a

particular way to understand those thresholds that still allows the distinction between judgment and judgmental belief, on one side, and functional credence or degree of confidence above the C+ threshold, on the other. On this view, the C+ threshold is where the subject acquires the judgmental belief, the disposition to judge affirmatively. (And similarly for C− and judgmental *dis*belief.)

4. Again, on this view there is often passivity, not freedom or intentional agency, in one's entering various states of confidence to some degree or other. Here one may just be functioning properly (or not), passively so. Compatibly with that, however, one can be free in the policies that govern one's correct, apt affirmation, upon reaching a certain degree of confidence. The point where one begins to be so willing is then the C+ threshold.

5. A distinction now becomes important. One's degree of confidence C on a certain propositional content P at a time t might be hosted passively, though it can of course be assessed for proper functioning. Even then, whether C lies above C+ or not is not just a passive matter, not if one retains agential discretion on how confident one needs to be in order to affirm (when one endeavors after truth and aptness). For C+ is then set not just passively but through one's own agency. So, even if the state of confidence itself is quite passive, whether it counts as belief—or as disbelief, or as suspension—is up to the agent and the confidence that they agentially require for willingness to affirm.

6. Note that on this view we still distinguish between (a) credence (the state of resultant degree of confidence), (b) whether that credence counts as belief, or as disbelief, or as suspension (all these being credential forms of epistemic attitude), (c) judgment itself (the act of affirming in the endeavor to affirm aptly), and (d) *judgmental* belief (as opposed to credential belief), or the disposition to judge upon consideration, when endeavoring to affirm aptly.

C. Two Sorts of Representation

1. Representation can take either of two forms. One is merely functional, with *no* direct agential control. Another is judgmental, *with* direct such control.

Seemings that p are attractions to represent that p. Some such seemings are merely functional (in which case the attraction can be causal without being conscious). They are just attractions to represent, where the representing is itself a merely functional state. Thus a low-level animal may undergo mutually meshing or clashing stimulations, until a resultant state inclines sufficiently in the affirmative direction (that p) to constitute a positive representation that p. This whole process can take place below the level of agential control. Nevertheless the process can still be functional in the sense that it has an aim: namely, correct representation.

Once we ascend sufficiently on the evolutionary scale, something new enters the picture: agency, agential control. Now we have intentions, and judgments, and reasoning, practical and theoretical. Human beings are still animals, of course, and this new element is not a replacement but an overlay. It must integrate with the parts of our animal nature that remain merely functional.

2. But now we also need to distinguish those positive representations that are *merely* functional, not only from those that are directly affectable agentially. We need to distinguish the merely functional *also* from hybrid states of a sort affectable by agency *but only indirectly*.

So, we have not just two but *three* distinct categories of representational states: (a) the merely functional, of a sort not *at all* penetrable or affectable through agential control; (b) the fully agential, of a sort *directly* penetrable or affectable through such control; and (c) hybrid representational states, of a sort affectable through such control, but only *indirectly*.

3. Once we reach the level of agency, moreover, we also find free acts, whether these be practical choices or cognitive affirmations.

Affirmation in particular is a distinctive act under voluntary control. It can be a public assertion delivered in a natural language, or a private act of affirmation to oneself, in silent soliloquy.

In affirming one might host one or more of a great variety of aims. Among these is the aim to get it right. The corresponding action, that of affirming in the endeavor thereby to get it right is an "alethic" affirmation. Once the affirmation *also* aims to get it right aptly, then it ascends epistemically to the level of *judgment*. An apt judgment is hence a fully apt affirmation, one that aims for aptness in alethic affirmation, and aptly attains that objective.

4. Positive representations aim to represent correctly, whether functionally or intentionally. They are then subject to the AAA normative structure. They can be accurate, adroit, and also apt (accurate through their adroitness).

Can a functionally apt representation be more than just apt? Can it be apt in a way that earns more relevant credit for the representer than the credit that it earns just in virtue of being apt? This is doubtful for the fully wired-in forms of representing that are distinctive of the *merely* functional. Rarely if ever does such a representation aim *also* for aptness and not just for correctness. To the extent that a creature hosts such representations, to that extent is it a rigid mechanism devoid of agency. *Merely* functional representations are doubtful candidates for full aptness.

By contrast, and at the opposite extreme, alethic affirmations under direct voluntary control often aspire not just to correctness but also to aptness. And these will then of course attain full aptness when they *aptly* attain the intended aptness.

5. What about the hybrid representations that are functional without being *merely* functional, since they are subject to *indirect* rational control? These too can be performances whereby the subject aims not just at correctness but also at aptness, even if the aiming is mediated through some regimen of indirect control. Take a player who reacts at the net with the quick punchy block distinctive of the good tennis volley. It may have taken much practice to be able to react automatically that way, and may still take much practice and a certain mental set when the net is approached. It is to the attributable credit of the player that through his years of diligent training he can now react that way. And this is so regardless of the player's failure to now act through a directly intervening choice based on a conscious meta-assessment of his competence and situation.

6. Consider next an epistemic example. One remembers a certain phone number, thanks not just to one's automatic semantic memory, but also to memory aids used deliberately, based on knowledge of their effectiveness. It is because of those measures—chunking, for example, or association, or repetition—that one now has that number right. By taking those measures one aimed to continue to represent not just accurately but also more aptly than otherwise, and altogether aptly. Since those measures were taken through voluntary choice and intention, moreover, the subject would seem

to derive some measure of corresponding credit for his now continuing to represent accurately. And this seems to be so despite how one's present representation of the number is owed to the involuntary operation of one's functional faculty of semantic, retentive memory. Such mnemonic performance is not subject to direct voluntary control. But it still benefits from the remote control exercised when the agent uses the memory aids.

D. A Theory of Competence

Finally, we turn to a theory of competence aimed to fit our AAA virtue epistemology, with its central notion of the apt belief, whose correctness manifests the pertinent *epistemic competence* of the believer. What follows will develop the initial sketch found in Chapter 1.

1. Competences (and abilities) as dispositions to succeed.[2]

   a. A preliminary sketch

A competence is a disposition (ability) to succeed when one tries. How are such dispositions in general constituted? When *complete*, they have a triple-S constitution with three components. But we can distinguish forms of competence that are less than complete. Thus consider the innermost (seat) competence, and also the inner (seat + shape). Beyond these there is the complete competence (including seat + shape + situation). With regard to driving competence (or ability), for example, we can distinguish between (a) the innermost driving competence: that is, the structural seat in one's brain, nervous system, and body, which the driver retains even while asleep or drunk, (b) the fuller inner competence, which requires also that one be in proper shape, i.e., awake, sober, alert, etc., and (c) the complete competence or ability to drive well and safely, which requires also

---

2. In my *Knowledge in Perspective* (Cambridge: Cambridge University Press, 1991), on pp. 281–4, the relevant conditions constitutive of epistemic competence are restricted to those "important and of interest" (282) to the subject's community. See also *A Virtue Epistemology* (Oxford: Oxford University Press, 2007), 137–9, and "How Competence Matters in Epistemology," *Philosophical Perspectives*, 24 (2010): 465–75. A similar approach is taken to epistemic *ability* by John Greco in his *Putting Skeptics in Their Place* (Cambridge: Cambridge University Press, 2000), ch. 9; and "The Nature of Ability and the Purpose of Knowledge," *Philosophical Issues*, 17, *The Metaphysics of Epistemology* (2007), 60–1.

that one be situated with control of a vehicle, along with appropriate road conditions pertaining to the surface, the lighting, etc. The complete competence is thus an SSS (or a SeShSi) competence.[3]

b. What is required for possession of a competence?

i. A competence is a certain sort of disposition to succeed when you try. So, exercise of a competence involves aiming at a certain outcome. It is a competence in part because it is a disposition to succeed reliably enough when one makes such attempts. A competence is hence necessarily a competence to ø successfully, for some ø. And it is thus tied to a conditional of the form: if one tried to ø, one would (likely enough) succeed.

ii. Competences come in degrees of reliability, along with a threshold. However, in order to possess a competence to ø it is not enough that the following conditional be true: that one would ø reliably enough if one tried to ø, that one would not too easily try to ø without actually øing. This could after all be true simply because, knowing one's limits, one øs rarely and only when in a narrow range where one would indeed succeed. Thus, you might restrict your shots as an archer to where you are two feet away from the target. This might show good shot selection, assuming that you are not reliable enough at any longer distance, and it might also display *some (minimal) degree* of archery competence, but it would not show archery competence period.[4]

---

3. Once we understand competences and dispositions in our threefold way, we can make the familiar distinction of finks from masks *for each component*. The trigger of the conditional corresponding to a given competence would prompt a "fink" to *remove* the competence. A "mask" leaves the disposition in place but prevents it from manifesting. Thus a mask might be an agent bent on stopping the manifestations, who would be provoked by the disposition's trigger to intervene in the process that normally leads to the manifestation, but without removing any of the relevant Ss (the seat, shape, or situation). By contrast, a fink would block the manifestations by removing one or another of the Ss. This might be the structural seat (innermost competence), or the shape, or the situation.

    Something can mask a disposition relative to some but not others of its relevant manifestations. Intervening winds might thus mask an archer's competence relative to the accuracy of a shot in hitting its intended target without masking that archer's competence relative to the adroitness of that shot, as manifest in the speed and orientation of the arrow speeding off the bow.

    A situation-fink masks both the inner competence and the innermost competence, finally, whereas a shape-fink masks the innermost competence.

4. Though whittled down to the length of a stub, a pencil would still be so many inches *long* without thereby being a *long pencil*. A pencil with some degree of length may lack enough degree to count as a long pencil *period*. Similarly, a performance may manifest some degree of (the relevant) competence without manifesting enough competence to count as a competent performance (of its sort) *period*.

iii. What then is required for possession of a competence? Required for archery competence, for example, is a "sufficient spread" of possible shots (covering enough of the relevant shapes and situations one might be in as an agent) where one would succeed if one tried, an extensive enough range. What constitutes this range? There must be a close enough sphere of possible worlds where one takes shots, varied enough across the relevant range, and these shots must easily enough succeed, extensively enough across the relevant range. (Alternatively, we might model competence through probability rather than possible worlds. In any case, here my focus is on the phenomena captured in "remoteness or closeness of possibility," however these are best modelled.)

It might be objected that even if one is tied down, so that, knowing one's condition, one would not try to shoot, this does not take away one's competence. But, on the contrary, that *does* bear on one's complete SSS competence, even when it does not affect the inner, SS competence, nor the innermost, S competence. *Moreover*, if indeed one is so disabled psychologically by a phobia that one cannot so much as try to shoot, this does take away even one's innermost skill S. One is now no longer so structured psychologically as to be competent to ø.[5]

2. Competence a special case of disposition to succeed.
   a. Take a soccer goalie who faces an opponent kicker in a tie-break attempt. Suppose the goalie anticipates with a jump to the left. If the kicker then attempts to score by kicking in that direction, the goalie is almost sure to make the save. But if the goalie chooses arbitrarily between jumping to the left, jumping to the right, and staying put, then her save is not nearly as creditable to her competence as it would be if prior experience with this kicker enabled her to anticipate the direction of the kick. If the goalie chooses her direction arbitrarily, then her anticipation of the kicker's choice is insufficiently reliable to qualify as fully manifesting competence. The credit due to the goalie is dampened by her lack of epistemically proper anticipation.

---

5. But here we have a choice. My own preferred choice is to say that one can have a "quasi-competence" to hit the target provided one is so propertied and situated that *if* one were to try to hit the target, one would likely enough succeed. But a *full, proper* competence would require also that one not be so disabled that one could never even try, no matter how desirable it might be to try or to succeed in hitting (a given suitable target).

b. Compare a rank beginner who receives service for the first time in a game of tennis. When the streaking serve comes at him, he swings blindly and wildly. If the coinciding trajectories of the ball and the racket produce a wonderful return, that does not reveal an unsuspected (reliable enough) competence seated in that receiver. Yet if he were ever to repeat that swing in those conditions, a successful return would result. A vigorous enough swing when ball and racket coincide that way will reliably produce such a return. But this does not reveal a competence, despite the fact that there is in that beginner a disposition to reliably return with success by so swinging in such a situation (when the ball approaches with that speed and direction). Even if it manifests *some (minimal) degree* of such competence, the degree is too low for the swing to manifest tennis competence *period*.

c. Flukey success will generally admit description similar to that of our lucky return of service. The performer will occupy a situation wherein he is disposed to succeed if he tries in a certain way; moreover, he is then *able* to try that way, and indeed *does* try that way in that situation, in the case at hand. There is a way of swinging available to our tennis receiver such that, relative to the specified situation of a ball traveling towards him at a certain angle and speed, if he were to swing that way, success would ensue.

d. In defining tennis-return competence we cannot relativize to the way the player happens to proceed in the situation of the fluke. Rather than his competence holding only *relative* to his proceeding thus in that sort of situation, his swing manifests competence precisely because of his ability to swing selectively that way, along perhaps with his competently bringing about the right sort of situation, for example by positioning himself well in preparation for receiving service.

Nevertheless, we cannot require of a performer that he bring about every aspect of a situation constitutive of a complete competence to succeed. Thus, the tennis player's competence is relative to certain lighting, wind, and precipitation conditions that he is not required to bring about, though relevant competence may still be manifest in his choice to play in given conditions, especially when the conditions are just barely acceptable.[6]

---

6. In *one* sense, you have the "ability" to open a safe if you have in your repertoire a sequence of basic acts whereby you would enter the right combination. But this does not give you a

Moreover, if a player tries to improve by practicing in challenging situations with high risk of failure, that cannot be held against him, if these situations are not included among those within which his competence is supposed to guide his performance to success. Thus, a tennis player might practice with a machine that feeds him balls much faster than any he would ever encounter in an actual game, or he might practice in lighting conditions that are significantly subpar. His risk of failure might of course rise dramatically in such circumstances, where he is still willing to test himself. But such a failure rate would not affect his possession of tennis competence.

Here's another way to see the point. Suppose player A prefers to play with far better players, whereas player B likes to crush weaker opponents. Player B thus has a *much* higher success rate for the various performances in a tennis player's repertoire, both actually and dispositionally (given his penchant for weak opponents). But player A may still be the more competent player nonetheless.

    e. Not every disposition to succeed when one tries constitutes a competence, then, although every competence will be constituted by a disposition to succeed when the agent is within certain ranges of shape and situation. How is a disposition to succeed made a competence? In the relevant domain of performance, there must be some prior selection of shape and situation, such that one seats a competence in that domain only if one is disposed to succeed upon trying when in that shape, in that situation. The sorts of shape and situation that are appropriate for a given competence will of course vary from domain to domain of performance.[7]

    f. A competence is a disposition to succeed, but it must be such a disposition properly restricted with respect to the three Ss—Seat, Shape, and Situation. At least the shape and situation must be restricted to the

---

competence to open that safe unless you know the combination. However, it is even doubtful that our rank beginner has any such sequence of basic acts *in their repertoire*.

7. For simplicity, I leave aside restrictions on *how you acquire* the relevant elements of competence, such as the seat and the shape, restrictions that have come to the fore with the cyclist Lance Armstrong (re artificially enhanced shape) and with the baseball player Alex Rodriguez (re drug-derived seat). Each of these athletes improved his performances by boosting his complete SSS dispositions to succeed, but these dispositions did not remain competences once thus artificially enhanced. They did not remain ways to attain fully apt performance, performance thus creditable to (proper) athletic competence and thus creditable to the athlete's relevant competence.

    Compare Descartes's restriction of how you must acquire and sustain your relevant cognitive competences, which comes to the fore with his fourth skeptical scenario, involving an inferior source of the meditator's relevant competences, a source inferior to a divine creator and sustainer.

appropriate. And these restrictions are imposed somehow within the domain of the relevant performances.

Again, all competences are dispositions to succeed, but not all dispositions to succeed are competences. Only those dispositions can be competences whose three Ss fall within the proper range.[8]

    g. The terminology of competence is flexible. Clearly one can be a good, safe driver, in possession of a competence to drive well and safely even when the nearby roads are all covered with oil. One's status as a good driver is not beholden to the condition of nearby roads. The fact that one is not competent to produce good driving on bad, even impassable roads does not take away one's competence as a good driver. Nor would one's skill be impaired by inebriation or sleep. None of this affects the fact that one has the competence of a good driver, which requires only that one Seat that competence, meaning that one hosts the seat: the seat/basis that, together with *appropriate* Shape and Situation, would dispose one to drive well if one tried.

It might be thought that we can distinguish (a) being a good driver from (b) having the competence of a good driver. The latter would require only that one have the skills required for producing good driving if one tried, while the former would require also that one at least normally *try* when one drives. Such innermost competence, which abstracts from appropriate shape and situation, would then constitute a so-called "skill." But this supposed distinction—between (a) and (b)—is put in question by the ways in which driving competence can depend on driving *goals and policies*, such as stopping at yellow lights, staying within the speed limits, and signaling one's turns. Competence can reside in the will.

3. More on the nature and epistemology of competences.

    a. Competences are a very special case of dispositions. Suppose a solid iron dumbbell would shatter upon hitting a certain surface only because a hovering fiend is determined to zap it if and only if it hits the surface, and just as it does so. This would make the relevant conditional true: the dumbbell would shatter on that occasion, but this would not make it fragile.

---

8. Many domains are set largely or wholly by convention, as are games, sports, and artistic domains. Other domains of human endeavor are set by our nature and needs, and by evolutionary teleology. Much is set by the approval of the group, or of the species. But there is surely room for the group to fall short: moral leaders, for example, can lead the way to recognition of competences previously overlooked.

Fragility is more deeply a matter of the degree of stressful external force required for sufficient loss of integrity. It is thus a "proximal" disposition, in respect of both trigger and manifestation. For such dispositions, and for such competences, the situational component may be null or nearly so. By contrast, a "distal" disposition will have targets and manifestations at a distance from the host of the disposition. So it will be a disposition to relate to the target in certain ways given certain inputs. For these dispositions, and competences, the situational component will generally be quite significant. This will apply both to perceptual and to actional competences, when the target is distal relative to the subject.

Distal competences require that the subject be in proper shape and properly situated relative to the target. The subject must be in a relevantly interesting combination of shape *and situation.*

> b. Just what makes a triple-S combination of skill, shape, and situation "interesting" is an interesting, and neglected, question. Such combinations constitute the innumerable competences of interest in the many performance domains recognized by human communities. Such domains—whether athletic, artistic, intellectual, medical, scientific, legal—contain performances aimed at certain distinctive aims, along with the competences whereby performers might succeed more or less competently. When a success manifests such competence, then it is apt, and only then. The SSS profile that constitutes any such competence is not always subject to full and detailed linguistic formulation, in which respect it joins much else of substantial human interest and importance, such as when conduct counts as polite.

What conduct does count as polite? This is much easier to discern by perception in a particular situation, than it is to formulate linguistically in full detail. This is so for politeness in general, as well as for particular matters of politeness, such as the distance that is appropriate for normal conversation in person, and such as the tone and volume of voice that in combination count as rude, to take just two out of many instances.

Moreover, that is not to say that rules of polite conduct are just a myth. Not all rules need to be formulated linguistically. If what is polite is defined by human convention, however, then there must be rules, in some broad sense, that communities agree upon ahead of time. There need not be a constitutional convention to institute those rules. Their institution may be more organic, less artificial than that. Moreover, the agreement within the community will not require so much as linguistic communication. It may be instituted more implicitly than that, through persistent profiles of approval/disapproval, praise/blame, and systematic and implicit manifestation in individual and social conduct.

  c. Returning to our own issues, this pattern of normativity seems applicable also to competences. Thus, the SSS profiles of the competences that acquire salience for communities may be determined not by antecedent, linguistically formulable convention, but rather by persistent implicit profiles of the sort that determine the content of politeness for that community.

What is more, that similarity is not a mere coincidence or analogy. There is after all such a thing as competence in etiquette, and even in morality. It seems possible to conceive of these domains either in terms of rules implicitly operative, or in terms of competences determined by proper community interest.[9]

  d. Competence, safety, and reliability
    i. In order to possess a performance skill (or the seat/basis of a competence), one need not satisfy any absolutely general reliability requirement. Again, one can exercise one's skill too often in inappropriate shape or situation, so that it fails (and would fail) with extremely high frequency, while of course remaining in place (to be thus frequently exercised).
    ii. Skill might be present and exercised, and its exercise might even lead to success without its being manifest in that success. Thus an archer might shoot skillfully, and the arrow might be deflected by an unexpected gust. However, a hovering guardian angel might happen by, determined to correct the trajectory of any well-shot arrow so that it would hit the target when (but only when) it would have done so but for the unlucky intervention of a gust. In this case, the archer's skill is exercised, and in the situation as pictured the skill does partly underlie a complete disposition to succeed. But this disposition does not amount to a true competence, since it is

---

9. That is of course *not* to say that all such domains have their normative source or basis in human convention. Nor need we suppose convention-based domains to lie beyond objective assessment in global or specific respects. They may still be subject to such assessment on how well they further any value they may be designed to secure.

situationally based essentially on the angel. And the angel's presence is a lucky exception, not a stable part of the relevant background.

What makes that innermost archery seat a true skill is that it would combine with appropriate shape and situation so as to dispose the archer to succeed reliably enough if she tried to hit a target. However, in the actual situation the archer's seat/basis fails to combine with an appropriate situation. The angel is an exceptional and ad hoc situational factor. No such angel figures in the situations of interest in the domain of archery, the situations relative to which we assess true archery competence and achievement. What makes that innermost archery seat/basis a true skill is that it would combine with *appropriate* shape and situation so as to dispose the archer to succeed reliably enough if she tried to hit a target, when so shaped and situated.

Consider the archer who shoots with the unexpected gust about to cross the field and the guardian angel poised to intervene, unbeknownst to the archer. This archer does not earn proper credit for his success, which does not really manifest competence.[10] And the reason for this, I suggest, is that the archer does not shoot when in appropriate shape, in an appropriate situation. The appropriate shape and situation for archery competence cannot be constituted by the potential interventions of an ad hoc guardian angel. The appropriate shape and situation must be taken for granted as background for archery shots. Relevant credit will redound to the archer only if his skill is manifest in the success of the shot. Such credit will normally accrue only if the skill produces success with the agent in appropriate shape and situation.

> iii. Skills do come in associated clusters. An archer who knows of the guardian angel, with her power and intentions, might have an enhanced archery skill that takes that into account. Such an archer might indeed manifest his enhanced archery skill when the gust comes along and the angel puts the arrow back on track. The success of his shot would thus be properly credited to that archer's enhanced skill, and thus properly credited to him.
> iv. Similarly, an archer could deliberately frustrate the attempt of a hovering demon to take his arrow off course. Here again an

---

10. Note well: The archer does not earn proper credit for the *success* of his shot aimed at a certain target. He may *still* earn plenty of credit for important qualities of the shot, such as the direction and speed of the arrow as it leaves the bow.

enhanced competence would be in play, to which the shot's success would be creditable.
  e. The bottom line is that the success of a performance in attaining its aim is properly credited to a skill—to an innermost seat of competence—only if that skill counts as such relative to pre-selected shape/situation combinations of interest in the relevant domain, and the performance's success manifests the skill: that is, only if the skill produces the success reliably enough in combination with the agent's relevantly appropriate shape and situation.
  f. Here, finally, is an ontological picture compatible with our view of dispositions and competences.

A given entity is subject to indefinitely many SSS conditionals of the following form: "If X were to host seat Se while in shape Sh and in situation Si, while triggered with T, then X would issue manifestation M." But only *some* such conditionals underlie dispositions and competences. Dispositions and competences are relative to community interest. The community (which could be just the default community of normal humans) will have a special interest in how entities would behave in certain situations while in a certain shape, when triggered by a certain trigger. And so it will pick out the seat Se of a disposition or competence of special interest, relative to the shape/situation combinations of special interest. This leaves it open that multiple Se conditions—Se(1) . . . Se(n)—could correspond to the same disposition or competence. All that is required of a potential seat Se(i) for it to seat a disposition or competence is that its conjunction with Sh and Si conditions of special interest, and with a trigger T, would constitute the antecedent of a true conditional with consequent M.

Thus can we define *positive* or *descriptive* virtues and vices, which would obviously be relative to the relevant community that does the valuing and disvaluing underlying the "special interest" of certain triggers, manifestations, shapes, and situations. The relevant community will then vary depending on which domain is in our focus, whether the domain of a particular sport, or discipline, or profession, etc., or whether it is just the basic human domain.

However, that also makes room for a more normative conception of vice and virtue, still relative to a given community and domain. A normative virtue is then a seat Se that gives rise to a manifestation M when the subject is triggered by some relevant trigger T in a certain Sh/Si combination, where M *should* be positively valued, and T, Sh, and Si *should* be of interest on the part of the community, with a view to the best attainment of the aims proper to the relevant domain. A normative vice is a seat that gives rise to a manifestation M when the subject is triggered by some relevant trigger T in a certain Sh/Si combination, where M *should* be disvalued, and T, Sh, and Si *should* be of interest on the part of the community, with a view to the best attainment of the aims proper to the relevant domain.

That all gives rise to issues interestingly similar to some pertaining to rule utilitarianism in ethics, though our view in epistemology has two important points of distinction. First, we focus on virtues and competences rather than rules. Second, we relativize to domains of endeavor. It is when we focus on the most general domains of human activity and endeavor that we make the closest approach to rule utilitarianism, though even here we keep the distance required for our continuing emphasis on virtues and competences, by contrast with rules.

Descending from that most general domain of competences pertinent to human action in general, down to the restricted domain of epistemology, we find options, two at least, which in fact seem compatible. We may opt for a relativism combined with the positive conception of virtues and competences. This option sets aside any absolute sort of "knowledge" independent of domain and epistemic community. Rather, knowledge is here always relative to domain and community. *Expert* knowledge is relativized to the standards of the particular domain of expertise involved. Compatibly, there can then be a more general *commonsense* knowledge still relativized to particular human groups. On this account, knowledge bears a similarity to politeness of the sort earlier suggested.

However, that is still very far from a relativism according to which what a group knows is simply what it intersubjectively believes, or some slight embellishment of that ugly basis. Also far removed is the view that the knowledge of a group amounts to whatever beliefs it arrives at in keeping with its recognized "ways of knowing." The sort of knowledge sketched by our positive account is much more circumscribed than any such wild relativism. It is relativized to epistemic competences understood as dispositions to get it right in certain Shape and Situation conditions of special interest to the group with respect to arriving at beliefs that will serve their alethic interests. But it gives standing to the *actual* standards of alethic reliability that the group settles on, even if they might have settled on standards that would *better* enable them to attain the true beliefs that would aid the flourishing of proper human interest to them (including attaining a view of things that satisfies proper human curiosity). It is only this that makes the knowledge attributed to them in a deep sense *relative* to them. So, it might be a knowledge that counts as such relative to a certain epistemic community because it manifests a real competence to get it right, in shape and situation conditions of interest to that community, and does so reliably enough *by their standards*.[11]

---

11. Again, a more properly *normative* conception of epistemic competence and knowledge is analogous to a rule utilitarianism of correct moral rules, with a conception of right action in terms of the rules *that would best serve* the community. On this option, we would reach a deeper way in which knowledge is a normative phenomenon. Conceivably, we might recognize both sorts of objective knowledge, both the positive sort relativized to domain of expertise and epistemic community, and also the normative sort on which knowledge is more deeply normative in its constitution. Both options would seem compatible with a competence-theoretic virtue epistemology.

5
Objections and Replies, with a Methodological Afterthought

A. Ten Objections and Replies

Objection 1

If first-order competence can be "blind" in the way of the clairvoyant, I do not see why second-order competence cannot be blind that way too, even if this second-order competence is directed at aptness on the first-order and the attitudes are judgmental.

The blindness we want to avoid is not simply the blindness of a guess. Moreover, the fundamental problem is not—or not entirely—about order. A suitably described clairvoyant could attain full aptness as far as I can see. She would be better off than the original clairvoyant, but she would still be missing something that has value from the epistemic point of view. Insisting that what is missing is a manifestation of some yet higher-order competence merely defers the problem; one is here reminded of the problem with higher-order-desire accounts of autonomy. Part of what is missing is what the normal perceiver has, which needn't ascend beyond the second order at any rate.

The worry may come down to this: unless fully apt beliefs are essentially based on reasons, they will be relevantly blind. Nothing in your picture entails that fully apt beliefs are essentially based on reasons. Yet it is clear that it is better for one's doxastic attitudes to be ex post justified by reasons. What explains this fact? Nothing within reliabilist virtue epistemology as such.

Reply

Unfortunately, I do not share the intuition that attitudes fall short unless based on reasons. I find it implausible that intuiting axioms, for example, must be somehow inferior to believing theorems based on the premises provided by the axioms.

Suppose moreover that, as suggested earlier, judgment is always based on (rationally motivated by) some degree of confidence (whether conscious or not). Can't we then conclude that, in cases like that of the clairvoyant, we *will* have a rational basis for judgment, after all, one provided by a corresponding credence? Yes, the credence itself might lack a rational basis, but are we to suppose that no rationally unfounded credence can be epistemically proper?

What should we then say of our knowledge upon arising in the morning that more than five seconds have elapsed since the alarm went off. Do we have proprietary temporal distance sensory states that keep changing with the passing of time? We *could* say that, most implausibly, in my view; but we needn't say any such thing. After all, some simple math and logic intuitions must be based on groundless seemings (attractions to assent). Accordingly, I see no need to require temporal phenomenal states, when we could again have recourse to non-sensory seemings issuing from subconscious mechanisms, with an alethic valence and a confidence magnitude.

Objection 2

But why the emphasis on the second order? Take anything whatsoever that might affect the likelihood of success, which might well lie on the first order. Isn't a performance better for taking that into account? Suppose the performance-affecting factor is the arrival of a tornado at this very spot exactly five minutes from now. Consider my performance as I shoot my arrow well ahead of the tornado's arrival. Isn't my performance made better by my taking that factor into account? If I wait five minutes and succeed even so, miraculously, my shot will surely be less well selected than it would have been but for my culpable neglect of the impending tornado. So, what is supposed to be so important about paying attention to second-order factors that might affect performance? Should one not avoid neglect on every level by trying to take properly into account whatever factors might affect reliability, whether on the first order or on the second?

Reply

That all seems correct, and it does pose a challenge to our emphasis on full aptness in evaluating attempts. The challenge now is to state the account correctly, giving full aptness its proper place. Here next is my attempt to do so.

First of all, yes, by taking into account more first-order factors that might affect our performance we enhance the reliability of that performance, and this of course makes it a better performance, and *perhaps* this need not involve any second-order phenomenon. True, one might choose what to do by taking positively into account reliability-boosting factors and taking negatively into account reliability-dampening factors. And in order to take such factors thus into account, one may not *need* to ascend to a second order so as to conceptualize the decision through second-order reference to our first-order performance. One could simply in fact be sensitive to those factors on the first order, either positively or negatively.

However, the insufficiency of that approach seems clear already in the case where the outcome of adequate sensitivity to such first-order factors leads to suspension rather than affirmation or denial. In such a case one double-omits intentionally by neither affirming nor denying, and one does so through adequate sensitivity to the relevant probabilifying and disprobabilifying factors.

So, at least in any case where pondering and judgment are involved and pertinent, the second order comes plausibly to the fore. True, someone might even here deny the need to ascend. Perhaps one can respond to the totality of relevant evidence directly with a low enough resultant seeming that properly supports one's suspension, a degree of confidence close enough to 0.5 to constitute suspension?

Two points should be made in reply.

First, even if that very degree of suspension does derive subconsciously from the possessed evidence and its overall weight, it does not follow that it derives with no second-order routing. The relevant second-order beliefs or commitments need not be conscious in order to be operative. Much of what goes on in quotidian reasoning occurs below the surface of consciousness.

Secondly, suppose the degree of confidence is based on the totality of possessed relevant evidence, with no ascent to a second order. This is a *de re* fact about that actual state of confidence. But this fact does not entail that the acquired degree of confidence constitutes suspension. For it to constitute suspension, it must at a minimum lie below the relevant threshold of confidence C+.

The suspension *constituted* by that degree of resultant confidence is, moreover, *not* the suspension of focal interest to us. Our suspension is rather the state at the judgmental level of intentional double-omission, whereby one neither affirms nor denies on the matter at hand. And this intentional state goes beyond the mere degree of confidence induced by the evidence in one's possession. The intentional state involves a kind of choice or, indeed, *intention*. And this seems even less plausibly a state that one can properly enter and occupy stably, absent any ascent to the second order.

On the contrary, now one seems required to consider the relevant risks in the light of one's pertinent, complete SSS competence.

What is more, that is not a peculiarity of cognitive, judgmental performance. The same can properly be said about performance of any sort. Whenever we perform we need to be sensitive to factors that boost or dampen reliability, even if the success whose probability is affected need not be cognitive, but can be, say, *athletic*. We can now see, also here in the general case, that it might be best neither to work towards p nor towards ~p. It might be best rather to stay neutral. This will mean that one does best here again through intentional double-omission. One neither aims to promote p nor to promote ~p. Thus, one might vote neither in favor, nor against; one might abstain instead. And such abstention is necessarily on the second order, since one thereby takes an attitude to the two forborne first-order attitudes.

Alternatively, one might of course arrive at a pro-state, or an anti-state, be it cognitive, as with affirmation or denial, or be it conative, as with promoting p, or promoting ~p.

Attempts *in general* are hence subject to assessment on the level of full aptness, since any attempt will be part of a structure consisting of <promotion, opposition, neutrality>. Now, in the case of interest to us, the most relevant neutrality is that of intentional double-omission, whereby one neither promotes nor opposes. Accordingly, here neutrality will be a matter of a second-order intention, the intention to neither promote nor oppose. And since the other two choices <promotion, opposition> are presumably on the same order as neutrality, since they too might properly result from such deliberation, they too are hence plausibly on the second order.

Consider, furthermore, the factors pertinent to full aptness, those that bear on whether one's performance will be not only successful but *aptly* successful. These factors concern the quality of one's complete SSS competence, and how likely it is that such quality will give rise to an apt performance. So, these factors bear on the reliability of one's relevant competence on the choice faced. And they generally bear and are known to bear on the aptness of one's performance. So, it would be negligent to give them no weight, not even implicitly, when deciding what to do.

That is not true *generally* about factors that might affect the reliability of one's attempts. Many factors *might* affect the reliability of an attempt while their relevance and even their existence lie beyond the agent's ken. And often enough this cannot be blamed on the agent, who pays them no heed, without negligence. Not even implicitly need the agent heed such factors, except possibly in the all-encompassing way of "Is there anything that might go wrong here?"

By contrast, our SSS profile is not like that. We need to consider factors that might go wrong *under this description*. We need to consider whether we are relevantly competent to pull it off: whether we have the skill, while in proper shape and well enough situated. We need to do so at least implicitly, even if we stop short of deep philosophical meditation. This speaks in favor of the pertinence of full aptness in general, and of its epistemic importance in particular.

Objection 3

A skeptical problem arises concerning an ordinary perceiver, Norm, who views a hand, or a fire, in a normal setting. You had earlier written as follows: "[Does] . . . ordinary perceptual belief sufficiently avoid the sort of danger that dooms the other. . . beliefs [including those of Barney in fake barn country]? Unlike being envatted or bedeviled, after all, dreaming and insanity are relatively familiar phenomena; these pose greater danger for ordinary perceptual beliefs. Is this danger low enough that ordinary perceptual belief is spared, unlike Barney's relevant beliefs? That is not beyond reasonable doubt."[1]

So, unless we now embrace skepticism, will the new theory be at odds with your earlier verdict, in requiring safety for "knowledge full well"? Won't ordinary Norm now be denied everyday knowledge of his hand or fire, since he cannot truly believe that his belief would be apt?

Reply

Granted, if ordinary "knowledge" aligns with *knowing full well*, and not with *mere apt affirmation*, that seems to favor dream skepticism. Suppose nodding off to be a nearby possibility when after dinner we settle comfortably into an armchair, and watch the flames flicker, hear the logs crackle, and feel the warmth. There is then a notable cognitive risk, since we might so easily have been dreaming at a moment when in fact we are still perceiving the fire. Even if we are thus awake and do see and hear and feel the fire, we might very easily have been dreaming instead. If we take ordinary knowledge to require full and not just bare aptness of affirmation, it would

---

1. "How Competence Matters in Epistemology," *Philosophical Perspectives*, 24.1 (2010): 465–75.

seem doubtful that in such a circumstance we do *know* we face a fire. How then can we respond to this skeptical challenge?

I respond by questioning whether in dreams we really form beliefs.[2] If, as I argue, we do not *really* believe when *in a dream* we believe, no cognitive risk is posed by the close modal proximity of dreams. This response to dream skepticism enables us to sustain the view that ordinary knowledge requires aptness of belief (full aptness of affirmation).

As for madness, it will depend on how near to it I am, so far as I know, at the moment of judgment. Too easily, perhaps, *might* one now be thus poorly *constituted*. Insanity, unlike being drunk or asleep, goes beyond being temporarily in bad shape for cognition.[3]

None of that bears on *animal* knowledge, which helps us to accommodate those who don't understand all the skeptical fuss (hardheaded reliabilists), even if their sight falls short of the reflective level.

Objection 4

A further kind of trouble derives from problematic examples.[4] Earlier you had presented the case of a subject who drinks from a cup out of several available on a table, where all the other cups contain a drug that much degrades subitizing ability. You had described that subject as follows:

> ... So our subject might easily have greatly lowered his subitizing competence. He might thus easily have believed incorrectly, since his competence might easily have been degraded. There were many equally available cups, after all; only by luck did he drink from the one without the drug. Does the fact that he might have suffered that fate deny him subitizing knowledge if in fact he does not suffer it? I can only report that to me that seems implausible.[5]

You now require knowledge full well, with its concomitant requirement that the first order affirmation would be apt (and thus would be true). But consider the subject who barely avoids the cup with the disabling drug. Don't we now risk denying him knowledge full well, since he "might so easily have affirmed incorrectly"? If he might so easily have affirmed incorrectly, how then can it be that his affirmation would then be true?

---

2. *A Virtue Epistemology* (Oxford: Oxford University Press, 2007), ch. 1.
3. Recall here Descartes's fourth skeptical scenario, where he considers that he might have been created by some lesser agency. He takes that to be knowledge denying, since we might then have been poorly constituted, so far as we can tell. And his theological reasoning is meant to reassure on that point of proper constitution, as well as on the issues of dreaming and madness.
4. As in section 9 of "How Competence Matters in Epistemology."
5. Section 9 of "How Competence Matters in Epistemology."

But can we really find it plausible that our subject is denied knowledge after all, because of the nearby cups with the disabling drug?

Reply

Here's a way to think of that case. The basis for a subject's disposition to judge correctly is a SeShSi (Seat/Shape/Situation) basis. Each of these three S components might be endangered, and the exact locus of the danger matters little, as Descartes saw so clearly. This emerges with his skeptical fourth scenario, wherein we might have been created by some inferior agency, so as to be ill conditioned, and indeed ill constituted. If one might too easily be ill conditioned, it seems a relatively minor matter just which of the conditions—which of the three Ss—is the target: whether the seat, the shape, or the situation. For full aptness, then, we need proper assurance that we are well conditioned *period*, no holds barred.[6]

Objection 5

Suppose I just managed to decline a strong drink at the end of a party (where that drink would have impaired my vision, which otherwise remains intact, because I remain well within my tolerance for alcohol). Now, on my way home, relatively sober, I notice a stop sign and pull up to a stop. I might easily have been impaired (I almost accepted that last drink): and if I had been impaired I would have mistaken the street sign (or perhaps the pedestrian) for a stop sign, or missed that sign and run it, or god knows what. But I rejected that last drink. Now, leaving aside a very general skepticism about knowledge, is there, plausibly, any failure on my part to know that there's a stop sign there?

If not, then how can knowledge full well be a useful condition for epistemology: doesn't it require that my affirmation would have been true? And if that requires, not just being well conditioned, but also an assurance that we're well conditioned, don't we lack that here?

Reply

True, I might easily have been impaired now, after I left the party and turned down that last drink. But it's another matter whether I can *now* judge that I am not *now* impaired, and whether I *would* now affirm correctly and aptly on that matter. If, after long enough, I've been doing well enough, I may now have what I need in order to know that, *although I might*

---

6. A fuller response to this objection is contained in the next reply.

easily have been impaired, I am now ok. I may now be well conditioned (SSS well conditioned), while also *assured* that I am well conditioned.

Suppose on the contrary that, as I head for the door, I am so close to the threshold of sobriety, that one more sip would have done me in. Yes, I might be sober enough to drive (and properly discern stop signs), but I don't really know that I am sober enough. Is there still nothing lacking in me as agent? (Compare the basketball player at a distance from the basket where she cannot know that she still has the required competence.)

So far we have covered just the shape (sobriety) and the situation (distance from the basket), but we can next see how the same reasoning will apply to the seat (or skill).

With age comes loss of memory, so that one properly hesitates when it seems that Columbus sailed in 1492. "Was it 1492 or was it 1494?" As the loss of memory becomes evident, even when one does perfectly well remember the right date, one's *judgment* may no longer be apt, since one can no longer assume aptly that one would affirm aptly. Here the problem concerns not just the shape one is in at the time, nor the situation that one occupies. It concerns rather the seat of one's relevant competence, the underlying faculty of memory, which one retains even when asleep or drunk, even when it cannot be exercised with complete competence, since one is then in bad shape. The elder in my example is perfectly alert and sober, however, and not in bad shape. In his case what may be lacking or degraded is the faculty itself, not the shape or situation.

Take again the basketball player in her zone of uncertainty, where she has no clue whether she still enjoys the competence required for a safe, reliable shot. It seems not to matter what gives rise to the uncertainty: whether it is low enough skill (or poor enough seat), bad enough shape, or unfortunate enough situation. Whatever the source may be, if a performer is unsure enough of having to a sufficient extent the complete competence required, then their performance will fall short in the way of the unsure basketball player, and of the guessing eye-exam subject. This applies to epistemic as well as to athletic performers. And people will track accordingly as we go through examples. Some will use the honorific word "knowledge" to mark the more demanding accomplishment, at least in certain contexts, while others deem sufficient some lower-grade accomplishment. These latter can see the good in the highly competent and reliable eye-exam subject, and award him the honorific.

The impairment that one might easily have suffered earlier is similarly related to one's present ability to judge that one is not now impaired.

The nearer and clearer the danger that one might now be impaired, the harder it will be to judge competently, as of the present moment, whether one would now affirm aptly on that first-order matter.

Finally, the meta-judgment that matters most at the moment of performance is the meta-judgment *as of that moment* answering to whether at that moment one would perform aptly. What matters then is what one's SSS condition is *at that moment*, and what dangers it may *then* still be subject to, as one performs. If so, consider Barney, or the partygoer, or the elder (*very near* the threshold of inadequate memory). Any such performer who *might easily have been* ill conditioned, through bad seat, shape, or situation, *may still in actual fact be* well enough conditioned at the moment of performance.

Such agents would seem to perform safely enough, even if they are out of position to *know* that they are well enough conditioned. And the way in which they fall short may be, *not* through lack of first-order safety with respect to their basic aim, but by failing to aptly discern such safety. That is plausibly what pulls us to withhold "knowledge" of Barney, and of the woozy partygoer, and of the elder at the threshold of knowledge-denying loss of memory, and of many other unfortunates in recent epistemic lore: Norman, Truetemp, blindsighters, chicken sexers, etc.

Objection 6

You have defended a conception of knowledge as not just individual but extended. This includes the way in which knowledge must be socially extended, given the status of testimony as an important epistemic source in its own right. You have long been committed in that way to a social virtue epistemology.[7]

If that commitment is correct, then the competences that bear most directly on much of our individual knowledge are socially seated. Moreover, they need not be seated in any organized group, such as a research group, or a company, or school. The relevant social competences may instead be seated in a motley group that extends through centuries, as in much of our knowledge about the remote past through surviving documents. There is no organized group that encompasses both the producers of those documents and the researchers who read them much later. So, the knowledge that derives from trust in documents, depends essentially on a complex competence seated partly in the writers from long ago and partly in the researchers who read them at a later time.

---

7. *A Virtue Epistemology*, 93–8; and *Knowing Full Well* (Princeton: Princeton University Press, 2011), 86–90.

This whole, temporally extended group still seats the competence that accounts for the epistemic status of the later readers' pertinent beliefs.

In that respect, the motley group is as creditable for the later correct and apt belief as is a motley group of tourists for the clean condition of a park at the end of a busy day. The tourists may vary greatly, and may act in minimal if any concert, and yet it may be their collective action that accounts creditably for that result.

Now, here's the problem for you. How can we know that our testimony-based beliefs would be apt? How can we know this when we lack any adequate grasp of the identity of the relevant motley group, and hence lack any way to determine how reliable they might be on the pertinent subject matter? How can we possibly arrive through testimony at fully apt belief?

Reply

Consider our implicit trust in fellow human beings to whom we can attribute specific testimony because we can understand what they say, either orally or in writing. Trust in such deliverances of testimony is as natural as is our default trust in the deliverances of our senses and memory. And, fortunately, it is also as generally conducive to the spread of knowledge and thereby to the flourishing of our species, and our communities. It is fortunate that both sorts of deliverances tend reliably enough to be correct, which is no accident. We relate to each other and to our physical surroundings so that all three channels of information are reliable to some appropriate extent. We trust our senses, our memory, and our fellows, and our trust in each sort of deliverance has a similar basis, a basis in our nature and our relations to our past, to each other, and to our environments, a basis that assures the sufficient reliability of all these sorts of deliverance. If this were not so, we would know far less. But since it is so, and since our trust reflects how we are relevantly constituted and interrelated, we do know through epistemic competence things that otherwise we could not know that way.

Our trust that we would affirm aptly if we affirmed in line with received testimony is thus like our trust in the deliverances of our senses or our memory. In all three cases, a basic default trust is founded on a basis of reliability. This default trust underlies our second-order assumption that we are well placed to affirm aptly, absent defeaters, which sustains our reliance on each of perception, memory, and testimony. And this makes it possible for us to judge aptly—to affirm with full aptness—in each of those three instances.

What we learn from the case of testimony is that the epistemic competence manifest in one's knowledgeable judgment need not be seated *exclusively* in oneself. It may be seated in a group of which one is a part, so that it is *partly* seated in oneself. Suppose the correctness of one's judgment *partly* manifests one's own competence, which is partly constitutive of the complete competence seated in the whole group. In that case the correctness of one's judgment can partly manifest one's constitutive competence, while it more fully manifests the complete competence seated in that group, one's place in which is essential for the aptness of that performance. When properly combined, this all suffices for the aptness of that judgment, and for the full aptness of the contained affirmation. Full aptness does not require detailed knowledge of how our first-order competence attains its sufficient reliability, nor detailed knowledge of its workings in the specific instance. For each of perception, memory, and testimony, full aptness requires only a proper trust *that* the pertinent competence *is* reliable enough and *would* work accordingly in securing aptness on the first order. And that trust can be proper when it is a default trust absent specific reasons for concern.

Objection 7

In a recent article, Duncan Pritchard defends a certain view of epistemic safety, and argues on that basis against the sort of virtue epistemology that you have defended in the past and in the present text. He takes the problem to require a solution that combines a virtue component with a separate safety component. Here first is the view of safety.

Safety (Pritchard's View)

S's belief that p is safe iff the way in which it is formed is a way of forming beliefs that would reliably yield correct answers.[8]

A very specific modal condition is in play here, however, and it is crucial to be clear on its content. Pritchard's solution to the lottery puzzle depends on that specific condition. He argues that one does not know, simply on the basis of probabilities, that one's ticket has lost, because one's belief then fails that very specific modal condition. The thought is that in a very similar possible world one's ticket wins, which suffices to make the actual-world belief that it has lost an unsafe belief. More strictly, in line with his Safety just above, what makes one's lottery belief unsafe and precludes its amounting to knowledge is this: that in a possible world similar enough to the actual world, one forms such a lottery belief on the same probabilistic basis and one's belief is nevertheless false.

---

8. "Anti-luck Virtue Epistemology," *The Journal of Philosophy* (2012): 247–79.

Pritchard thinks that, in order to constitute knowledge, a belief must be safe that way and must also be formed virtuously or competently. In his view only thus can we properly resolve a tension for virtue epistemology when it tries to combine a proper treatment of Gettier examples, such as the fake barns example, with a way to accommodate knowledge by testimony.[9] And that takes us to the heart of his newly distinctive combination of anti-luck and virtue-epistemological components, as follows.

Anti-Luck Virtue Epistemology

S knows that p if and only if S's safe true belief that p is the product of her relevant cognitive abilities (such that her safe cognitive success is to a significant degree creditable to her cognitive agency).

On this account, Jenny knows the directions to the Sears Tower in Chicago when she receives them from a passer-by. Jenny is said to know because her belief is safe while its correctness is sufficiently creditable to her cognitive agency (which notably does not require that it be primarily *so creditable). As for Barney in fake barn country, he fails to know because, although the correctness of his belief is indeed to a significant degree creditable to his cognitive agency, still his belief fails to be safe, given the barn façades populating that neighborhood.*

Reply

That way of understanding safety does help Pritchard's account deliver both of his desired results: first, that Jenny knows through testimony the directions to the Sears Tower; second, that Barney fails to know he faces a barn. The reason for the latter is that, in at least one close-enough world, Barney would form such a belief in the same way while his belief was false. This would happen when he viewed any of the mere barn façades so common in that neighborhood.

However, that account has a weak point in its modal notion of luck, explained above. According to anti-luck virtue epistemology, the belief that one has lost the lottery, when based just on the probabilities, fails to constitute knowledge. This is because of how unsafe it is, since there is a close-enough possibility where one's ticket in fact wins. Or rather, more strictly, one's lottery belief is unsafe because of this: *because in a close enough*

---

9. My own solution to that tension has now been published separately, in a publication that Pritchard's paper does not take into account: namely, section 8 of ch. 4 of *Knowing Full Well*. Although I will not reprise that solution here, objection 4 above is relevant, along with my reply.

possible world a belief is false despite being formed the way that this one is formed in the actual world.

The view clashes with our intuitive reactions to cases of clear enough knowledge. Here is one such case.

A Bad Apple

I assume that technology would enable us to make a zillion tickets equally close to winning at the time of a lottery drawing. In that case the lottery intuition says we don't know our ticket will lose (nor can we know it has lost, once in fact it has, unless the result has been announced).

Pritchard's Safety would explain all of that by requiring a kind of safety according to which there cannot be even a single possibility of failure that is as close as any relevant possibility, even if there are a zillion-minus-one equally close possibilities within which one succeeds.

But take now a world where Apple has grown so large that a million operators stand by constantly to provide answers to any simple Apple question, and suppose technology randomizes in such a way that there are a million-minus-one operators no farther modally from me than the one I actually reach when I place my call. And suppose there is *one* bad apple in the lot, a liar who would give me an incorrect answer. But suppose further that Apple's service continues to be great, so that all the other million-minus-one operators are infallibly reliable in their answers to such questions. Is that enough to preclude me from learning the answer to my question from the operator I actually reach?

Here again the new "anti-luck" safety requirement entails the wrong answer.

Objection 8

Your view implies that Lottie knows that her ticket will lose its zillion-ticket lottery, simply based on the probabilistic information that enables her to form a highly reliable belief that it will lose. Suppose it is true that her ticket will lose, and suppose Lottie bases her belief quite competently and reliably on the probabilistic information. She is not just guessing, nor is she basing her belief on any fallacy, nor does her belief derive from improper trust in a lying testifier, nor does it come from the past through a memory weakened by Alzheimer's. Et cetera. On the contrary, her belief seems competently and reliably acquired, so that beliefs thus acquired would be very likely correct.

True, there is a belief thus acquired that is false in a very close possible world: namely, the belief about the winning ticket, that it will lose. But, as we have seen, this sort of unsafety cannot be allowed to block knowledge. If it did so, then our Apple customers would be blocked from knowing what they do so plausibly know.

So, isn't your virtue epistemology refuted by this simple lottery case?

Reply

1. What needs explaining in the epistemology of lotteries is our reluctance to think that one knows one has lost a lottery (before one sees the results), even when there is an enormously high probability that one's ticket *did* lose. Here next is a proposal.

In essence, I would now respond to the lottery problem as I once did to Nozick's sensitivity-based skepticism.[10] Can a proper treatment of lotteries perhaps be as simple as the following two-paragraph argument?

> Robert Nozick thinks we fail to know that we are not in a skeptical scenario, and that we so fail because our belief is insensitive. But subjunctive conditionals do not contrapose, and we are misled into accepting a sensitivity condition by confusing it with a safety condition. Plausibly, then, we do know we're not in a skeptical scenario, since this belief is safe enough, no matter how insensitive. So, the response to sensitivity-wielding skeptics is to respectfully suggest that they are led into error by the foregoing confusion of sensitivity with safety.

> Now I'd like to respond to lottery skepticism in close parallel to that earlier response to a skepticism of radical skeptical scenarios. Consider those who think we fail to know that our ticket has lost even in a lottery scenario where the odds of winning are minuscule. Here again we can argue that they are misled by the evident insensitivity of their belief, in just the way the sensitivity-based skeptic above is misled. The right requirement is a requirement of sufficient safety, of truth in enough of the near-enough worlds. And this is a requirement that our lottery belief does fulfill. So, really we do know well enough that our ticket has lost, despite the insensitivity of our belief, just as we know well enough that we are not relevantly bedeviled or envatted, despite the insensitivity of these beliefs. Sensitivity is epistemically noxious in its power to mislead. It misleads us not only with regard to skeptical scenarios, but also with regard to lottery scenarios. Sensitivity is easily confused with safety, because of how plausible it is that subjunctive conditionals contrapose. Once we are clear that they do not contrapose, we can then countenance basis-relative safety while discarding sensitivity. And this enables us to reject both errors: the error of the skeptic about skeptical scenarios and that

---

10. I mean the response in "How to Defeat Opposition to Moore," *Philosophical Perspectives*, 13 (1999): 141–54.

of the skeptic about lottery propositions. By replacing sensitivity with safety we can begin to defend a more acceptable and commonsensical view in both instances. (Of course, we do need a proper understanding of safety.)[11]

2. Moreover, I would now cast a gimlet eye also on Vogel-style lottery propositions.[12] True, we are somewhat pulled to say that we do *not* know that our car has not been stolen from where we parked it in the morning. But the misleading sensitivity idea is here again to blame. We are again led to think that we do not know, by the same misleading confusion of the bad sensitivity condition with the good safety condition. And the same reaction is appropriately in place generally with respect to Vogel-style lottery propositions. Moreover, the insensitivity of inductive conclusions should not lead us to worry about induction, if it is safety rather than sensitivity that really matters.

3. Some who speak of lotteries, and of lottery propositions more broadly, may thus have a sensitivity condition fixedly in mind, and may hence properly deny us knowledge that the ticket has lost. Some philosophers may even properly deny us knowledge that one is not in a skeptical scenario, if they too have fixedly in mind a sensitivity condition. This may be the case of Nozick, and of others. And they are of course right to recognize an objective phenomenon of sensitive belief, and right to think that we lack that condition in our belief about the skeptical scenario and about the losing ticket. Thus they can be led to properly question closure, or to turn contextualist, etc.

Compatibly with that, they may also be led to overlook the alternative—*and compatible*—view that there is a kind of "knowledge" in those cases. And they may overlook that subjunctive conditionals do not contrapose, and thus overlook safety-based approaches. (However, again, we will need to ask what sort of safety would be most appropriate, and we may eventually need to make room also for aptness: for belief correctness that manifests epistemic competence.)

---

11. The sensitivity conditional can provide this explanation even if there are cases of sensitivity that do not elicit the ignorance intuition. There might be special countervailing reasons at work in the exceptions, while perceived insensitivity might still retain a very strong and explanatory *tendency* to elicit a denial of knowledge. (This is a view defended by Keith DeRose.) Even in all the cases where the tendency is present, however, a "no knowledge" intuition might derive erroneously from confusion with a more nearly correct safety condition, where sensitivity and safety are still thought to be equivalent through a powerfully tempting fallacy of contraposition.

12. Jonathan Vogel, "Are There Counterexamples to the Closure Principle?," in M. Roth and G. Ross (eds), *Doubting: Contemporary Perspectives on Skepticism* (Dordrecht: Kluwer, 1990).

4. I have claimed that lottery propositions are knowable, which may provoke incredulous outrage. And yet, about someone's infidelity after twenty-five years of marriage, I might say: "You see, you never know!" This I might say commonsensically even if it would be wrong to add that no one ever knows that their spouse is faithful. And to someone in tears because their hopes were dashed when their ticket lost in a zillion-ticket lottery, we can say: "Why are you surprised? You should have known that you would lose. You knew the odds!" And to someone who trusted their shaman's prediction that their ticket would win, and is surprised when it loses, we can say: "Aw, come on, you should have known better." Finally, consider someone anxiously holding their ticket as they look expectantly at the screen where the winner is about to be announced. It seems perfectly appropriate to tell them, seriously and with no hint of jocularity: "Don't set yourself up for disappointment. Trust me. Your ticket has lost."[13]

In line with my methodological paragraph earlier, and in line with the preceding paragraph, it seems occasionally commonsensical to attribute to people knowledge of lottery propositions, and especially of Vogel lottery propositions. If by "commonsensical" we mean that many or most ordinary English speakers will go along in *some* ordinary enough contexts, then obviously both a given sentence and its negation could be commonsensical.

5. Everyone is well aware that subjunctive conditionals don't contrapose. And most everyone now sees safety as independent from sensitivity. That is all true, I agree, on appropriate presicifications. But to agree on that much is not to draw an explanation from that fact.[14]

Sensitivity becomes extremely attractive when we see how well it explains our tendency to say that only once the results are announced can we know our ticket has lost, even if the probability of a miscommunication is much higher than that of our ticket's winning. The difference is said

---

13. Alternative explanations may of course be proposed for these cases, but they will be attempts to explain away what is said *in competition with* the straightforward interpretation according to which people are just reporting what is just obviously true. And two can play the same game, as in our attempts to counter the straightforward interpretation of the widely shared claim that one cannot know or even reasonably believe based merely on probabilities no matter how high.
14. Compatibly, we may add a similar explanation for good measure. When deniers of lottery knowledge appeal to the fact that one always *might* win the lottery even if the chances are so low, and conclude from this that one never knows one has lost, the strong plausibility of this may correlate with a similarly strong tendency to confuse the epistemic with the metaphysical "might."

to reside in the fact that, before we perceive the results, our belief is not sensitive, whereas, once we rely on a newspaper (for example), our belief is sensitive. Initially, if the ticket had won we would *still* have believed that it had lost, since the win would *not* have affected our purely probabilistic basis. But once our belief is based on the newspaper, then if the ticket had won, we would not have believed it to have lost (on plausible assumptions, in a normal case) since the newspaper *would* then have published something different. So, sensitivity is undeniably attractive, but it also has execrable consequences, so its attraction is a siren call.

6. Let us next return to the more general issues of epistemology to which Pritchard's account was addressed. Now we have an alternative take on lottery examples such as that of Lottie (above), now welcomed as a knower. With this result, we can now opt for a more reasonable and commonsensical account of safety. We can require, for the safety of a belief, not that there be no single close enough, similar enough case in which the believer goes wrong. We may require instead the following more forgiving condition: that the belief be reliable *enough*: that in enough of the close enough cases in which the believer forms similarly enough a similar enough belief, he again believes correctly. And we can plausibly conclude that through my phone call I can come to know the answer to my simple Apple question.

Objection 9

Imagine that there is a great but underconfident street saxophonist. He now faces the choice either to pick an easier but lower-paying piece or a more difficult piece. He decides—recklessly by his own lights—to play the hard piece. What makes his decision reckless is an ill-founded belief that the piece lies beyond his competence. He plays it flawlessly, nevertheless, thus manifesting his sublime competence, and makes a lot of money, as he had hoped.

Did his performance of the difficult piece fall short here because of its etiology? This is entirely implausible. I can't see how one could say "yes" without being deeply in the grip of a theory. His performance was flawless. Still, there is something that fell short. What? Well, the saxophonist himself is open to criticism for choosing the piece he chose, a reckless choice. Here it seems right to separate the evaluation of the agent and his decision to perform from the evaluation of the performance. We can criticize the saxophonist's choice to perform the harder piece. But the performance does not fall short.

Yet, according to your view, the performance must fall short in virtue of failing to be fully apt. This looks like a problem for thinking that there is any such category as full aptness. The category conflates two distinct loci of evaluation that should be kept separate.

Reply

I focus on performances but have long tried to make it clear that these are assumed to be performances *with an aim*. Here's a capsule statement of the relevant reasoning, which for simplicity I will state in its abstract form, though its bearing on the particular example should be obvious.

1. Performances are of two sorts: (a) deeds, and (b) aimings. Kicking one's spouse in one's sleep is a deed, an attributable doing (unlike squashing a rabbit at the end of one's fall off a cliff), but it is not an aiming, something one aimed to do.
2. Aimings are of two sorts: (a) functional or teleological (whether biologically, socially, or psychologically, whether by a whole animal or by an organ or subsystem), and (b) intentional.
3. Moving to epistemology, consider alethic affirmations, aimed at truth. An intentional action can have more than one end, constituting more than one *attempt*. So, an attempt constitutively involves a particular aim. It is this distinctive aim that makes it subject to the AAA normative structure of such attempts, which can be accurate, adroit, and/or apt.
4. A full attempt is an attempt that aims not only at its basic goal but also at the *apt* attainment of that goal. A fully apt attempt is an attempt that *aptly* attains *both* of those aims.
5. Alethic affirmations are sayings (in public or to oneself) of a special sort, since they must be aimed at truth.
6. To judge that p is *at least* to alethically affirm that p (aiming at truth), but it is more than that. Judgment also aims at *aptness* of alethic affirmation.

Any successful attempt is of course a deed (an attributable doing). Thus, when Diana kills her prey, there is the successful attempt, but there is also the deed (the attributable doing). The choice and intention are constitutive of the attempt, but not of the deed. So, if "the shot" is just the *deed*, then the shot may be perfectly fine without being fully apt. But this leaves it open that Diana's *attempt* is better when fully apt than when merely apt.

In any case, the whole AAA structure properly applies, not to doings or to deeds, but to aimings, and especially to attempts. So the sort of "shot" that can be apt at all is Diana's attempt. This is the "shot" that seems better when fully apt than when just apt, since the quality of its constitutive choice-plus-intention plausibly matters to the quality of the constituted entity, the successful attempt.

In judgment (unlike mere affirmation, or even alethic affirmation) the agent aims not just at truth but also at aptness. So, the fuller attempt that constitutes judgment is so much as apt *only if* the constitutive alethic affirmation is *fully* apt.

Rejoinder (Objection 10)

Consider another case that might be clearer:

> Davy hasn't been on a skateboard in fifteen years, though he was a pro in his teens. He has just encountered some friends from his past. They bet him $200 that he can't do a certain trick on the skateboard. He accepts the bet out of sheer brazenness. He has little reason to think that he still knows how to do this trick. He's in excellent shape, though—he just ought to worry that he's forgotten how to turn the trick. As it turns out, he still remembers how and he manifests this knowledge by performing like a pro.

Because his doing of the trick manifests his know-how, the doing of it is an intentional action. It isn't merely an attributable doing, like kicking someone in one's sleep.

True, he did not know that he still had the know-how. Does that reflect poorly on the quality of his performance of the trick, an intentional performance that exercised his know-how? I don't think so.

But the same claims then apply to Diana. It is not her shot that is better in virtue of being guided by her apt belief that it would be apt. She is more praiseworthy and her choice of shot is better, granted. But that is a different claim than the claim that the shot itself is better. Theory-neutral reflection makes it seem far more natural to make my different claim.

These points raise several worries. If the first-order belief that you call "knowledge full well" is analogous to Diana's shot, I worry that the belief doesn't get any better in virtue of being motivated through risk assessment and the like. If so, there isn't really another grade of knowledge to which this belief ascends. Rather, there is a distinct epistemically praiseworthy locus of evaluation—the believer and the believer's doxastic decision-making procedure (as it were). But then we shouldn't call the first-order belief a piece of "knowledge full well."

So something has to go.[15]

---

15. Many thanks to Kurt Sylvan for pressing objections 9 and 10.

Reply

This rejoinder makes it clear how intuitively compelling is the present line of objection. Granted, a fuller reply is required. Fortunately, there *is* more to say.

First of all, the aiming at aptness involved in fully apt affirmation must guide the constitutive alethic affirmation *at the time of affirming*. And the point applies to performances generally, including those spread out in time. It is not enough that one adopts a certain aim when one decides to perform in a corresponding way. After all, that decision might lapse before the moment of action. If it is to provide the guidance required for full aptness, the relevant second-order intention must be concurrent and coordinate with the first-order action, which might involve a procedure over some span of time. Absent such concurrent guidance, the first-order action might possibly be aborted at various times within that span. Or it might suffer the fate attributed by Santayana to the fanatic, who "redoubles his effort when his aim is forgotten."[16]

Secondly, we need to recall that many performances unfold in constitutive domains. A chess move is not just the player's grasping the piece and moving it from one square to another. A player might have that merely "geographical" intention, of course, and *that* attempt (performance with a constitutive aim) can then be evaluated with respect to its success, which might manifest an unexcelled competence to make such motions with success. Nevertheless, the move might be an abysmal chess move, leading to checkmate in the opponent's next move. Here the geographical attempt comes nested in the chess attempt (to do what will best help the player towards winning, or at least toward averting immediate defeat). The nested attempt can be apt even though the nesting attempt is inapt.

There are innumerable such domains of human performance, some more formal and rule bound than others, but every such domain will have its proper objective(s), and its correlated standards of success, and of proper competence. This seems obvious for the various formal sports, including chess, with their rules and goals, and with their standards of success and of competence. Our archery and basketball examples already implicitly bring this out. But it is true also, though more vaguely so, in less formal sporting activities, such as an afternoon's hunt. And it remains true in uncountable domains of successful and proper performance made available to humans through convention or evolution.

What is crucial for my argument now is that, for any given domain, there will be a standard of competence, a standard of *reliable enough* disposition to

---

16. *Life of Reason: Reason in Common Sense* (New York: Charles Scribner's Sons, 1905), 13.

succeed. This tends to be a rather vague matter, generally at the upper end of the vagueness ubiquitous in human common sense. And it will depend on the particular sort of performance, and the specific situation.

In a match, for example, the tennis player will have various options when the ball comes at him across the net. Each option will have a risk/reward profile as *the player aims for his relevant objectives*, such as that of winning the point.

The good player will always be mindful of that profile, as he chooses stroke after stroke. So, his objective is not *just* attaining the desired immediate effect of the shot he settles on speedily: say, the objective of lobbing with topspin over the opponent at the net. No, that shot is in a deeper sense assessable with respect to whether it was a well-selected shot. If the opponent was far enough back from the net and the player was close enough to the net, it may be blindingly obvious that he should hit an angled passing shot instead. The lob may be far too risky, although the risk will diminish in proportion to how much closer within the court the opponent is to the net and how much farther the player is.

That is just an example of how complex the assessment of relevant risk can be, even given a fairly simple objective proper to a given domain, as is the objective of winning a point in tennis. And that remains so in the details of this case, even if in general the player must simply opt for *a shot that is likeliest to help him win the point*, period.

Note, moreover, that the shot might be an excellent choice even if it is *very* unlikely to win the point, since it may still be as likely as any of the options then available to the player. If against all odds it wins the point cleanly, then it will be creditable, even highly creditable to the player. However, if in our example the player opts for a shot (the lob) far more risky than another available shot (the angled passing shot), then the winning shot will be criticizable. Despite being a winning shot, it might still be poorly selected in the extreme, and an inferior shot in that regard.

Human performance *can*, however, escape the constraints of critical domains, such as sports, artistic performance, and any other domain where there are formal or quasi-formal rules or standards. Human performance can also escape the standards set for the species by evolution, as to what performance conduces to normal human flourishing. Human performance can be carefree and spontaneous, or otherwise escape any such standards or boundaries. Indeed, the relevant objective may be entirely subjective and selected by the agent in near-total freedom. There is just no limit then to what is *reliable enough* or *too risky*.

Accordingly, the counterexamples proposed are more troublesome for our virtue-theoretic account if detached from any normal objective, such as that of making money from a passer-by, or that of winning a bet. Suppose instead that the saxophonist and the skateboarder simply come up with the idea of producing a pleasing and difficult performance, which might not even involve any existing musical or skateboarding composition. Rather they will perform improvisationally in complete freedom, the only objective being that of producing a performance that will be pleasing, at least to themselves and perhaps also their friends, and pleasing in the aesthetic way distinctive of the sort of performance involved, with originality included as a major factor. For *this* sort of free performance, there is no domain-internal standard of reliability enough, and hence no standard of proper risk. This therefore seems a limiting case of full aptness. It is a case where full aptness is automatically attained with simple aptness. Since here no risk is *too* high, the agent can aim for first-order success while implicitly aiming for aptness in attaining that success. Since aptness will there be attained aptly whenever it is attained at all, there is no way for such performance to fall short once its simple success is apt.

In order to see the relevance of all this to epistemology, we need only recognize the epistemic dimension of human performance, with domains containing distinctive standards, whether these be the standards set by a particular discipline or profession, or those required by normal human communities, or those demanded for the proper functioning of the evolutionarily designed faculties of our animal nature.[17] Consider knowledge, therefore, of whatever sort, whether expert, commonsense, or of the functional animal sort. Any such knowledge will involve performance within a relevant epistemic domain that will import standards or boundaries, in the light of which we can see that—unlike spontaneous, improvisational performance—the aptness of alethic performance does not entail its full aptness.

B. Methodological Afterthought

A fuller response to the foregoing objections—to objections 3–8, in particular—may require us to move away from metaphysics to semantics

---

17. We will go more fully into this in Chapter 8, "Social Roots of Human Knowledge."

and conceptual analysis: *from* metaphysical inquiry as to the nature and conditions of knowledge *to* semantical inquiry on the terminology of "knowledge" and its cognates, etc., or *to* conceptual inquiry into the content of our related concepts.

Full-aptness virtue epistemology offers a unified account of performance normativity across the breadth of human performance. A unified treatment of our *epistemic* intuitions then flows from the general account to that special case. Philosophers divide on BonJour's clairvoyant Norman, on Lehrer's Truetemp, etc. But even these divisions now receive a unified treatment. How so?

We rely, first, on a framework of the normativity of performances that encompasses all of the following:

> attempt; successful attempt, competent attempt; competent and successful attempt; apt attempt; reflectively apt attempt; fully apt attempt.

Applied to epistemology, we then have:

> (alethic) affirmation; successful affirmation, competent affirmation; competent and successful affirmation; apt affirmation; reflectively apt affirmation; fully apt affirmation (apt judgment).

Philosophers and common sense pick and choose, while our epistemic vocabulary is subject to ambiguity, contextual variation, contrastive factors, etc. (including epistemic versus metaphysical modals, and safety conditionals). Suppose now that we're more interested in the metaphysics of knowledge than in the linguistics of epistemic vocabulary. So long as we can see what sort of epistemic status people may be attributing (by whatever linguistic devices), therefore, and so long as we can place the attribution of such status within the framework of performance normativity, we might be reasonably content at least initially.

The new virtue epistemology of knowing full well can more fully explain the divergence of intuitions than did the animal/reflective account. Consider again the examples of notorious epistemic controversy that repeatedly arise in the Gettier tradition. Why do these cases divide philosophers into persistent ostensible disagreement? We can now suggest that while some of us focus on mere animal knowledge and *affirm* accordingly that those subjects "know," others may focus rather on reflective knowledge or on knowledge full well, and *deny* that those subjects really "know."

PART III

Knowledge and Agency

6

Knowledge and Action

What follows will draw inspiration from Aristotle's virtue theory for an account of how human knowledge and action are related.

A. Aristotle

1. We begin with a passage that illuminates Aristotle's ethics, from Book II, Chapter 4, of the *Nicomachean Ethics*:

> It is possible to do something that is in accordance with the laws of grammar, either by chance or at the suggestion of another. A man will be a grammarian, then, only when he has both done something grammatical and done it grammatically; and this means doing it in accordance with the grammatical knowledge in himself. (*EN* II 4, 1105a22–6)

This provides a key to Aristotle's view of human flourishing as the fundamental ethical value. Please note that the second "in accordance with" cannot mean simply "coinciding with the content of." After all, what one does might coincide with the content of one's knowledge entirely by chance. But Aristotle means to rule out such accidental coincidence, as is clear in the first sentence of the passage. There must be a tighter connection than just coincidence between one's knowledge that a certain sentence is grammatical and the being grammatical of one's utterance, in order for the utterance to be "in accordance with" the knowledge. The sentence may be known to be grammatical, for one thing, but its grammatical utterance may be due only to the assurance of a liar (to the "suggestion of another"), while the knowledge remains implicit *and* inactive.

The view is further specified in the capsule statement found in Book I, Chapter 7, according to which

> ... human good turns out to be activity of soul in accordance with virtue, and if there are more than one virtue, in accordance with the best and most complete. (*EN* I 7, 1098a16–17)

Chapter 8 adds:

> Yet evidently, as we said, it needs the external goods as well; for it is impossible, or not easy, to do noble acts without the proper equipment. In many actions we use friends and riches and political power as instruments ... (*EN* I 8, 1099a31–b8)[1]

And Chapter 9 explains further:

> [Happiness] ... has been said to be a virtuous activity of soul, of a certain kind. Of the remaining goods, some must necessarily pre-exist as conditions of happiness, and others are naturally co-operative and useful as instruments. (*EN* I 9, 1099b26–8)

One last important component appears in Book IV, Chapter 1:

> Now virtuous actions are noble and done for the sake of the noble. Therefore the liberal man, like other virtuous men, will give for the sake of the noble, and rightly; for he will give to the right people, the right amounts, and at the right time, with all the other qualifications that accompany right giving; and that too with pleasure or without pain; for that which is virtuous is pleasant or free from pain—least of all will it be painful. (*EN* IV 1, 1120a23–7)

2. Beyond his own main statements, Aristotle's view stands out more clearly by contrast with the Stoic alternative, which seems diametrically opposed. Aristotelian flourishing involves the exercise of one's virtues, moral and intellectual. However, some virtues require external aids for their exercise, as when liberality requires money. By contrast, all that the Stoics require for a full measure of happiness (faring well) and virtue is that one properly order one's preferences and choose rationally on that basis.

---

1. It might be thought that external goods further happiness the way a good scotch furthers a pleasurable internal state, as a mere means to real happiness, which is internally constituted. But this cannot be right, given that for Aristotle faring well is *constituted* by noble action, such as the liberal handing over of a gift, and not just the simulacrum in a Matrix scenario. Nor is it plausible that happiness consists of virtuous activity *plus* possession of external goods, since human good *is* virtuous activity, and external goods are, not virtuous activity, but instruments used *in* some such activity.

True virtue resides in the perfection of one's rational nature, and it is the exercise of such virtue and only this that makes a life good.[2]

This paints a stark contrast. Who is right?[3]

B. Aristotle and the Stoics

1. Take a culture where sheep are sacred and wolves evil. Sheep are to be protected, wolves to be killed. Suppose you shoot and kill a sheep in wolf's clothing. Your action is "in accordance" with virtue. Nevertheless, it falls short. We are focused on your doing in killing that sheep—that very doing, not things done whereby you do that doing. This doing is distinct from any action of yours, strictly speaking. An action of øing must implement an intention to ø, as such, and you do not intend *to kill a sheep*, as such. You do intend to kill that animal (clothed as a wolf), and that animal *is a sheep*, but you do not intend to kill it under *this* description.

Suppose next you shoot and kill a wolf in wolf's clothing. Now you do intend to kill this animal, and this animal is a wolf, and you do intend to kill it under this description. Now your full endeavor is in accordance with your virtue, as is its success. You do intend to kill that animal before you, as it happens a wolf, and you do intend to kill it as a wolf. In a way this success *is* "in accordance with" your relevant competences, practical and cognitive. You endeavor to kill that wolf by shooting it, when you spot it, and believe it correctly to be a wolf. You thus bring to bear a complex combined competence. This includes your ability to tell the look of a wolf, and it includes also your shooting competence. So, your lethal shot at that wolf manifests relevant virtues and competences seated in you. Nevertheless, your killing

---

2. The article on Stoicism, by Dirk Baltzly, in the *Stanford Encyclopedia of Philosophy* contains a brief account. Also relevant is the ostensible contrast with the supposedly Socratic view that wisdom is sufficient for happiness (for flourishing). But see Russell Jones on "Wisdom and Happiness in *Euthydemus* 278–282," *Philosophers' Imprint*, 13(14) (2013): 1–21, for a compelling critique of adducing that passage in support of the thesis that Socrates (or Plato's Socrates) really held the view that wisdom is *sufficient*, and not just *necessary*, for happiness.
3. I have tried to cite only some central passages important for the account of Aristotelian ethics that is standard, at least in the respects highlighted. Of course, a full account would contain more detail. (See for a start the article on Aristotle's ethics by Richard Kraut in the *Stanford Encyclopedia of Philosophy*.)

of that wolf falls short. The performance of your basic action (say, pulling the trigger) aimed *to kill a wolf* does manifest those perceptual and executive competences on your part. But that *aimed performance* still falls short, in that *its success* does not manifest competence, not fully, depending as it does, essentially, on luck.[4]

Compare your performance of a basic action (again, pulling the trigger) aimed *to kill an animal that looks like a wolf.* Here success does fully manifest competence, and is fully apt.

The basic action (pulling the trigger) must trivially succeed, since one pulls the trigger as a basic action if and only if one aims to pull the trigger simply by doing so. By contrast, consider the action of pulling the trigger *not only* in an endeavor (or with the aim) *to pull the trigger,* even if one does have *that* aim in doing so. Suppose one aims (also) *thereby* to kill an animal that looks like a wolf. This is not just a basic action. It has a larger means-end structure. The end is *to kill an animal that looks like a wolf.* The means is *to pull this trigger* (since one knows it to operate a gun properly aligned with the wolf-looking animal before one). The success of *this* more complex action requires that one indeed kill an animal that looks like a wolf, and that one's intentional aiming with the following content play a suitable rational role in one's decision to perform that basic action: *to kill an animal that looks like a wolf.* Here one's competence operates properly enough that one earns full credit for the success.

Perhaps one also intentionally kills a wolf, in killing that animal (a wolf) that looks like a wolf. But one's competence is now diminished, as it relies on an important element of luck: namely, on one's belief that the wolf-looking animal is indeed a wolf. This belief does turn out to be right but only by credit-diminishing luck.

2. When Aristotle extols activity in accordance with virtue, does he mean to include your shooting of the sheep in wolf's clothing? Surely not. It is even questionable that he means to include your shooting of the wolf in wolf's clothing. The kinds of luck involved in these killings—bad in the case of the sheep, good in the case of the wolf—seem inimical to his virtue-based view of the human good. For, recall, Aristotle explicitly

---

4. Or on chance, or accident, or mere coincidence. In what follows, this further elaboration is meant to be attached silently to occurrences of "luck." The sort of agential luck intended is inversely proportional to the degree of competence manifest; it is a credit-reducing or even credit-removing sort of luck.

means to rule out success by chance. How then should we understand his ethics in keeping with the view that neither killing is action fully in accordance with virtue? Two very different ways deserve to be considered.

One way introduces italics in the capsule statement of Aristotle's view that ". . . human good turns out to be activity of *soul* in accordance with virtue." Having seen the animal before you in the field, you intend to kill it, and settle quickly on a plan. By shooting it you would kill it; by aiming your gun at it, situating your trigger finger properly, and pulling the trigger, you would shoot it. So, once you have aimed and situated your trigger finger, then by pulling the trigger you would shoot it. And now you pull the trigger by choice. You are free to so choose, and if you do so choose you thereby endeavor to kill the animal. Given your epistemic and practical perspective on the situation, you choose through virtue. You endeavor to kill that animal, you freely choose to do so, and you work your will through intervening means.

Let us focus now on this "activity of *soul*," namely, the free choice, freely determined. Here there is no slippage of the sort found in the killing of the sheep in wolf's clothing, nor in the killing of the wolf in wolf's clothing. In *those* killings an essential means-end belief turned out to be *false* or at least *not known to be true*. Such luck, whether bad or good, is irrelevant to the case of the choice. Either the choice requires no means at all, and you just choose, or the choice counts as a limiting case of means-end action, in which case the limiting means-end proposition could not possibly be false, nor even unknown to be true. That by choosing you would choose is trivially true and known to be so. In the case of a basic action, moreover, little or no gap separates the choice and the doing. Even if one pulls the trigger *by choice, by free choice*, no priority—of time, space, or efficient causation—distinguishes the choice from the doing. (It is after all possible to change one's mind right up to the very moment in which one intervenes so as to cause the death.)

According to this interpretation, we avoid the prima facie problems for Aristotle deriving from his formula that the human good consists in activity in accordance with virtue. The relevant activity is activity of soul, namely choice, and no spoiler luck is possible in that case.

On this interpretation, no deep difference seems discernible between the Peripatetics and the Stoics. Both sides will surely recognize preferences, both will recognize properly ordered preferences (in accordance with virtue) and will recognize choices that properly express these preferences (in keeping with deliberative virtue). For neither side will there be the sort of luck (bad or good) that affects action in our sheep and wolf cases.[5]

That interpretation clashes, however, with Aristotle's emphasis on the need for external instruments and settings for properly virtuous action. What follows will thus explore a different interpretation of Aristotle, and a different way to connect knowledge and action.

C. Aptness and Flourishing

1. The statement of the alternative option does not italicize "soul" in the statement of Aristotle's view. It does of course need to cohere with that statement, but it does so in a different way. The earlier interpretation pales with increasing understanding of the concept(s) of "soul" among the Greeks.

I cannot improve on the following brief statement of Aristotle's view:

> The soul of an animate organism, in [Aristotle's] . . . framework, is nothing other than its system of active abilities to perform the vital functions that organisms of its kind naturally perform, so that when an organism engages in the relevant activities (e.g., nutrition, movement or thought) it does so in virtue of the system of abilities that is its soul.[6]

By contrast, the Stoic view restricts

> . . . rather dramatically the proper subject matter of a theory of soul. In fact it is arguable that the Stoics, in limiting the functions of soul in the way they did, played an important role in a complicated history that resulted in the Cartesian conception of mind . . .[7]

Whereas the activities of the Stoic soul are plausibly restricted to inner acts such as choices, that is not Aristotle's view. Aristotelian activity of soul can be constituted by externalia such as the actual handing over of goods

---

5. It simplifies theoretical formulation to allow, as a limiting case of the "by" relation, the case where one øs by øing. But for our purposes this is optional. We could opt for a conception of basic action defined not as "øing simply by øing" but as "øing where there is nothing else by intentionally doing which one øs." And this would not significantly affect the relevant reasoning in our main text, though it would require some reformulation.
6. From the article entitled "Ancient Theories of Soul," by Hendrik Lorenz, in the *Stanford Encyclopedia of Philosophy*.
7. From "Ancient Theories of Soul" in the *Stanford Encyclopedia of Philosophy*.

in accordance with liberality.[8] True, the physical giving of the gift derives from choice. But the action itself encompasses not only the choice but also its proper implementation, through the intention involved (since choice entails intention). In developing this option it will help to understand more fully what is involved in hosting an intention. Though this option is inspired by Aristotle, and though it seems a plausible way to understand his view, it is no less interesting to develop it on its merits than as a way to understand Aristotle.

2. Let's begin with pro-attitudes in general. These will involve favorings generally, including physical appetites but also resistible attractions to choose that may derive from the advice of others, for example, or from reasoning of one's own. Favorings in this general sense may also be emotional without being physical, in that they derive from, or help constitute, our emotions, including those that are social without being physical. Conative dynamics, "deliberation" in a broad sense, whether conscious or unconscious, is a balancing act, whereby favorings are weighed on the scales of choice until a resultant results.

In deliberation, such a favoring may be either initial or resultant. If initial it might take the form of a hope or a wish. Will such a hope or wish rise to the level of intention when future directed? Not necessarily. Intention is restricted to distinctive contents, whereas one can hope or wish for just about any outcome. Intention is at most a favoring *that one bring about* a certain outcome.

If one does resultantly favor that one bring about a certain outcome sometime in the future, as opposed to merely wishing or hoping, must one not assume that the necessary costs are worth paying? In the many cases where means are required, must one not presuppose that these will be economically enough available? Of course, one need not be sure. But you could hardly be seriously committed to bringing about the relevant outcome, while convinced that you could bring it about only at prohibitive cost. This could not be a serious commitment, not rationally anyhow.

One needs at least that much, even if one does not yet have a detailed plan in mind. The plan at that point may amount to little more than a plan

---

8. It might be argued that Aristotelian "activity of soul" is narrowly restricted to activities of nutrition, movement, or thought, so that these are not just *examples* in generic form. But, for one thing perception will be included, surely, and with perception (of the environment), and nutrition (ingestion of food), externalia (the object seen, the food ingested) will be constitutive of the activity.

to make a plan, maybe even a detailed plan for how the plan will be made. Real commitment, real intention to bring something about, in any case seems to require that one think one will succeed, even if this thought falls short of outright judgment and judgmental belief.[9]

3. Let us here focus on a simple means-end action; say, turning on a light by flipping a switch. If one intends to do this in the next while, one must have some idea that the necessary costs will be worth paying. Getting up from where one sits will entail more or less cost: for example, one may need to look for the switch that is normally to be found in such a room. If unwilling to implement some such plan, one is not serious enough to be a real intender.

That of course does not mean that there must be some such plan that one is prepared to implement, except insofar as looking for a plan at some future time counts as already having a plan. If one has no aim to adopt such a plan, then one is only wishing or hoping that one will bring about the outcome. In order to upgrade that favoring so that it constitutes intending, one must have more by way of an actual or potential plan that will take one from where one sits to attaining the outcome.

Aristotelian action involves choice based on a resultant favoring of one's implementing a plan to attain a goal at which one thereby aims. One chooses, one acts, in the endeavor to attain that goal, which attempts to implement one's plan. We focus here, for simplicity, on simple endeavors, such as turning on a light, where an initial choice is all it takes, if all goes well. A competently made choice would then be "in accordance with" competence (virtue). This is why the choice to shoot the wolf-looking animal is competent.

Suppose we think of the action as involving not just the choice, but also, say, the physical handing over of the cash, in a liberally generous action. In this case a competent action can still be disastrous, as in the killing of a wolf-looking sheep. Moreover, the action can even be competent and successful while still falling short, as in the killing of the wolf in wolf's clothing, where an essential means-end belief is Gettiered.

Is not the shooting of the wolf in wolf's clothing *in accordance with* virtue? Would it not do all that a particular action can do to constitute flourishing? Arguably, it would not. Once we include the externalia involved in that full action, including the death of that wolf, once we say that this is part of what

---

9. But we shall eventually turn up reasons for doubt on this score.

constitutes the flourishing of the agent through the success of his action, the momentum is hard to stop until we reach the proper Aristotelian view. This view would include, among the factors relevant to such flourishing, not just the success of the outcome but also the aptness of the agent's performance. Only thus is the success not just "by chance" in the way Aristotle deplores. Aptness would require not only that the agent's plan be implemented so that the desired outcome does come forth. The outcome must *also* manifest the agent's relevant competence. In particular, the agent must competently implement his full plan, which includes the competent adoption of the relevant sequence of steps, and its sustainment as it unfolds.

Of course, the shooting of the sheep in wolf's clothing does not attain the agent's aim, so it is not an action in accordance with virtue: it does not even result in the success of the agent's main first-order aim, which is to kill a wolf, not a sheep. What of the killing of the wolf in wolf's clothing? Why is this not an action in accordance with virtue? Because, although the action succeeds in its main aim, it succeeds by luck, so that relevant competence is not sufficiently manifest in the killing of that wolf.[10]

4. So much for distinctions relevant to Aristotelian flourishing. Did Aristotle opt for one rather than another of these options? Why think that only apt action is "in accordance" with virtue, unlike merely competent, adroit action? Why think that in our example only the apt killing of a bare wolf would qualify, and not the competent killing of a wolf in wolf's clothing mistaken for a bare wolf? The stronger requirement, that of aptness, is made reasonable by the intuitive thought that an action falls short if it succeeds too much by luck rather than (manifest) competence. That is why the grammatical utterance falls short because of how its grammatical character is owed to chance or to the suggestion of a liar.

Aristotle's prominent example of Olympic success also encourages this thought. Aristotle points out that our admiration and prizes go to the

---

10. Essentially involved in such supposed competence is the agent's belief (explicit or implicit) that if the animal he sees looks like a wolf, then it is a wolf. But this is something our shooter does not know. Because he is Gettiered, he does not really *know* how to bring about the following outcome: *that he kills the wolf before him*. (Which, in the intended sense, leaves it open that there be a wolf before him that he knows how to kill.) This *specific* know-how is missing despite his retention of a *general* ability to kill wolves. He does not know that by shooting the animal before him that looks like a wolf he would kill a wolf. So, he lacks the required situation-specific competence. His success in killing a wolf, by shooting the animal that looks like a wolf, is hence not a success that manifests relevant competence. Our agent lacks the complete specific competence.

competitor who actually competes and succeeds, and not to those who stay on the sidelines, no matter how much more gifted they may be. Relevant, admirable goodness is fully present only in the action that succeeds. Only derivatively, secondarily, might the competence, the disposition, also be admirable. Even if there were no recognition of our distinctions in Aristotle's writings (which, as we have seen, there is in fact), it would seem natural to distinguish between the Olympic athlete who succeeds only by luck and the one who succeeds aptly, through competence. Only the latter flourishes fully.

5. Finally, thus interpreted, Aristotle enables a solution to the Meno puzzle as to the value of knowledge over mere true belief. The traveler who reaches Larissa through competence acts "in accordance with" virtue—virtuous competence—in a way denied to someone who picks the right road but gets it right only by luck, not knowledge. The ignorant traveler does of course reach Larissa. In that respect his relevant doings succeed, and might even qualify as competent if properly based on reason for his choice of road. Nevertheless, the success of his means-end action does not more fully manifest competence as opposed to luck. He no more deserves full credit than does the limping, fainting Olympic runner who wins from way behind only because the other runners are all struck by lightning near the finish line. To reach Larissa through ignorant luck is not to flourish.

D. Knowledge and Action

1. The importance of knowledge derives in good measure from how it relates to human achievement generally. This emerges through examples like the following:

> Hopeful Hunter is a tribesman lost in the woods on a moonless night. His hunt has been fruitless so far. Out of boredom he takes a shot in the dark, hoping to hit some prey. Amazingly, he does thereby kill a rabbit. The shot has of course a kind of success, but little credit redounds to our hunter.

> Similarly situated, Superstitious Hunter interprets a light breeze as encouragement from his god of the hunt to take a shot in the dark. He believes that the god will guide his hand and that his shot will succeed. On that basis, he takes his shot in the dark and does succeed, but thanks only to Lady Luck.

Is either hunter, poised to draw and shoot, able to shoot and thereby kill their prey? If this means whether it is logically possible that the shot succeed, then the answer is, obviously, yes. Nothing precludes the logical possibility that such a shot kill some prey.

2. Does Hopeful Hunter at the moment of shooting have the ability to then kill some prey? Well, again, if this means only whether he is "able," whether it is *logically possible* that he shoot and kill, then the answer is just as obviously yes. However, our talk of ability often requires more. A shot in the dark would not normally be thought to manifest ability. If the dark night is also silent and odorless, if nothing can guide the hunter's hand, if the shot is randomly directed, then, even if success is logically possible, it would manifest little if any ability. Hopeful Hunter does not even believe that shooting as he does has much chance of succeeding. In his opinion the chance is near zero, which seemingly precludes any real ability to succeed by shooting.

3. But is that only an illusion? Why not say that he does have that ability, even if he is not aware of it? A basic action is available to him, one he could perform, by performing which he would bring about the killing of some prey. And this is all it takes for him to be able to kill the prey, for him to have that mere ability. Of course, Superstitious Hunter shares that ability, even if he too lacks the relevant knowledge. By hypothesis he does believe he has it, indeed believes he knows what gives it to him, but the source of his belief is not a source of knowledge.

Neither Hopeful Hunter nor Superstitious Hunter *seems* to attain success creditable to the agent. In each case, one might plausibly reason as follows: "The success is gained only through a kind of luck incompatible with relevant credit. Neither hunter's success manifests their competence. Poorly situated as they are, neither hunter so much as *has* the required competence."

4. On the other hand, what is a competence if not just a disposition to succeed when one tries? Why doesn't Superstitious Hunter have such a disposition? Surely he would succeed if he tried. He would apply his true belief as to efficient means, would act accordingly, and would thereby succeed.

The intuition persists, nonetheless, that even Superstitious Hunter does not succeed through (relevant) competence. His ability to then shoot some prey is constituted in essential part by an incompetent, unjustified belief. If he were to succeed on that occasion, it would be a lucky accident. If he relied generally on the way in which he then formed his belief, he would in general fail to attain a true belief, and would fail to shoot any prey.

What is the competence that can make the success of a shot relevantly, fully enough attributable to the shooter? Even if there is no clear general answer to this question, it may be thought, Superstitious Hunter has no apparent disposition that can constitute such a competence. It is true that he has a disposition to succeed when he tries to shoot some prey on that specific occasion. But this disposition is so inadequately based as to constitute no relevant competence to succeed *creditably*.[11]

5. How might Superstitious Hunter arrive at his true belief that his shot in the dark would succeed? He might believe that his god of the hunt would ensure that the shot would succeed, regardless of its direction or speed or timing. Alternatively, he might have an imaging ability that enables him to believe that if he next shot thus, in a certain specific way (with that imaged orientation and speed), his shot would succeed, and that this is so because this belief is guided by the god (although in fact it's just what first came to mind, with no reliable basis whatsoever). In neither case is it plausible that Superstitious Hunter now has a relevant competence to hit prey. He does have a disposition to do so, based essentially on his superstitious belief, but this belief cannot constitute a competence that might make the success of his shot *creditable* to him.

6. Why is it that Superstitious Hunter would lack relevant competence to shoot prey with shots in the dark? A relevant competence would seem to require a broader field of accomplishment. The supposed competence of Superstitious Hunter is stipulatively restricted to the particular occasion involved. If he tried to succeed similarly with other shots in the dark aided supposedly by the god of the hunt, his success ratio would be near zero. No competence of relevant interest is thus seated in him.

---

11. No "relevant" competence, which is compatible with the agent's having some quite minimal competence of too low a degree to earn him more than negligible credit. (At least he gets the shot off competently enough, with the arrow speeding off the bow.) In what follows, an important distinction will come to the fore. We must distinguish: (a) the degree of credit due to an archer, such as Hunter, for the success of his shot, from (b) the degree of credit due to him for getting food for his family through killing some prey by means of such a shot. It may be that there was absolutely no better available means, and that this shot with its known non-zero probabilty of success was the very best option available and better than any other. If Hunter's shot is driven by such reasoning, then he might still earn substantial credit provided the shot does succeed.

Competences are a special case of dispositions, such as the simple disposition of fragility. Suppose a pewter mug would shatter upon hitting a certain surface but only because a hovering fiend would zap the mug as it hit the surface. This would make the relevant conditional true: the mug would shatter on that occasion, but this would not make it fragile. For the latter to be the case, one would need at a minimum that the mug would shatter when in a relevantly interesting combination of condition and situation. The essential presence of the determined fiend makes that situation irrelevant to the mug's fragility.

7. What a hunter needs for her relevant full competence is know-how. Sometimes this know-how involves knowledge of what means can be used to kill a prey. Competence can be constituted by a belief that means M will bring about end E, but only if this belief is true, competent or justified, and, indeed, a case of knowledge. In a slogan: When knowledge-how is constituted essentially by a means-end belief, this belief must be a case of knowledge-that.

That is *not* to commit to the view that competence is *always* so constituted, however; in my view, it isn't. An immense amount of our competence *is* of course knowledge constituted, but not all, not plausibly. There is much basic competence that comes with our brains, or is soon acquired through early child development. There seems no compelling reason to insist that it too must always amount to knowledge-how, especially if such knowledge-how is understood to amount not just to ability, but to some sort of implicit knowledge-that.

Though I see no need to do so, we *could* also recognize a kind of know-how that is not constituted by propositional knowledge of means. Thus, it seems to me that I can be said correctly to "know how to bend my forefinger," even without propositional knowledge of means whereby I can do so (other than the limiting case of my just doing it by doing it). Nor do I lose that knowledge when my forefinger is immobilized by force or paralysis or numbness. Now I still know how to do it despite being (temporarily) unable to do it. Yet, my knowledge how to do it is not constituted by any substantial means-end belief of any sort. On this tack, knowledge-how need not be constituted by any substantial knowledge-that, and hence we *might* still be able to analyze knowledge-that in terms of competence, *and* understand competence as knowledge-how, with no vicious regress. But defending against vicious regress on this tack would be non-trivial, since for one thing we'd need to consider the competence whereby one can obtain the insubstantial knowledge that one can ø by øing, under a practical mode of presentation. (Someone who can wiggle their ears at will would have the insubstantial knowledge that he can do so by doing it, and can implement that knowledge at will, but others lack that knowledge-how under a practical mode of presentation. What is the difference, and how does the ear-wiggler gain his distinctive knowledge? Does he acquire an apt belief, at least a functional one? What then is the competence that is manifest to the effect of his having that knowledge-how?)

So, the easiest way to avoid the regress is to understand competence as a certain sort of disposition to succeed, which need not in turn be understood as knowledge-how constituted by knowledge-that, so that it lies beyond sheer ability.[12]

E. Does Apt Means-End Action Require Knowledge of Means?

1. The view of knowledge as apt belief faces the case of Simone—a pilot in training who might easily be, not in a real cockpit, but in a simulation, with no tell-tale signs. In this thought experiment, trainees are strapped down blindfold in their cockpits, and only then is the blindfold removed. Let us suppose Simone to be shooting targets accurately while flying a real plane. She now justifiably believes that her training is long over, that every morning she goes up in a real plane. In fact, however, most of the time she is still in the simulation cockpit. On the occasions when she is aloft shooting missiles, her shots can still be not only accurate, surely, but also competent, and even apt.

So much for Simone's physical shots and for how their aptness is affected by the danger to her competence posed by her situation. What of her intellectual shots, her judgments and beliefs? She *is* flying her real plane, recall, and takes herself to shoot a certain target. Suppose this belief to be accurate and competent. Can it also be apt? That is to say, can it be a belief whose accuracy manifests Simone's epistemic competence? Can it be apt despite the threat to her competence posed by the simulation cockpit?

---

12. We would then have the option either to deny that such competence is a kind of knowledge-how, or, alternatively, to deny that the knowledge-how that is tantamount to such competence is itself a kind of knowledge-that.

2. Simone does have a kind of knowledge, it might be insisted, since she does have an apt belief, a robust sort of knowledge beyond the "knowledge" of an electric-eye door.

Recall Simone's shot when she hits her target from her plane up aloft. Her shot is clearly successful. It hits and destroys its target. Moreover, its success manifests her competence, and is therefore apt.

Consider now her relevant full competence. This would include her ability to aim properly and to pull the trigger when the target lines up properly with her equipment. She believes that if she pulls the trigger when things line up that way, she will hit, or is very likely to hit, the intended target. Acquired in her training, this belief is integral to her shooting competence.

A competence will often include as a constituent some such means-end belief enabling action by specifying a means available to the agent that, with sufficient reliability, will lead to the desired outcome. And now we may reason as follows.

> Suppose the belief is false. You cannot *aptly* attain an outcome by taking means that you believe will lead to that outcome, when it is false that they will do so.
>
> What if the belief is *true* though incompetent? Suppose it is formed with no adequate evidence although it is the sort of belief that requires evidence. An incompetent means-end belief could hardly help to constitute a competence fully creditable to the agent, one whose exercise might yield creditable success. This agent's success again manifests no relevant competence.
>
> Consider how much of our action is means-end action, especially if we include here not just causally efficient means, but rather any case of the "by" relation, where we do something *by* doing something. The competence required for apt performance of such ordinary action would very often involve apt means-end beliefs.

3. Such competence is constituted by knowledge how to attain one's objective. What constitutes the competence is this know-how, but included in it is then the knowledge that the means would yield the outcome. Suppose that Simone aptly hits her target in important part through knowing that her means would yield her end. If she *does* know that by pulling that trigger she would hit that target, however, and if she does know that she pulls the trigger, then she must know that she will hit her target. This is something she must know despite how "unsafe" her belief seems, since she might so easily have been in the simulation cockpit, where pulling her trigger would produce only an abortive shot.

When Simone aptly hits her targets up aloft, she seems to enjoy animal knowledge of her surroundings, and of how she can affect them through her basic actions. What is true of Simone is true of all animals whose conduct is thus explicable through means-end, belief-desire psychology. It is through apt beliefs about our surroundings that we gain the know-how that makes us effective animal agents.

That is all it takes for us to have animal knowledge, even in cases where we may intuitively incline to think that the subject somehow does not *really* know. *This* intuition can *also* be accommodated, but perhaps only by invoking a *reflective* knowledge that can be lost with no loss of animal knowledge.

F. Reflective Knowledge

1. A belief amounts to animal knowledge provided it is apt, but it amounts to reflective knowledge only if it is also meta-competent. This promises to solve our Simone problem. We had reached the conclusion that if Simone is to hit her target aptly when aloft, she must then know that by pulling the trigger she would hit her target. Otherwise her complete competence to hit it at that time is in doubt. But how can she possibly know herself to be flying a real airplane, when she might so easily have been acting under simulation. It is hard to see how she could really know that much, thus situated.

We can now respond that Simone's knowledge is on the animal level but falls short. Knowledge full well requires apt belief, or fully apt representation. It requires, therefore, not only apt representation, but also, on the second order, apt grasp (at least in the form of apt presupposition) that one's first-order representation is apt, where the accuracy of this second-order attitude must then manifest the believer's second-order competence.

2. Let us next tweak our example, so that the simulation includes an indiscernible screen that is only sometimes transparent, allowing Simone to see the scene beyond and shoot real targets. Just as often the screen contains only a movie, however, which corresponds to nothing beyond it. What if at a moment *when the screen will just happen to be transparent* Simone wonders whether she would *then* be safe and competent in forming certain

perceptual beliefs about what she *does* see through the screen? Can she now answer with affirmative correctness even though just as easily the screen might then reflect only a film, with Simone unable to tell any difference? At the moment of interest she might indeed see the scene before her, seeing that things are thus and so, even though just as easily she would be seeing no such thing, but only the contents of a movie.

Plausibly, Simone could *then* (at that moment) competently affirm that things *are* indeed thus and so before her, based on her apt visual experience as of their being (indeed) thus and so. The scene is perfectly visible in normal sunlight, as it is when she looks out the window some fine morning. And the knowledge thus acquired could of course help constitute her competence to shoot a target that she sees. Nevertheless, it is hard to credit her affirmation as really knowledgeable. And we can now offer an explanation.

Simone plausibly enjoys first-order "animal" knowledge of the scene before her, as she views it through the perfectly transparent screen. She then seems to exercise her first-order visual competence to get it right. She exercises (a) perceptual competence to form visual experiences through her visual systems, and (b) conceptual competence to host appropriate visual seemings on that basis, and to form visual judgments thus based in turn. And this animal knowledge then helps constitute her competence to shoot the targets that she sees through the screen. Nevertheless, she is missing something epistemically important. For, she is unable to believe aptly that as she forms her judgment she has any such access to the scene before her. This is because it is then random whether the scene is at that moment transparent or illusory. As she is about to judge, she might just as easily then (at the moment of judgment or infinitesimally thereafter) view a film as a real scene, and she has no way to tell the difference. For this reason, she is unable to judge or presuppose—at that very moment as she decides whether to affirm—that her visually based affirmation would be likely enough to be correct. She is unable to know whether at the moment of interest she has or will have the SSS competence required.[13]

Consider then her judgment that it is sunny outside at a moment when the screen *does happen to be* perfectly transparent, enabling her to see that it is indeed sunny at that very moment. The mere *affirmation* in the endeavor

---

13. We can assume that, at the moment she made her judgment, her situation could switch instantaneously and *seamlessly* from transparent-screen to screen-with-movie.

to affirm correctly is then plausibly competent on the first order. It is based immediately on the apt visual experience and the apt visual seeming that p. In affirming accordingly, she thereby functions appropriately. The affirmation then does get it right, and in so doing manifests a first-order competence to make such correct visual affirmations. So, the affirmation is not only competent but also apt. However, the affirmation might too easily have been inapt, since the screen might so easily have been opaque (while seamlessly segueing into something now quite divergent from the reality yonder). Something is thus seriously amiss in the relevant judgment, which falls short in the following respect.

To judge is to affirm in the endeavor to affirm aptly. But when she takes it that in affirming as she does she *would* then affirm aptly, our subject is incorrect. Given the random behavior of the screen, given that it is just as likely that it would be transparent as opaque, she is wrong to think that she *would* then affirm aptly, if she affirmed at all on the matter at hand. Only by luck can she at that moment get it right with her relevant first-order perceptual affirmations aimed at truth. True, her *affirmation* that p is correct at that moment, when the screen happens to be transparent (at least for a moment). Her affirmation is correct, and even apt, as apt as would be her affirmations based on her perceptions through an open window some sunny morning.

Why are they apt that way? Because she happens to satisfy the interesting Shape and Situation requirements whose combination with her visual sorting skill gives her the competence to sort the things she sees clearly displayed under the sun before her.

Nevertheless, Simone's perceptual *judgments* through the randomly transparent screen are not apt, since her affirmations are not guided to aptness through an apt appreciation of the conditions. Therefore, when she happens to view the scene before her through the transparent screen, and affirms about that scene in the endeavor to affirm aptly, she will affirm aptly, but her attainment of *this* aim will not be apt. This is because the randomness of the screen precludes her believing aptly that her affirmations about the scene beyond *would* then be apt, that if she then affirmed about that scene, her affirmation *would* be apt. This is made false by the fact that the screen might as easily be transparent as not on that occasion. So, it is not so that her affirmation *would* then be apt. It may be that the screen *will* by chance be transparent, so that her affirmation *will* then be apt, but compatibly it is not so that her affirmation *would* then be apt. On the contrary, it might too easily then be *inapt*.

3. In line with the foregoing reflections, we need to distinguish affirmations that are judgments from those that are not. An affirmation is a judgment only if it is in the endeavor to affirm reliably and indeed aptly. It may just be alethic, in the endeavor to affirm correctly, or it may have only some pragmatic and non-cognitive aim. The guesses of a game-show contestant can then be thus alethic affirmations in the endeavor to get it right without being judgmental affirmations in the endeavor to get it right aptly.

Recall how our eye-exam example shows that animal knowledge need not be credal. Suppose I have been flawlessly right for years in my eye-exam guesses at a row far down the chart. The statistics assembled over decades by the technicians show that it has been no accident. *Somehow* I can know the letters at that row even when I take myself to be guessing. Of course, I am *trying* to get it right. That is what I am supposed to do in order to undergo the test properly so as to yield a correct eye-glass prescription. So, why is it that I have been guessing? Because one can guess by affirming in the endeavor to get it right, as one does in a game show, and as one does when one takes the eye exam. What then prevents the guess from being a judgment? What is the missing ingredient? Recall our proposal: In a judgment one must aim to get it right reliably enough, even aptly. If so, then there is a kind of animal knowledge that does not require belief at all (whether judgmental or not), since it requires only guessing.[14] The knowledge attained by our eye-exam subject is then a subcredal knowledge constituted by no credal affirmation, by no judgment or judgmental belief.

Subcredal animal knowledge requires apt affirmation, but judgment requires more. With judgment one aims for more than just getting it right. One aims not just for success but for reliable enough, even apt success. And to succeed with this aim, as one affirms, it is required that one be able to tell that one *would* then get it right aptly, or at least that one *would likely enough* get it right aptly. The judgmental knower must have a second-order grasp—a belief or presupposition—that her first-order affirmation would then be apt. Suppose again that she faces the randomizing screen when the screen happens to be transparent at the moment of affirmation. In that case, Simone does seem to have the subcredal animal knowledge that partially constitutes her competence to shoot straight. Because the screen happens to be transparent, she does get it right when she affirms in line

---

14. This remains so in our example, where the guess is not a *sheer* guess.

with the perceptual competences made possible by the transparency of the screen. But she lacks the second-order competence required for judgmental knowledge. She lacks the required competence to *judge*, not just to affirm, aptly. This required competence would enable her to succeed aptly in the endeavor not just to get it right, but *to get it right aptly*.

4. *That* is then what we may be tracking commonsensically when we deny that she *really* knows even when the screen is perfectly transparent so that on the first order she forms apt perceptual affirmations (and representations). *Those* affirmations (representations) fail to be guided to aptness by the subject's awareness that they *would* be apt. Even though they *are* apt when the screen happens to be transparent, their *attainment of aptness* is not itself apt; it is spoiled by credit-limiting luck.

5. There is however a difference between our two Simone cases. Simone in her plane up aloft does have credal animal knowledge of the scene before her on the ground, despite how easily she might have been in the simulation cockpit instead. By contrast, when she faces the transparent screen, Simone lacks any credal knowledge of the scene before her.

That contrast between our two Simones derives from the following corresponding contrast. When up aloft, Simone's perceptual affirmations are unsafe in one way: as she makes her perceptual affirmations, she *might easily have been* ill placed to make them, since she might so easily have been in the simulation cockpit. Call this *backwards-unsafety*. Despite the backwards-*un*safety of her perceptual affirmations as she makes them, Simone's affirmations when aloft still seem safe in another way: if she were to ask herself whether her affirmation *would then* be apt, as she contemplates a perceptual affirmation, she can answer correctly in the affirmative. So, her affirmation then is *forwards-safe*.

If Simone aloft lacks credal animal knowledge, then, it is not for the reason that the screen-dependent Simone lacks it. It is not because it is *false* that she would affirm aptly on the scene before her. If Simone aloft lacks credal animal knowledge it is rather because, even if it happens to be true that if she affirmed perceptually, she *would* affirm aptly, this is not something she is in a position to know, given how easily she *might then have been* under simulation, indiscernibly so.

Consider on the other hand Simone as she faces the randomly transparent screen. Her perceptual affirmation at that point is not only backwards-unsafe. It is also forwards-unsafe. As she considers at that very moment whether her affirmation *would* be apt, she cannot correctly answer yes, since the screen might then as easily give transparent access to the scene beyond as opaque access only to a movie. And this fits with denying Simone even credal *animal* knowledge when she depends on the randomizing screen.

6. Given that result, what are we to think of Simone's successful shots when the screen happens to be transparent? To my mind she does shoot her targets aptly, with success that manifests the shooting competence required for relevant credit. If so, then no sort of *credal* knowledge-how is required for aptly successful, relevantly creditable intentional action. That still leaves it open, however, that at least *subcredal* knowledge-how be required. Even when she faces the randomizing screen, Simone may still enjoy subcredal knowledge of the scene before her, so long as the screen happens to be transparent as she makes her perceptual affirmations.

7. Yes, *that* example leaves it open that at least subcredal animal knowledge is required for aptly successful, relevantly creditable intentional action. So, that general claim is left open by the example. But is it a quite generally true claim? Chapter 7 will begin with a focus on this issue.

7

Intentional Action and Judgment

A. Taking Stock

1. We have explored a connection between knowledge and apt action, action whose success manifests pertinent competence. We have focused on action that takes a means-end form, a form human action so often does take. Consider the complete competence required for such action to be competent and for its success (in attaining its aim) to manifest competence. Such competence seemed initially to require the agent to believe *knowledgeably* the relevant means-end proposition.

On further reflection, that now appears too restrictive a view of apt action, which may after all require nothing more than a good guess, especially if one must act when nothing epistemically better is available. In response we may reduce the level of knowledge required to that of simply *thinking* that the means-end proposition is true, so long as this thought is competently enough sustained, even with competence whose reliability lies well below 50 percent. We need not even insist that this is literally knowledge. We can allow that we speak metaphorically in calling such guess-like thoughts "knowledge." This need not concern us if our interest is not so much semantic as metaphysical analysis. But we have seen how proper it seems to recognize in English a kind of subcredal animal knowledge, as in the case of the flawless eye-exam subject.

If credal animal knowledge is not required for a competence to succeed, perhaps subcredal animal knowledge can suffice? And perhaps knowledge of at least this low level is *required*?

2. Even that much is made doubtful by actions still to some extent apt and creditable without anything properly called knowledge to serve as the means-end connection. Not even subcredal knowledge seems required.

Take a case in which we need to choose arbitrarily by just supposing that a certain means-end proposition is true. We may need to act on that assumption just as an arbitrary choice among 360 equal options, one of which must be chosen. We might just barely guess by opting for straight swimming in one of 360 directions, and we might reach land that way, and our doing so may be apt to some extent. Our guess is minimally competent. At least we do not swim in circles! So that seems a way to get it right on the direction of reachable land, in a way that manifests some degree of aptness.[1]

On the other hand, we need not even positively guess. We need not positively think that the choice we have made is right, and that our choice *will* be a successful means to our end. We can instead just *suppose* and *hope* that the chosen option will yield success, while acting on that assumption. Here one's action might be successful and even apt to some extent, despite the element of luck owed to the arbitrariness of our supposition. Here again, what may enable the action to attain some degree of aptness is that it succeed (one reaches land) in a way that manifests (sufficient) competence, so as to be a success somewhat creditable to the agent.

3. That concludes our inquiry into whether apt action requires knowledge of at least the animal level. *Arbitrary* supposition cannot constitute knowledge of any sort.[2] Apt action connects with epistemology more tenuously than by requiring knowledge of the means to one's end. Nothing more is necessarily required than arbitrary supposition on which one is willing to risk action. Such supposition will sometimes enable apt attainment of one's end by connecting it to some means, helping thus to constitute a much fuller competence manifest in successful attainment of that end.

A value of animal knowledge hence resides not in its being *necessary* for apt intentional action, but rather in its often being a constitutive part of what is

---

1. Compare the pitcher who luckily hits a home run without manifesting competence (period) as a home run hitter (unlike the unique Babe Ruth). It still seems possible to say that his success manifests some (slight) degree of competence, and instantiates some (correspondingly slight) degree of aptness.
2. Here we should interpret the "arbitrariness" of the supposition to preclude the sort of subliminal reliability that enables our eye-exam subject's guesses to constitute a sort of subcredal knowledge.

sufficient. This status it often attains by constituting the subject's grasp of relevant means-end information, however tenuous that grasp may be, whether through a reliable-enough though subcredal thought that the means will yield the desired end, or through a more substantial judgment to that effect. Moreover, such "knowledgeable" success is *more fully creditable* to the agent than is the success due to suppositional luck. And the relevant *credal* animal knowledge would bring credit beyond that of its *subcredal* correlate.

4. Compatibly with that, we can nevertheless uphold the Aristotelian view of human flourishing as a life of accomplishment, while activity of soul relevantly avoids luck to the extent that it is in accordance with virtue, and at the limit in accordance ". . . with the best and most complete."

B. What Is an Intentional Action? A Preliminary Account

1. Have we now stumbled on a problem for our analysis of intentional action in Chapter 1? An *intentional action* was said to be constituted by the apt success of an intention of the doer's, one that manifests the doer's competence to succeed with such intentions.

What now shall we say about the swimmer who manages to reach shore? Does he reach shore intentionally? It would seem so. At least, he does aim to do so. And he does attain that aim. But does he do so aptly? Does the attainment of the aim manifest a competence to do so reliably enough?

Very plausibly it does not. At first the swimmer just guesses at random one of 360 directions in which he might swim, and the guess, as we saw, need not even rise to the level of a thinking, however tentative, that land lies in that direction. It may be nothing more than an arbitrary supposition for the sake of trying something as likely to succeed as any of the other directions.

Shall we conclude that the swimmer reaches shore intentionally without manifesting any competence to do so? The success does seem a matter of pure luck, which ostensibly refutes the account of intentional action as *apt intention*.

But it is far from clear that the swimmer's success does *not* manifest a specific competence to reach shore. Competences need not be infallible, after all. They can be just reliable to some degree, which can be extremely low. A home run hitter might aim for the rafters, exercising a gift unmatched in the history of the sport. Here reliability is still quite low, while attainment is nonetheless intentional and creditable to say the least.[3]

If our swimmer's shore is distant and the crossing difficult, success may manifest competence that is outstanding. And he does certainly aim to reach safe shore. This is the aim that keeps him swimming for hours.

Outstanding competence is then manifest, yes. Competence to reach shore given the swimmer's capabilities *and know-how*? This is not so clear. According to our account, however, it is this sort of *specific* competence that a success must manifest in order to be intentional. But why deny to our swimmer the specific competence to succeed upon trying in those conditions?

Compare the tennis novice who swings wildly as he receives a thunderbolt serve. There are many ways he might have swung, many arcs that his racket might have traced at many different angles. And there *is* of course one such way of swinging vigorously that will yield a winning return. Suppose he happens to swing that way, and does score a winning return. Is he then competent to hit a winning return?

Why not say that he does have *a* competence to do so, though not a very high competence? After all, he does aim to hit a winning return, and he does secure various elements of competence in his performance. His eyes are open. He is alert and focused. He faces and swings in the right direction. Et cetera. His overall competence to return that serve is of course extremely low; nonetheless he has *some* degree of it. And this degree *is* then exercised in pursuit of his firm and present aim to make the return. He does succeed in doing so, moreover, and his effort with that degree of aptness is crucial to the success of his attempt. Here again it seems rather plausible that the aim is attained intentionally, as was the aim of the swimmer.

2. Competence does come in degrees, within a dimension reflecting one's probability of success, in relevant conditions of shape and situation. One has a degree of such "competence" proportionally to how likely one would be to succeed if one tried when so shaped and situated.

Compare the "length" of a piece of writing. A novel can attain some degree of length without counting as a *long* novel. Similarly, an agent can attain some degree of (relevant) competence without counting as a (relevantly) *competent* agent. So, we must distinguish (a) attainment of success

---

[3]. But please recall that my "intentional" is tantamount to "by design," and is thus stipulatively restricted from its wide latitude in ordinary speech.

that manifests some degree of (relevant) competence in a given domain, from (b) attainment of success that manifests *competence* (period) in that domain. Attainments of sort (a) may qualify as intentional actions, and for this they need only attain some degree of aptness, corresponding to the degree of pertinent competence then exercised by the agent. Only with attainments of sort (b) do we reach success that is *apt* (period) in that domain. In this sense a domain will normally allow a distinction between (c) attainments to some degree apt, manifesting some degree of relevant competence, and (d) attainments that are apt (period), and manifest competence (period), in that domain.

3. The foregoing account accommodates our swimmer who reaches safe shore, the golfer who scores a hole-in-one, and also the following compelling case.

> A prisoner is told by his jailer that throughout the coming night his jail cell will be unlocked, but the jailer's testimony is only a cruel joke. The prisoner does form the belief, though, and by acting on it that night, he escapes, since completely by accident the door *was* unlocked. Is his escape intentional? Is it apt?

It is hard to deny that the prisoner escapes intentionally (by design). Moreover, his escape does seem plausibly enough to manifest a degree of competence already seated in him as he lay in bed prepared to make his move. And that degree of competence seems also to be manifest in his successful escape, even despite the important element of luck involved. A competence need not be infallible, after all.

Note in any case the sharp contrast between the prisoner and Davidson's waiter. The waiter does intend to upset his boss, to do so by knocking over a stack of dishes. So he arranges the tall stack in the kitchen in preparation for the execution of his plan. But before he can execute, his nervy intention makes him nervous, which makes him stumble onto the stack, thus knocking it over and upsetting the boss. Here there is a clear and powerful intuition that the waiter upsets the boss *un*intentionally, even though he does so because of his intention to do so. What then makes the difference between this case and our earlier cases? Is it not true in all of them that the agent succeeds in doing what he intends, and succeeds according to plan? It is by knocking over the dishes that the waiter upsets the boss. And it is by swinging in certain ways that the tennis novice and the golfer attain success, and by swimming in a certain direction that the swimmer reaches safe shore, which is his goal. So, why is our intuition so much more powerfully and decisively that the waiter succeeds *neither* intentionally *nor* aptly?

4. Here is a proposal. Suppose that intentional and apt action each requires that there be a set of spatiotemporally arrayed basic actions such that the agent takes it (at least in practice), with respect to each, that *partly by* doing it will he attain his goal. And suppose that the agent must attain his goal minimally *sufficiently by* performing all members of this array of basic actions. Here I mean "actional minimal sufficiency." That is to say, although each member of the set is essential to the set's sufficiency, no other basic action is required for the goal to be attained. The attaining of the goal then constitutes an intentional and even somewhat apt success provided it is a success that manifests some degree of specific competence on the part of that agent.

In addition, the agent must have a plan at least implicitly in mind, at least a determinable plan, by implementing which he intends to reach his objective, such that the goal *is* attained in line with this plan.

The desirability of this last component may be appreciated through our golfer. If he does hit a hole-in-one, there will inevitably be a substantial amount of luck involved. But the hole-in-one success may still derive from the intentional and apt success of the golfer's plan to drive the ball to the green as close as possible to the hole. And the golfer's determinable plan may be executed properly. But there's a special case wherein the golfer's hole-in-one would not so plausibly amount to an intentional and apt success. Suppose the shot is hooked far to the side, but ricochets off a tree so as to end up as a hole-in-one. *This* way of attaining success would not only fall outside the golfer's vague plan, as a specification of it; rather, this way of fulfilling the plan's ultimate objective would *conflict* with the plan. Intentional success would seem to require that the agent attain his objective, manifesting in so doing a degree of competence to do so. But it is also required that the attainment not be *contrary* to plan, and the competence manifest must be a competence to successfully implement the plan.

5. Finally, it is important to distinguish an action's being intentionally successful from its being *apt*. Intentional success requires that the action manifest a degree of aptness, but aptness *period* requires *sufficient* reliability, for actions of that sort in the pertinent domain. *Apt* intentional success thus requires not just some degree of aptness, which suffices for the being intentional of that success. Its being an *apt* intentional success requires more that just some degree of aptness; it requires *enough* aptness.

What determines whether an intentional action is apt period in its domain of performance? This would vary from domain to domain. When is a basketball player's shot reliable enough to count as apt? What about a baseball hitter's swing? A chess master's gambit? A comedian's risky joke? A detective's following of a lead? A scientist's line of inquiry? In each case some judgment of appropriate risk must be made, one that takes into account the relevant skills, shape, and situation of the performer.

C. Two Further Problems

1. Take again a golfer's hole-in-one. Competence to hit a hole-in-one specifically (or at least reliability at doing so), in his conditions must of course be very low. But that ostensible problem we have already surpassed. The golfer nonetheless does hit the hole-in-one intentionally. If in so doing he does not manifest competence, moreover, it is not necessarily because the competence manifest is too low. We have already seen low reliability to be no insuperable obstacle to intentional success.

More problematically, however, golfers normally do not aim at *hitting a hole-in-one* specifically. It need not be through so aiming that the golfer attains his success, though the success is attained intentionally nonetheless. We must hence relax the condition that in order to attain X intentionally one must have aimed to attain X specifically. One must have aimed to attain Y, for some Y related appropriately to X. In the golfer's case, here is a likely Y: coming as close as possible to the hole (with sinking the shot being the limiting case). Of course, that does not provide a general solution to how Y must be related to X in general. One suggestion is this: X must be a determinate of Y. Better yet, X must be a determinate of Y such that the agent favors Y&X over Y&~X in such a way that he aims to attain more specifically the following: [Y, *preferably X*]. In this way, an aim can be a complex, hierarchically ordered aim.[4]

---

4. Recall in any case the shot in the dark whereby Superstitious Hunter happens to kill a rabbit. I now see no good way to deny that hunter as much credit as is due our lucky golfer and our lucky swimmer. It seems best to grant that Hunter does "intentionally" kill that rabbit, as does our swimmer reach shore, and as does our golfer sink his shot. In each case important competences are exercised to the effect of an aimed-for success. Compatibly, it seems a matter of degree how much the success is due to luck nonetheless, and how much due to competence. Some degree of causal credit seems due the agent in any case. As to what degree of consequential credit/discredit is deserved, that seems a contextual matter contingent on relevant practices distinctive of the pertinent domain of action.

2. Second problem. Suppose I play chess regularly with my young grandson, and I can see the fast improvement, but also the low confidence and the nervous anxiety. Hence I continue to play so that (as I fully expect) he may start to win more and more of our matches, and gain confidence and enjoyment in the game. Let us suppose that to be my master intention as we play our next game. I aim to lose by playing, since I feel confident that he is now definitely the better player, to the point that by playing him I will likely further his winning. But I want the game to be real and fair, so I play to win, but with the overarching and guiding intention to lose. If I did not aim to lose I would not play, since I've been fearing I may damage his fragile confidence, and discourage him to the point of quitting the sport altogether.

Suppose I win the game. Do I win intentionally? I do intend to win. And I attain my aim aptly, through the exercise of competence. What if I lose? Do I lose intentionally? Again, I aim to lose, and if I attain that objective, I will do so competently as well. It will not be a fake loss. That is not what I want. No, it will be a real loss, where I am really trying to win. Yet, my *overarching* aim is to *lose* by so trying. Paradoxically, it appears that one can seriously aim *both* to win, *and* to lose. How can this be?

How? In the way of our example, with one aim being subordinate to the other. But the subordinacy is special, not the usual. The usual way in which one aim is subordinate to another is through one's intention to attain the latter by means of the former. Our special way in which one aim is subsidiary to another is through one's intention to attain the latter by *hosting* the former. Thus, it is not that I aim to lose to my grandson by *winning*. Rather, I aim to lose to my grandson by seriously *aiming* to win. Still, the questions remain: If I win, do I win *intentionally*? If I lose, do I lose *intentionally*?

I am not sure what to say. My own inclination is to distinguish and label. Perhaps the thing to say is that my losing would be *overarchingly* intentional, my winning *derivatively* intentional. Why so? Well, the master intention here is the intention to lose. That is what most deeply explains my conduct. But in pursuit of that aim, I do seriously aim to win, as I do want my grandson to score a win that is real, not just fake. If I unexpectedly win, however, then my win *is* still intentional, but only derivatively so, since the guiding master intention is the intention to lose, not to win.

Alternatively, one might say that only the master, overarching intention with which one performs a doing is capable of making that doing intentional. But I see here nothing more than just a verbal issue. The structure of the relevant phenomena is now in plain view, and it remains only to apply labels. True enough, that is not to say that labels cannot be misapplied, by the standard of the natural language. But nor is it given a priori that the language will always stand ready to deliver already dedicated labels that appropriately distinguish what is there to be distinguished. Ours, I sense, is a case of the latter sort. Is it really a determinate issue whether I win "intentionally" when my master intention was to lose, my intention to win only derivative?

In the appendix to this chapter, we take up what it is to intend, which deserves our attention through its central involvement in our account of intentional action. But for now we continue to develop that account.

D. Intentional Action: A Further Development

1. Let us next explore more fully the metaphysics of intentional action, via a metaphysical "by" relation.

When someone has ten cents in their pocket this could be by having ten pennies, or by having two nickels, or by having a dime. These are all ways of having that amount of money in one's pocket. When someone makes the light go on, this could be by activating a sensor, or by flipping a switch. These are alternative ways of making the light go on. If one activates the sensor, this could be as passive a doing as when, pushed off a cliff, one *does* fall to the ground below. Alternatively, it could be a deed, a doing of one's own, and perhaps even something one does intentionally. This could in turn be done by the raising of one's right leg. Of course, one might raise one's leg as a mere doing, under the doctor's mallet.

One's raising of that leg is not just the rising of the leg, which could be forced up by someone who seizes it, or could rise in a surgeon's hands once amputated. There seems a difference between those ways in which one's leg might have risen, and one's raising that leg. The latter is *perhaps* something that one *does*, even though one cannot help doing it once the mallet strikes. If a nurse is in the way, one does kick that nurse; that is something one surely does. If one *does* roll downhill when pushed from the top, then in a similar way one *does* raise one's leg when the mallet strikes. These are things that one does even if none is properly owned as "one's own doing."

By contrast, the rising of the leg that is amputated, or forced up physically by someone else, or by a gust of wind, corresponds to nothing that one *does*, not even to anything that one does passively. Still, one does *perhaps* raise one's leg passively under the mallet, and *very plausibly* one might raise it thus passively in one's sleep. In this last case a doing is one's own doing—is thus a "deed," let's call it that—even though it is not *intentionally* done.

There are thus things done by one's body, or its parts—as when the leg is forced to move up—without being things done by oneself. The leg *does* move up, even if it is made to do so by the force applied. And there are things one does passively, *deeds* done without being done intentionally, as when one moves one's leg while asleep.

2. Competence aligns with none of that, since it requires intention, which is absent in those cases. A competence is a disposition to succeed in attaining certain aims that one might have in a certain domain. A competence is a disposition to attain those aims if one tried to attain them. Trivially, I would say, it is a disposition to attain them intentionally, even if this does not entail that the attainment must be *consciously* intentional.

We are proceeding on the assumption that in order to do something intentionally one must do it in accordance with one's most determinate relevant plan, one that begins with a set of basic actions and eventuates in the aimed-for outcome. How the outcome comes about must not clash with that plan, as it does when a golf ball ricochets off a tree for a hole-in-one. Moreover, the execution of the plan must consist in the performance of a spatiotemporal array of basic actions whereby one means to attain the objective via the plan. The plan might gain specificity as the time for action approaches, if one thinks that one can still affect the outcome. That is why the basic actions can be spatio*temporally* arrayed.

3. We are thus relying on the notion of an action that is *basic*. This I understand as simply a deed D that one does intentionally, there being no *other* deed D' *by doing which* one intentionally aims to do D (alternatively: there being no such D' that one does intentionally *in the endeavor* to do D).

One important notion to be used below is that of an aim A's being attained *partly-by* one's doing deed D'. The aim might be a deed of one's own, deed D, as above. But other aims might also be attained *partly-by* deeds of one's own.

When one aims to do D, there is a deed D' *by* which one intentionally aims to do D, where D = D' in the limiting case. When one is competent to do D successfully, moreover, that is because one is competent to do D by doing D′, for some D′; which is compatible with the possibility that one do D by doing D″, for some D″ distinct from D′. One may be competent to do D by doing D′, moreover, but *not* competent to do D by doing D″. In that case, if one always tried to do D by doing D″, one would not really be competent to succeed when one tried to do D. In order to be competent to successfully do D when one tried, there must rather be a D′ such that one would succeed reliably enough when one tried to do D by doing D′, *and* such that one would try reliably enough to do D by doing D′. (Or, rather, there must be some set of actions like D′ such that, in trying to do D, the agent would reliably enough pick one or another of the members of that set as the deed by doing which they would try to do D.)

For a particular example of the above, let D = putting some water in a certain basin, D′ = twisting open the right faucet with one's right hand, and D″ = twisting open the left faucet with one's left hand.

Normally, however, one must coordinate one's own basic deeds so as to bring about one's objective. One's basic deeds must form a spatiotemporal array such that one attains one's aim only through the combination of the members of the array, where the array suffices for the attainment of the aim. Here the aim is attained sufficiently-by the combined doing of the basic deeds in the relevant array. So we have:

> Attainment A is attained sufficiently-by set (array) X iff X is a maximal set of deeds D partly-by each of which is A attained.[5]
>
> Attainment A is an *individual* attainment *by individual* I iff A is attained sufficiently-by a set X, all deeds in which are deeds of I.

Thus, one may fill the basin quickly by first opening the right faucet with one's right hand, and then opening the left faucet with one's left hand. If no other basic deed is required for the actional sufficiency of that set, then the quick filling of that basin is an individual attainment of one's own.

---

5. A is a *collective* attainment iff X is a set such that A is attained sufficiently-by set X, and there are at least two deeds in X done by disparate agents. Attainment A is then a collective attainment by group G iff G is the set of all agents such that each does at least one deed in X.

Because an outcome might be agentially overdetermined, more distinctions are relevant here, but this initial sketch will omit a full display of them. Moreover, we can now make use of the ideas here in order to analyze collective action, possibly involving agents spread broadly in space and time, whose respective basic doings are essential to the sufficient array whereby the relevant outcome is produced. Here we shall not go into such social issues. For initial simplicity, we restrict our focus to a single agent, though his relevant basic activity may be spatiotemporally widespread.

E. Intentional Action in Epistemology

Next we continue to apply our ongoing account of action to the special case of epistemology.

1. A judgment that p is by our account an affirmation that p in the endeavor to affirm aptly on whether p. Affirmation is normally a basic action, or at least so is affirmation to oneself, in the privacy of one's own mind. Therefore, if the epistemic agent succeeds normally in getting it right aptly on that subject matter, they will attain that apt affirmation by affirming that p. Moreover, if the *judgment* not only attains success but does so aptly, then the agent must attain not only the truth but also the aptness of their affirmation by affirming that p. This means that in order for the judgment to be apt, the alethic affirmation involved must be *fully* apt. It must be one that attains aptness in its aim of attaining truth, where this aptness must be aptly attained as well.

As we have seen through examples, it is possible for someone to affirm aptly on a certain question without doing so *fully* aptly. Their affirmation may attain truth aptly without attaining aptness aptly. And it is the latter that is required for the *full* aptness of the affirmation, and for the aptness of the associated judgment. Since a judgment is an affirmation in the endeavor to answer the corresponding yes/no question aptly, a judgment will not itself be apt if it simply attains success as a judgment. Given its constitutive aim, a *judgment* will attain aptness only if the *aptness* and not just the truth of the *alethic affirmation* is attained aptly.

When a judgment succeeds, it is an intentional action. It is an intentional apt affirmation. But intentional action requires only the attainment of that action's constitutive aim through *some degree* of competence. This degree need not lie above the threshold of reliability required for epistemic competence. So, the apt correctness of that affirmation need not itself be aptly attained. In order to *aptly* attain such *aptness*, one needs a second-order competence to attain it reliably enough. (Aptness can be attained intentionally, however, without being attained reliably enough.)

> Thus, an apt judgment qualifies on our account as an apt intentional action. It is (a) the action of intentionally getting it right (on a certain whether-question) with an apt positive affirmation, where (b) that action of *aptly* succeeding is *itself* performed aptly, such that *its* success manifests pertinent competence on the part of the epistemic agent.

We may thus conclude that a judgment is an intentional action of affirming aptly, where this apt affirming might itself be attained aptly. A judgment is apt if and only if its constitutively contained affirmation is *fully* apt.

2. Finally, judgment is a particularly simple sort of apt intentional action.

> In a "simple" intentional action, the agent aims to perform a deed D at t partly-by performing a basic action B at t.

Correct alethic affirmations and correct judgments are thus by our account simple intentional actions. But they are different in the following way.

In a *correct alethic affirmation*, the agent affirms in the endeavor to (thereby) affirm correctly. (So, an alethic affirmation cannot be motivated *exclusively* by pragmatic ends. It must have at least the minimal epistemic objective of getting it right on the content affirmed.) If the agent does get it right with their affirmation, then, we have the following structure: the agent *affirms correctly* that p at t partly-by *affirming* that p at t. If our agent's affirming that p at t is a basic action, their alethic affirmation is then an *intentionally correct* affirmation, which thereby qualifies as a simple intentional action.

In a *judgment*, the agent affirms in the endeavor to (thereby) affirm aptly. If the agent does attain that objective, then, we have the following structure: the agent *affirms aptly* that p at t partly-by *affirming* that p at t. Since, again, affirming that p at t is a basic action, the agent's affirmation is an intentionally apt affirmation, and constitutes an intentionally successful judgment. Since the judgment is a structure constituted by a basic action of affirming aimed at *apt* affirming, and since it succeeds in this aim by means of that basic action of affirming, the judgment too is a simple intentional action.

Appendix: What Is It to Intend?

We might think of intention as a resultant favoring of one's attaining a given goal, accompanied by at least a minimal plan for doing so, where this favoring will then guide one's endeavoring through that plan. The initial plan will normally acquire specificity as one gradually approaches the time intended in the goal. The proposal is emphatically only that such a plan is necessary for intending, not sufficient, since the full plan might be resultantly favored without being adopted.

Consider now a relation between such intention and the means-end action involved in implementing a plan:

> Xing in the endeavor that one attain E involves an intention to bring about E: that is to say, it involves a resultant favoring that one bring about E by implementing a certain plan for doing so, where this plan includes one's now Xing.

Such resultant favorings (resultant attractions to choose) might be subconscious, and might then have a standing in the domain of the conative analogous to the standing of credences (resultant attractions to affirm) in the domain of the cognitive. These are not necessarily attractions to freely choose or to freely affirm. Some of the strongest attractions may be irresistible, as when they derive from a forceful conscious experience or appetite. And some may be irresistibly *binding*, as when one is viciously addicted.

Some choices are freely determined, in any case, as are some judgments or acts of affirmation. A resultant favoring might or might not be intense enough to constitute a disposition to make a conscious choice. Moreover, the favoring that turns out to be resultant may be bound to thus result, with binding force, and may also force the choice. But if the force is that of binding reason, then the choice can still be free, and this is a sort of freedom that judgment can also share.

These conscious choices have advantages similar to the conscious judgments that constitute conscious beliefs. Entering one's conscious reasoning, for one thing, they can help coordinate collective action, when expressed in the course of collective deliberation. For a social species, such advantages are considerable, even essential.

Our resultant favorings, including those that determine conscious choices, or dispositions to so choose, are only a subset of a much broader set of favorings. This broader set includes all resultant favorings that correspond to affirmable optatives, of the form "Would that p!" The propositional contents of these optatives may concern the actions of others, and not only one's own. So why do we here focus on our particular resultant favorings? Why more specifically do we focus on the choices, or dispositions to choose, that are based on favorings *that one act* in certain ways? Because we are interested in Aristotelian action, and on how it can help constitute flourishing, individually or in society. Such action is goal directed, and the pursuit of a goal involves intention.

8

Social Roots of Human Knowledge

Social factors affect epistemology in at least two ways. They bear on an important sort of belief, and also on a corresponding sort of epistemic competence. This concerns a kind of value possessed by knowledge, and concerns also how the pragmatic can properly encroach on epistemology. We begin with this latter issue.

A. Pragmatic Encroachment

The Risk of Pragmatic Encroachment

What *sorts* of factors bear on the hunting-relative evaluation of an archer-hunter's shot? This involves how well that shot contributes to the overall hunting-relevant objective: say, a good afternoon's hunt. One way it can contribute is by being successful, by aptly hitting a target of high (hunting) value, and killing that prey. Such aptness does not require that the shot be also meta-apt. A shot can aptly kill its prey, manifesting the archer's skill, even though it was too risky a shot, and betrayed poor judgment. An apt shot can thus fail to be meta-apt. On a meta-level we ask whether the risk undergone is appropriate. What might this involve? How can we understand a way of managing and assessing risk while bracketing such practical objectives as how much it matters to that hunter or to his tribe that he not misuse his energy, time, and resources?

Suppose *a successful hunt* to be the primary objective in the domain of hunting, and the correspondingly primary value in the critical evaluation proper to that domain. Yes, of course, but what is it that constitutes "success," i.e., *hunting* success? As it stands this objective is formal and must gain content with the specifics of the particular hunt. What is the size and character of the hunting party (down to the limiting case of an individual)? What is the sort of prey involved? Is it a sporting event or is it a hunt for needed food? For present purposes, however, we abstract from all such detail and focus on the formal objective. The hunter's assessment of proper risk then plausibly depends on how his shot, with its chance of success, is combined with other shots he might take, and what shots others in the hunting party might take, and also on the resulting pattern's likely contribution to a successful hunt.[1] The evaluation hence needs to go beyond the single probability assessment, to the assessment of patterns containing that shot. A shot whose probability is too low, if considered in isolation, can *still* be meta-apt, if it contributes appropriately to an overall pattern that, while containing some such shots, still probably enough results in a successful hunt. (That can still be so, even if what is involved in a hunter's successful hunt is not sharp and determinate, especially if she is part of a hunting party. Each hunter might then aim for a successful hunt, which might involve the hunt of either the individual hunter or the hunting party.)

The like is found across otherwise disparate domains. Take a tennis champion in the heat of an important match. Gathering up all his might at a crucial point, he blasts a very flat, extremely low-percentage second serve past his opponent. An excellent serve, of course, on one dimension: a successful ace owed to the champion's skill. His shot has a 15 percent chance of success, let us say, while a hacker who tried a spinless serve hit so hard would have a nearly zero percent chance. Nonetheless that shot may show extremely poor *tennis* judgment. He should never have taken such a risk at that crucial juncture, judged by the tennis-relative objective of winning the match.

Here is something that does not help: that the champion noticed his girlfriend entering the stands and wanted to impress her. The shot did impress her, but that fact does not make it *a better tennis shot*. Another serve would have been more appropriate: a high-percentage spin serve kicking high to the opponent's weaker backhand side. This would have been a more appropriate shot even if it had just missed the service court, thus losing the point.

---

1. We must be flexible on how, in a given context, the proper ultimate hunting-relative aim is set: whether, for example, the good hunt is relative to an afternoon, or relative to a days-long hunting trip. Either way, the aim will be domain specific; it will not vary generically over the full range of aims that a subject or a community might have.

Not that the flat hard serve is never relevantly appropriate. It might be appropriate despite being low percentage. This will depend for one thing on how it fits within a pattern of shots over the course of the match. (It might unnerve the opponent, for example, or lead him to receive farther back.)

Something similar is true of the archery hunt. The average reliability required for archery competence in a hunt will depend, for example, on the hit/miss differentials compatible with a successful hunt. But a shot can still be apt by manifesting a competence that is not reliable outright, and even when its reliability is quite low, so long as it is reliable *enough*. What matters is how the shot, with its individual reliability, fits within some broader pattern that coordinates with the agent's past and future selves, and with other agents altogether.

We turn next from performance normativity in general to virtue epistemology more specifically.

Pragmatic Encroachment through Norms of Assertion and Belief

When we are told that knowledge is the norm of assertion, this can be understood as advocating a necessary condition for *proper* assertion, namely knowledge.[2] What is this propriety? Arguably, it involves social epistemic norms. These may or may not derive from human convention. They may rather be norms set, not by convention, but by the needs of an information-sharing social species. Leaving open the exact source, content, and nature of such norms, I rely only on the plausibility of their existence.

Without going further into the source and objectivity of epistemic norms, we can still wonder: What sort of thing determines their correctness? Let's suppose for the sake of argument that in some important sense

---

2. This is then defended as a way of explaining how repugnant we find certain Moore-paradoxical claims, such as "p but I don't know that p" or "p but I don't believe it" or "p but I'm not justified in believing it." What makes knowledge *the* norm as opposed to, say, truth, or belief, or justified belief? Arguably, what is distinctive is that knowledge is the most general such norm that explains the others. Yes, truth, belief, and justified belief are also norms in that it would be incorrect to assert when one lacks any of truth, belief, or justification, but that is plausibly because in lacking any of these one lacks also knowledge. So it is knowledge that thus unifies the relevant set of norms. However, if this is the argument, then knowledge that one knows may be a more plausible candidate for being thus *the* norm of assertion. This is because there are several Moore-paradoxical claims covered not by the knowledge norm but only by the knowledge-that-one-knows norm, notably the following: "p but I doubt whether I'm justified in thinking that I know it." But these issues are peripheral to our present concerns.

knowledge *is* a norm of assertion, that one falls short if one affirms, whether publicly or privately, what one does not know. Such affirmation can be an act either of thought or of speech. *Judgment* in particular is an affirmative act of thought.[3] Knowledge then is a norm of judgment. And this is of course compatible with knowledge being apt belief, or belief whose correctness manifests (sufficient) competence and not (too much) luck. The conclusion to draw is then that aptness is a norm of belief. And this fits our picture platitudinously. A belief does surely fall short if it fails to get it right through competence. It falls short in the way any performance with an aim falls short if it fails to secure its aim through competence. That knowledge is a norm of belief is then a special case of the fact that *aptness*, success that manifests *competence*, is a norm of *performance*.[4]

What, however, does such competence require? Core epistemic competence is a dispositional ability to discern the true from the false in a certain domain. Infallibly so? Surely not: that is asking too much. Reliably? Well, yes, reliably *enough*. What then is the standard? How much reliability is required for it to be, epistemically, reliability enough?

Is it really appropriate, however, to require a precise specification of a threshold? Is this not as inappropriate as it would be to insist on an exact threshold for justification enough to constitute justification, or an exact threshold for confidence enough to constitute belief? We are content to assume that *there are* such thresholds (or twilight zones) for justification and for belief. Why can't we extend that tolerant attitude to the supposed threshold of reliability for epistemic competence? Can't we just assume that there is such a threshold, even if we cannot specify it more precisely?

Fair enough. But we might still wonder about the dimension of epistemic justification and that of epistemic competence (whether these are different or at bottom the same), and even about the dimension of confidence. All three are magnitudes, each plausibly involving a threshold.

---

3. This is a temporary expedient for expository purposes; in due course we will find reason to distinguish more elaborately between the state of believing and the assertive act of judgment.
4. This provides an understanding of the knowledge norm of assertion different from that found in Timothy Williamson's *Knowledge and Its Limits* (Oxford: Oxford University Press, 2000). See especially ch. 11, "Assertion," where the knowledge rule is understood as governing *assertion* constitutively, by analogy with the ways in which the rules of chess constitutively govern the pieces. Our account is in terms of the constitution of judgment and assertion as actions, but the constitution is teleological rather than normative. Judgment is not for us *constitutively* affirmation that is subject to certain norms. Even if affirmation is *necessarily* subject to such norms, it need not be *constitutively* so subject. Judgment is for us constitutively affirmation with certain *aims* (hence the teleological constitution), namely: truth and aptness.

We might still wonder how such a threshold is set. What *sorts* of considerations determine it? In particular, is the epistemic threshold invariant across the practical situations of both subject and attributor?

How reliable is reliable enough? Will this vary depending on how much is practically at stake for the subject? For the attributor? Take a fact that p. Earlier we distinguished (a) the degree of reliability required for an appropriate public assertion of that fact (or for the *claim* to know it) from (b) the degree required for the subject to just know it, regardless of whether he claims to do so, and also from (c) the degree required even just to believe *competently* that p, to manifest in so believing a reliable enough competence. These degrees may well coincide, determined as they all are by what we can appropriately store for later retrieval even when the original basis is gone from memory. If we put aside pragmatic concerns such as whether a check will bounce, or whether one will be late for a meeting in another city, what then determines whether a competence is epistemically reliable *enough*?

How can we assess risk of failure (false belief) once practical concerns are set aside? The concerns that remain would be cognitive or theoretical. Using a catchall label, let's call them "(purely) epistemic."[5] What is distinctive of these? They presumably involve truth, and its reliable acquisition. A competence is epistemic only if it is an ability, a disposition, to discern the true from the false in a certain domain. But infallibility is too much to require, which triggers once again our persistent question: How reliable is reliable "enough," and is this something that varies from subject to subject, or from attributor to attributor, or both?

When we bring in extra-epistemic concerns about physical safety, or bouncing checks, or importance of timely arrival, in the *epistemic* assessment of a belief, are we proceeding as inappropriately as when we assess the tennis appropriateness of a serve by how well it impresses a friend entering the stands? There appear to be domain-internal standards that determine proper risk in tennis. And the same seems true of hunting, and of indefinitely many other domains of human performance. These admittedly resist precise formulation. They presumably concern how success is assessed internally to the domain. Domain-internal standards of such success would help determine

---

5. In a fuller account we may need to rule out other concerns besides the prudential and moral, such as perhaps the aesthetic. I leave that open for now, and assume for simplicity that any other such concerns fall in with those I am gathering under the title of the "practical or pragmatic."

domain-internal standards for "reliability enough." For a hunt we have the successful hunt, for tennis the winning match. Whether a particular performance is appropriate within either domain depends on how appropriately that performance is meant to contribute—and how appropriately it does contribute—to a pattern of activities with enough probability of attaining domain-internal success, such as that of the hunt or of the match.[6]

As humans and as fellow members of our communities and of our species, we depend crucially and variously on the acquisition and sharing of information. The epistemically successful life is a difficult thing to define in general terms, as is the epistemically successful history of a community or species. It seems a matter of collectively attaining and sustaining a picture of the surrounding world that enables a level of prediction, control, and understanding within an acceptable range, given the possibilities and tradeoffs proper to the constitution and situation of the subject and/or his group.[7] Here non-epistemic factors do plausibly bear. What determines the acceptable range depends on the needs of that life and community, and on the range of possible success allowed by participants' constitution and situation.

Epistemic competences are analogous to tennis and hunting competences. The latter abilities or dispositions attain their status as competences by how they bear on the proper objectives of tennis and hunting respectively. Whether a tennis or hunting ability is reliable enough depends on whether its exercise can sufficiently further the relevant objectives over the span of a match or of a hunt. This is compatible with the failure of many instances of that exercise. And assessment of proper performance must also take into account how effectively that particular performance joins how successful a pattern by that subject or group over the span of a match or hunt.

Competence and Reliability

In our two comparison cases, hunting and tennis, an *unreliable* ability can still be reliable enough to constitute a competence. Despite its low reliability,

---

6. And we will need to allow also a derivative sort of appropriateness for performance under simulation, as when a device is tested without being properly situated. Through similar flexibility we can also assess how good a *practice* serve is, one that is not part of a match; its quality is presumably correlated with how hard it would have been for an opponent to handle it in a match.
7. This is success on a basic level, one analogous to the shot's hitting its target; or, more directly relevantly, to a belief's hitting the mark of truth.

such an ability can be manifest in the success of the hunter's kill or the champion's winning ace, making this an apt performance. But it seems quite otherwise in the epistemic domain; or at least so it seems initially.

A speculative hypothesis that a detective, or a lover, or a meteorologist feels in his bones to be correct, can be based on a considerable ability that nevertheless falls well short of being 50 percent reliable. An affirmation on such a basis is thus analogous to the long shot by the hunter-archer or the blasting serve by the tennis champion. These latter seem properly assessable as apt, so long as they succeed within the hunt or the match. Suppose the long shot does kill the prey and the blasting low-percentage serve does win the point, and suppose these performances to be part of a pattern reliably enough predictive of success over the course of a hunt or of a match. That particular hunting shot, and that particular serve, would then each be assessed as both apt and meta-apt, as one whose success manifests a domain-specific competence of the performer, and one that runs appropriate risk (perhaps when viewed as part of a relevant overall pattern), even if the risk of failure for that isolated performance is quite high.

It seems otherwise, however, in the domain of knowledge. Take the speculative belief-in-one's-bones based on an ability to discern truth, though with low reliability. That belief will not be considered an instance of knowledge, surely; nor will it be thought to hit the mark of truth through a reliable enough epistemic competence exercised by the believer. If that ability falls very far short of reliability, if it falls near the server's 15 percent rate of success, then it will not be granted the status of a knowledge-level epistemic competence. When taken at face value, its deliverances will provide neither knowledge nor reliably enough apt belief.

Why is a batter's 15 percent competence deemed outstanding, as is a basketball player's 40 percent three-point percentage, while an epistemic ability at those levels is dismissed as subpar and inadequate to provide knowledge? True, those athletic percentages top the relevant distributions among humans and even among players. Suppose however that the ability to speculate correctly on the part of the detective or the lover or the meteorologist also tops its relevant distribution. All three of them are as good at such risky, speculative thought as is anyone, and far better than most. Nevertheless, this would not make their pertinent competences reliable enough to give them knowledge of the truth. Even if we did not always require epistemic reliability above 50 percent (as we do), still 15 percent would hardly suffice. The correctness of unreliable speculation cannot manifest epistemic competence sufficient to constitute knowledge.

Take a thought that manifests a disposition with low truth reliability. Why might such a thought be deemed insufficiently reliable? Should this be explained through our membership in an information-sharing species, and in more specific epistemic communities? Why does apt belief and judgment require more reliable competence than the baseball hit or the basketball field goal? At least in part, I suggest, the answer is that epistemic competences are relevant not only to the attainment of a good picture of things for the believer, but also to informing others, enlarging thereby the pool of shared information. Risky informed guesses do not pass muster as objectively endorsable apt attainments of the truth, properly stored for later use, and transmissible to others through public assertion.

Why not? Why would our need to inform others have so much explanatory payoff beyond that of our need to know things ourselves? And why might the social dimension of epistemology import a requirement of reliability higher than seems proper in other domains, where performance is recognized as apt despite the low reliability of the competence manifest? What follows will gradually develop an answer to these questions.

Aptness versus Reliable Aptness

Take the Hail-Mary shot by a player in the last seconds of a basketball game. The shot goes through the hoop and earns credit through the player's apt performance, even though this long shot had a very low chance of success. A social entity, the team, is involved, and the player's performance is assessed as part of the team's performance. Nevertheless, his unreliable shooting competence (from that far out) might still be manifest in a performance that attains a degree of aptness, his game-winning field goal. That shot can manifest competence, even if from that distance his percentage is quite low, say 10 percent. The percentage of the average player, after all, even the average pro, may fall well below that.[8] Even if his relevant competence is not at all remarkable, moreover, it does involve some skill. He at least threw in the right general direction. In addition, there was no alternative play

---

8. Note also that the per-pitch or per-swing success ratio of a good baseball hitter (as opposed to the per-at-bat ratio) is similarly low.

that would have had greater chance of success, as there was no time to pass to a teammate. The team-involving social dimension of basketball hence does not preclude that a performance might attain an impressive degree of aptness while manifesting very unreliable competence. Why not allow similarly that aptness of belief might be based on unreliable competence?

The foregoing suggests a distinction between:

> *somewhat apt thought*, whose correctness manifests some degree of competence on the part of the believer, and on the matter at hand, and in the circumstances,

and

> *reliably enough thought that is apt (period)*, above a threshold of reliable competence set by the needs of human flourishing in information-sharing communities.

Given this distinction, we might well allow that a thought can attain some degree of aptness without amounting to knowledge. Thus, the well-informed hypotheses of a self-confident Sherlock Holmes or Albert Einstein can amount to somewhat apt thoughts (affirmative thoughts), while falling short of knowledge. In a way they *are* somewhat apt affirmations, whose correctness does manifest competence far above the average for the sort of question and the circumstances involved. Nevertheless, they are not *reliably enough* apt affirmations. They need to be confirmed—in some cases through more pedestrian, reliable ways—before they can attain the status of outright knowledge. Only through such confirmation could they finally attain the status of reliable enough apt belief. And only thus can they be really *apt (period)*.

Note further how this might help explain the standing of norm-requiring competence (or epistemic justification) for assertion. There is a norm of assertion that derives from a default reliability requirement imposed on members of human communities. We are accordingly required to assert only what manifests reliable enough competence. What is properly asserted is only what is underwritten thus reliably. The standing of this norm derives in turn from the requirements for *appropriate* sharing of information, conducive to human flourishing through mutual reliance. So, the explanation of the norm's standing will derive from the requirement of reliability if sharing is to conduce properly to such flourishing.[9]

---

9. The *sharing* relevant here is that of co-temporal intersubjective testimony, but includes also the cross-temporal mnemonic sharing of earlier with later selves.

A Better Solution: Understanding Judgmental Belief Properly

An example used earlier is relevant here once again.

> When I go for my yearly eye exam, I am asked to read the lines of a chart with letters that shrink line by line from a huge single letter at the top, to those barely visible at the bottom. At some point I start to lose confidence that I am getting the letters right, but I keep going until the technician tells me to stop and then records some result. At that point there are many cases where I am quite unsure as to whether it is an 'E' or an 'F', say, or a 'P' rather than an 'F', etc. Suppose, however, it turns out that I am in fact flawlessly right year after year at a line where I am thus unsure. At that point I am in effect "guessing." I do affirm, to myself in private and to the technician in public, and I do so in the endeavor to get it right. And surely we can stipulate that I thereby manifest a competence that I do not recognize as reliable enough. That is why I resort to guessing, when I affirm as I undergo the eye test. Unbeknownst to me my affirmations are surprisingly reliable, as it turns out. How then do we assess my performances? We are here conflicted. In a way I *do* know those letters, as shown by my impressive reliability. But there is also a pull to say that I do not *really* know. What accounts for this? Quite plausibly, what is missing is my assessing my "guesses" as reliable enough.

That being so, we can draw a distinction concerning the first-order act or attitude involved in one's question as to whether the letter is an 'E' (or an 'F'). The act or attitude that we retain even once our confidence wanes sufficiently is the affirmation, or the willingness to affirm, that the letter is indeed an 'E', where one affirms in the endeavor *to get it right on that question*. The act or attitude that we no longer perform or host is the affirmation, or willingness to affirm accordingly, in the endeavor to get it right *reliably enough, indeed aptly*.

Accordingly, we can distinguish two sorts of affirmation. Affirmation in the endeavor to get it right *reliably enough, and indeed aptly*, on a certain question is *judgment*—let us call it that. To affirm in the endeavor to get it right, *without* affirming in the endeavor to get it right *reliably enough* is, by contrast, only to *guess*. (This leaves it open that you can also guess in other ways: for example, by merely *supposing* or *assuming* in the endeavor to get it right, without so much as affirming.) Of course, either a judgment or a guess can in fact get it right, and if it does get it right, the judgment or guess might or might not get it right reliably enough.[10] Either of them can thus amount to

---

10. However, the success of a guess may be attained reliably *enough* as soon as it is attained at all.

an apt intellectual performance, a performance that attains its aim in a way that manifests the performer's competence.

The knowledge that we are reluctant to attribute here requires full-fledged judgment, not just a guess. Compatibly with that, we can allow a lower grade of "knowledge," whether metaphorically or literally, one that requires only apt guessing, and not apt judging. Apt judging, moreover, requires that the performer attain his aim, and do so in a way that manifests *"enough"* relevant competence. Accordingly, to really know (judgmentally) one must affirm in the endeavor to get it right aptly (and reliably enough), and one must attain *that* objective in a way that manifests one's relevant competence. Since the eye-exam guesser does not even judge, he cannot know judgmentally.[11]

Encroachment and Invariantism: What Is Reliability "Enough"?

Aptness then is success through competence, where the competence must be reliable enough. This enables a distinction between the things we know full stop, and the things we know well enough to act on them. One might know something, after all, even though in a special context, e.g., where one's expert opinion is required, one does not know it well enough for action. Just think of the stakes involved in the context of a nuclear reactor, or a law court, or a surgery room. How more specifically do we understand this variation?

We might try saying that to know well enough in a high stakes situation is to have a reliable enough apt belief. If we applied our earlier formula, then, we would have to say that as the stakes rise, the subject's knowledge dwindles or even disappears, provided his competence does not rise.

More plausibly, however, there is no such outright loss of knowledge; what changes is only whether the subject knows well *enough* in the new context, with its higher stakes, whether he knows well enough to enable proper reliance on that belief as a premise in practical reasoning. *This* threshold does rise: reliability enough for deciding about something unimportant need not be enough when the stakes rise. (This chapter's appendix goes further into this.)

---

11. Although we have focused on judgmental belief, with its constitutive aim, functional belief also aims at getting it right reliably enough, so that there are functional correlates of judgment and of judgmental belief, correlates that require only functional aimings, and not intentional, conscious endeavorings.

The following example might help make plausible how the standard for knowledge can remain stable through variation in the stakes.

> Suppose that H(igh) is in a high stakes situation and has excellent evidence for his belief that p, but not good enough to give him knowledge that p. L(ow) for his part also has good evidence for believing that p, but not nearly as good as H; yet L's evidence is good enough to give L knowledge that p, since the stakes are so low in his context. Suppose H and L both store their beliefs in the normal way we do all the time. Weeks later they both believe the same thing based just on their retentive memory, now while asleep and quite removed from any high stakes situation. Should we now say that L knows while H does not, even though L's evidential basis is weaker than that of H, and there is no other relevant difference beyond the different stakes at the time of acquisition of the respective beliefs?

Although that is a persuasive reason in favor of invariantism, here we may just find ourselves conflicted.[12] If we still find remaining plausibility in subject-sensitivity and variantism, we need to reconsider how best to accommodate whatever makes these as plausible as they are.

My suggestion is that "human knowledge" is not tied to the stakes at the time of acquisition, nor at the time of evaluation. What we "know" period is a matter of what we believe with reliable enough aptness for storage of that belief. And the reliability required for such storage is the reliability pertinent to belief and assertion by members of our information-sharing social species. Asserting things that you do not believe with enough reliability would thwart human communities, since we cannot possibly keep track of the evidential etiology of people's beliefs. So, we need some agreed measure for assessing how much weight to place on the *testimony* that crosses from one subject to another, and on the *retention* that crosses from our past selves to our present selves.

According to the present suggestion, then, one "knows that p" *period* if and only if one aptly believes that p reliably enough for storage of the belief even after forgetting the original basis for its acquisition. No mere guess is good enough to be stored, so as to remain in place even once its initial credentials are gone; only knowledge is suitable for such storage.

---

12. Would the proponent of pragmatic encroachment not simply deny preservationism about memorial knowledge? True, proponents of pragmatic encroachment already seem implicitly committed to denying preservationism, but that seems prima facie not just a feature of the view, but an intuitive problem. To fully resolve the conflict, we would of course need to consider any independent arguments against preservationism, but I myself know of none that seem convincing, not against a properly formulated preservationism.

That, moreover, is compatible with the fact that what you know well enough for storage may *not* be something you know well enough for it to provide a proper practical basis for action when the stakes are high. So you might know something "flat out" even if you do not know it well enough to act on it when the stakes are high.

On the flip side is the apt Hail-Mary shot, or its intellectual correlates in the beliefs of our imagined Holmes or Einstein. Your affirmative thought might be apt even when it is not even flat-out knowledge. It might still admirably get it right through competence, with a competence reliable enough for speculative thought, or thinking in the dark. Your thought might still fall short: it might not be reliable enough for storage, nor, accordingly, reliable enough for human knowledge, plain and simple.

B. Knowledge and Judgment

Belief and Its Relation to Judgment

Earlier we distinguished two varieties of belief: first, credence above a certain confidence threshold; second, affirmative judgment or the corresponding disposition. This latter "affirmative" variety is belief as a kind of disposition to affirm alethically, in the endeavor to answer the pertinent question correctly, reliably enough, and indeed aptly. Such affirmation is an on/off act of judgment that takes place in the privacy of the subject's mind. Denial is then affirmation of the negation, and suspension is the intentional omission both of affirmation and of denial, an omission that can be either provisional (while one deliberates or ponders) or else conclusive, settled.

Why however should we think that there is any such all-or-nothing act of affirmative thought? If only we could make sense of this act, related acts could then be explained in terms of it. (Thus, denial of <p> is affirmation of <not-p>, and suspension on the question whether p is intentional omission of affirmation that p, along with intentional omission of denial that p.) How then should we make sense of the supposed act of private, mental affirmation? How more fully and explicitly should we understand this supposed act? Why should we so much as allow that there is or might be any such?

Undeniably, there is of course the on/off act of *public saying that such and such*, performed through the use of a natural language. Through such a saying we can endeavor to attain one or another of a vast number of aims, including pragmatic aims divorced from disinterested intention to inform. Fortunately, there *is* very often the intention simply to inform—to inform and not to misinform—as a dominant aim in human communication. Given our capacity for strategic self-deception, a similar distinction seems in order for judgment and belief as for public assertion. Despite how susceptible we can be to epistemically irrelevant pragmatic factors, there is such a thing as disinterested belief influenced purely by the aim to get it right, to believe correctly.

Consider the importance of proper assertion for an information-sharing social species. A newscaster or a teacher might assert with testimonial propriety even when they do not voice their own beliefs.[13] If the speaker plays no role in any such epistemic institution, however, no such role as that of newscaster or that of teacher, then their assertion is epistemically proper only when it voices their own belief. Otherwise it would be improperly insincere. But what sort of belief is at issue here? Is it belief as confident enough credence or is it rather *judgment*, an act of affirmation or a disposition to affirm with the aim of affirming correctly, with truth, reliably enough, and indeed aptly?

Suppose such judgment to be what most directly determines proper, sincere public affirmation. A speaker's affirmation of what he does *not* in this sense judge to be true would then involve an epistemically improper clash: what he is willing to say publicly then clashes with what he says to himself *in foro interno*. In order to avoid such impropriety, what the speaker affirms publicly must comport with what he would affirm to himself in the privacy of his own mind. Otherwise there would be either some speech flaw, or some failure of sincerity. Fully epistemically proper affirmation requires the avoidance of any such flaw or failure. It must express in unflawed speech what the speaker thinks (in act or disposition). The speaker speaks with epistemic propriety only if he speaks as he thinks, with sincerity and without linguistic flaw.[14]

Is there an account in terms of credential threshold that rivals our account in terms of judgment? According to such a rival account what assertion

---

13. As Jennifer Lackey has made clear, in her *Learning from Words* (Oxford: Oxford University Press, 2008) and in earlier papers.
14. In counting as epistemic any such linguistic flaw, I am assuming that flaws in the channel of testimonial communication so count. Suppose someone makes an error in manipulating symbols as they work out a proof on paper, a proof meant to determine belief through inquiry. In my view, that would count as an epistemic flaw. Compatibly, of course, epistemic flaws come in different sorts.

requires by way of sincerity and avoidance of flaw would be *proper expression of a credence above a certain threshold of confidence*. But what will set that threshold? Would it not be what the subject is willing to affirm to himself in the endeavor to answer correctly? Maybe so, but why the privacy restriction, why the restriction to what the subject affirms to himself? Why not just understand belief as a disposition to assert publicly when one faces the corresponding question and one endeavors to answer it with the aim of answering correctly? Well, for one thing, no one radically "mute" could then hold any beliefs. Moreover, our answer in terms of private affirmation is unaffected by the fact that epistemically irrelevant pragmatic factors might so easily influence what one is willing to say in public. And, finally, ours is the account of belief that will most smoothly bear on the subject's conscious reasoning, as he invokes premises in his practical deliberation or theoretical pondering, all of which can take place in the privacy of his own thought.

When Is a Belief Sufficiently Reliable to Constitute Knowledge?

Consider a stream of thought or speech clean of pragmatic factors. You perceive that p, store that belief, and when later you field a relevant question, your answer is in line with that stored belief. Consider next the reasons, perceptual or otherwise, that prompted the initial storage of your belief, which is then retained long after the lapse from memory of the basis on which it was formed. After that point your accessible basis will be reduced to whatever still supports your continuing to so believe, often just the fact that you do still believe as you do, along with the reliability that you can properly attribute to your relevant memory.

Despite having acquired such a belief with a very high degree of confidence, this confidence may well fade in tandem with dwindling awareness of one's original basis for so believing. In fact, such later confidence will align not with the original confidence and its basis but rather with synchronic confidence in one's present reliability on the subject matter of that belief. What is the degree of reliability that is appropriate for retention of a belief? This can differ crucially from the degree of reliability later required for reliance on that belief either in the subject's private conscious reasoning or in his public assertion. What one is later justified in premising privately or asserting publicly will of course depend on the question at hand and on the amount at stake for oneself or one's community in the correctness of so premising or asserting.

But our question abstracts from such special contexts, where the risk exceeds what is normally at stake in conveyance of information or reliance on a premise. Indeed, our question applies even when one is asleep, or unconscious altogether. At that point one is still storing immensely many beliefs. What determines whether a belief is thus stored with epistemic propriety?

What is the use, the epistemic use, of such stored beliefs? Largely it is the use they still have even when we have forgotten the bases on which they were initially stored, or retained over time. However, we do want our beliefs to be reliable beyond some minimum. We want to be able to appeal to them properly at any arbitrary later time when they may become relevant. So, we are allowed to store a belief when its basis endows it with at least that minimum level of reliability. Moreover, we want to store potentially useful beliefs when they do reach that level, to the extent possible, without overloading our memory banks. We are now considering the subject and his indefinite future, and the uses he may find for his stored beliefs. Even just for an arbitrary subject in isolation from his group, some level of reliability is required if he is to store a belief with epistemic propriety. We would want such a level in his stored beliefs, so that we can in the indefinite future trust those stored beliefs to have that level given just their storage in his memory.

What is pragmatically at stake in a particular situation can vary enormously, of course, and the degree of reliability required in a belief worthy of trust *as a basis for action* will depend on the stakes in that particular situation. Consider extraordinary situations where the stakes are abnormally high and where reliability is at a premium. These must be distinguished from ordinary situations with normal stakes. A reasonable degree of reliability is required for normal questions in ordinary situations of quotidian interest. This is the degree of reliability required for ordinary human knowledge. As the stakes rise, we need knowledge above such ordinary epistemic quality. We now need knowledge for sure (or for more sure). And we cannot just draw a belief from storage and trust it simply on that basis, once we are in a context that demands additional reasons for trust. These special reasons could take either of two forms. They could amount to first-order reasons synchronically in view for a certain answer to our high-stakes question, or they could amount rather to special reasons for believing that we are particularly reliable on such subject matter, when situated as we are when we then consider our question.

Such contexts, we say, require abnormally high reason for trust. But what is this "trust"? How do we manifest our trust in a high stakes situation? Do we manifest it by what we are willing to judge affirmatively even to ourselves in the privacy of our own thoughts? If so, then the stakes *do* after all affect what we know, for they affect what we relevantly believe. They affect how we are willing to think affirmatively, what we are willing to affirm to ourselves. And this affects what we believe in the sense of judgment, or affirmative belief.

There is however an attractive alternative option. We might deny that the mere heightening of the practical stakes affects what we are willing to affirm to ourselves, or how we are willing to judge. What reasons might there be for this denial? First of all, the stakes may not affect what we are willing to affirm to ourselves in the simple endeavor to get it right on that question. Not even what we are willing to guess privately, to ourselves, is affected that way.

Even more plausibly, moreover, we might deny that the mere heightening of the practical stakes affects what we are willing to affirm in the endeavor to affirm correctly *and reliably enough, above the threshold set by our social epistemic norms, and thus aptly*. This is because the social epistemic norms pertain to what judgmental beliefs we can properly store for appropriate later retrieval and sharing, in quotidian contexts with normal stakes. What the stakes may happen to be at that moment is hence not relevant to our willingness to judge, not if judgment is defined as affirmation in the endeavor to affirm reliably enough for normal stakes.

What is affected instead by rising stakes, we might counter, is how we are willing to *choose* on a given basis. Thus, we might feel confident enough to judge and even to affirm publicly that the ice is solid enough to bear our weight, while still hesitant to step on it, if the water is too cold and we fear for our lives or even just for our comfort. On this view, we are still willing to think, and even to say, that the ice is solid enough, while considering this too uncertain to justify relevant action. What is more, our judgment might even constitute ordinary, commonsense knowledge, even though this knowledge is not relevantly "actionable."

The considerations bearing thus on the mnemonic channel from one's past self to one's present self apply similarly to the testimonial channel from one subject to another. When we take at his word someone who speaks in his own person, we can very often believe accordingly with epistemic propriety, and we can reason practically on that basis, and we can assert thus in turn when speaking in our own person. When this happens, the testifier is often voicing his stored belief, one stored and retained reliably enough, and the speaker communicates competently to the hearer.

However, one cannot *always* take a speaker's say-so on trust, making the knowledge so attained actionable. It depends on the question and situation, and what is at stake. As the stakes rise, so do the requirements properly imposed on speakers in determining how worthy they are of our trust in the specific situation, and whether their testimony yields knowledge that is relevantly actionable. The normal human reaction is to accept testimony at face value, even without specific knowledge of the speaker's credentials.

Compare how memory operates unimpeded, properly so, even once the subject's awareness of the initial basis fades and disappears. This is how it is for the great bulk of our body of beliefs. This is how it must be, given human limitations. It would be cognitively disastrous always to relinquish beliefs as soon as our awareness of their source dwindled, or to reject all testimony unsupported by known credentials. We are built to retain beliefs even after we have lost awareness of their initial basis and of how reliable that basis may have been. And we are built to trust testimony absent special reasons for distrust.

A further interesting question concerns the degree of confidence that attaches to a belief when it is initially acquired. When that belief is stored and retained, what exactly is retained? Is it a credence *with its initial degree of confidence*? Not so, and properly not so, at least in most cases. A high degree of confidence is retainable only with retained awareness of the belief's excellent enough basis. On pain of vicious regress, however, this latter must be a kind of pseudo-retention. What "remains" is rather a related but fresh belief, of some degree of confidence, that one's synchronic first-order belief is properly based on some reliable basis. Confident enough endorsement from one's I-now perspective is required for proper retention of a first-order belief with a corresponding degree of confidence. That is at least required once that belief is challenged, even if, absent special reason or occasion for reconsidering, it properly remains by default.

Any reduction of your ability to endorse that first-order belief, from your synchronic I-now perspective, is correlated with a corresponding reduction of your epistemic right to retain your high degree of confidence. The retained belief now remains only as a belief once acquired. Only through features of one's synchronic I-now perspective can one now endorse it with a corresponding degree of confidence. And the credence's degree of confidence will properly fade in tandem with reduction in the subject's ability to endorse that credence properly from his ongoing second-order perspective. And it will eventually dwindle below the degree of confidence required to sustain the subject's first-order belief. But what is that degree of confidence? Plausibly, it is the degree of confidence required for proper synchronic affirmation.

What then is the degree of confidence epistemically required in a normal context for such affirmation? What is required at least for affirmation to oneself? Is this degree of confidence the same as the degree required for proper synchronic affirmation to an interlocutor? This is made implausible by how misleading public affirmation can be, if speaker and hearer each knows that the other knows the stakes to be high. In such a case, confident assertion is likely to convey not just where one takes the truth to lie, but also where one takes it to lie surely enough to make our knowledge relevantly actionable.

Consider the need to guide oneself individually while allowing for one's cognitive and mnemonic limitations. Consider also our need to guide ourselves cooperatively, with proper allowance for those same limitations. Some threshold of reliability is thus required for storing our guiding beliefs, so that our continuing disposition to affirm will satisfy that minimal degree of reliability. This requires the subject's ability to remember without excessive distortion. We must guard against a memory that reduces reliability below the required minimum when the belief is later drawn from storage in a normal setting.

We need a store of beliefs, of stored dispositions to affirm to oneself or to others in normal settings: i.e., in ordinary settings of human reasoning or communication. Given human storage limitations, we cannot always or even often store awareness of how our beliefs are initially acquired, nor can we retain a running awareness of their continuing basis. Moreover, what is most relevant to our epistemic cooperation is the act of assertion, normally just flat-out assertion. This is how propositions can figure as premises of reasoning, practical or theoretical. Proper cooperation requires sincerity, moreover, "sincerity" to oneself (avoidance, for example, of wishful thinking) and sincerity to interlocutors.

In sum, there is a minimum level of reliability required in the epistemic deliverances trusted in our daily lives. This includes the many gauges used in a technological civilization. We do not require infallibility, since little if anything could then be trusted. But we do require a high level of reliability. We are ourselves among our main sources of information. This includes not only our fellow human beings but also our own past selves. Just the fact that such a source delivers a proposition is a good reason to believe that proposition, absent special reasons for mistrust. Without implicit trust in the testimony of our neighbors or our own memories, we would be greatly reduced epistemically, well below the level of an isolated Robinson Crusoe reliant on his memory at every turn. Indeed it is hard to see how any human could live once so radically reduced epistemically.

Accordingly, we need some consensus, whether natural or conventional, on what is a minimum level of confidence (and corresponding reliability) required for storage of a belief (making allowance for the inevitable dampening of reliability that will come with later reliance on memory). *This*, I submit, is the level coordinate with *ordinary human knowledge*, the level required for proper assertion, and for properly endorsed synchronic judgment (absent special reason for mistrust).

That is all compatible with heightened requirements for trust when the stakes rise. This is perfectly in line with the similar rise in our requirements for trust in any relevant gauge as the stakes rise. Ordinary gauges may not suffice in a nuclear plant, in a surgery room, or in a Formula One car. Much higher reliability is required for our trust in such special contexts. Someone who uses an ordinary gauge in some such special context may still know what his gauge delivers, even if he should not there guide his conduct by what he knows. He needs not just such ordinary knowledge but knowledge *for sure*, or for *more* sure. He might have knowledge all right, while still lacking *actionable* knowledge.

Communication and the Value of Knowledge

A crucial component of our collective epistemic life is the act of sincere affirmation, which could take the form of either sincere private affirmation to oneself, or sincere public assertion to others, in the endeavor to affirm with epistemic correctness, with truth.

Two critical domains are here important. First, there is the domain of epistemic communication. Acts of communication are subject to epistemic assessment in various respects. They are assessable in respect of clarity, conciseness, and also audibility or legibility (and even readability), and more. When we speak we often aim to communicate information, to convey it from speaker to hearer. What the speaker knows becomes thereby knowable to the hearer. This knowledge involves belief in the sense of disposition to affirm. What is affirmed becomes thus available to others, and perhaps usable in their own reasoning, and as a basis for their rational action, provided the stakes are appropriate. Various features of the act of communication become relevant to this aim to communicate. Communicative acts are subject to such varied assessment concerning the appropriate conveyance of information. They can be better or worse in these various respects. This fact holds a lesson in the study of the value of knowledge, to which we turn next.

We have taken note of the fact that an intended act of communication can be assessed in various ways: in respect of clarity, for example, or if aural in respect of audibility, etc. This does not require that acts of communication must have some objective final value. Not even successful acts of communication need have any such value. I may write in my diary in beautiful cursive "Today I had eggs for breakfast," or I may tweet this to the world at large. My act can then be assessed in various communicative respects: legibility, for example, spelling, grammar, and so on. One such act can certainly be *better* than another. But none of this requires that there be some distinctive, objective *communicative value* that constitutes a distinctive sort of final value, not even one that is prima facie or *pro tanto*.

The same is true, of course, for critical domains generally. There is no distinctive final archery value, or chess value, even though archery and chess performances can be assessed as better or worse *as performances of the relevant sort*. It might be replied that there is a crucial distinction between archery shots and chess moves, on the one hand, and beliefs on the other hand. Archery and chess are just invented domains of amusement for human beings. The domain of beliefs is not at all like that. Beliefs and the broader epistemic domain are unavoidable for human beings, and crucial for our individual and collective success. Our participation in that domain is crucial for the flourishing of our lives individually and in society.

Compare however the domain of speech. Utterances in speech can of course be assessed. Some are better than others in a great variety of respects. Most of these respects of evaluation do not require any consequentialist understanding according to which there would be some distinctive communicative final value, some final value that successful communicative utterances would need to have. There is no such distinctive final speech value any more than there is a distinctive chess final value or archery final value. Nor is any such communicative final value made any more plausible by the fact that communication is not optional for humanity, unlike chess or archery. True, without communication there would be no humanity. Communication in fact seems barely less important to our social species than is knowledge. Yet we can still assess human communicative acts without committing to any distinctive final communicative value. So we should similarly consider whether epistemic assessment of beliefs requires any distinctive final doxastic or epistemic value.

Why not think of it as follows instead? Human communication is important for human flourishing, for the flourishing of individuals and for the flourishing of groups. This does not require that there be any distinctive communicative final value. It requires only that communication be a sufficiently important component of enough human ways of flourishing, which can take many and various forms. It is hard to imagine a flourishing human life that will not involve communication in some important ways at some stages at least of that life. Moreover, communication enables flourishing not only instrumentally, but even constitutively, as shown by the place of communication in human relationships. No human society can flourish while deprived entirely of communication. But from this it hardly follows that so much as a single act of communication need have any final value distinctively its own, or indeed any final value of its own at all. Much less does it follow that *all* successful acts of communication must have some such final value.

Just so, human knowledge is at least as important for human flourishing as is communication, both for the flourishing of individual lives, and for the collective flourishing of groups. But this no more requires any distinctive epistemic final value than does the importance of communication require any distinctive communicative final value. It is required at most that knowledge be an important component of enough human ways of flourishing, which can take many and various forms. We have found it difficult to imagine a flourishing human life or society that will not involve communication in some important ways. Similarly, it is hard to imagine a flourishing human life or society deprived entirely of knowledge. Knowledge of various sorts will surely figure as a component of the flourishing of individual lives and of the flourishing of human beings in groups.

But is it really true that human flourishing requires knowledge in the ways suggested? We face the *Meno* problem and its variations. Why is knowledge better than merely subjectively competent belief? Why is knowledge better than merely true belief? Well, compare this: Why is well-based happiness or pleasure better than the equally subjectively pleasant tone of the subject in an experience machine victimized by a controlling demon? The life of such a hedonic victim is no more a flourishing human life than is the illusory life of a Matrix dweller, which indeed can itself include much illusory or false pleasure. The subjective character would be real enough, of course, but its content would be illusory nonetheless. Victims of experience machines and Matrix frameworks would have subjective enjoyment, true enough, but their lives would fall horribly short nonetheless, as is revealed by our wholehearted preferences when a choice is forced. Better truth than falsity in a human life, better competence than incompetence, yes, but better yet what is required for the full human flourishing of that life, which is incompatible with a life of illusion, in the various forms canvassed.

Appendix: Actionable Knowledge

If one knows that øing is the best thing for one to do now (out of its relevant reference class of options), does one act wrongly if one does not ø? What if one *also* knows that there is a non-zero objective chance (relative to one's basic evidence) that øing is not best, and indeed that there is a non-zero objective chance that øing will be horrendously bad. What if by comparison what one knows is that only a minuscule margin of value is secured by øing? By hypothesis one knows that øing is best, so øing is of course best, and in fact those horrendous consequences will not ensue upon one's øing. It might still be appropriate for one to hedge one's bets, however, by not øing. Just consider the enormous risk that one runs by øing, when this risk is assessed relative to one's basic relevant evidence.

Suppose for example that one knows one's ticket to have lost, even without having seen the lottery results. Is it now appropriate for one to sell one's ticket for a penny, since this will mean a net gain over the other relevant options? But what if one knows that one's irascible partner will react very badly if in fact one's ticket has won and one has sold it for a penny. Or suppose one knows or believes justifiably that God would punish with eternal damnation those whose actions turn out so badly? Would one act appropriately by disregarding the objective chance (relative to one's basic evidence) of such untoward results? Suppose one acted in accord with what one knows to be best, however small may be its margin of positive value. Would that be appropriate? Surely not.

We are thus prompted to take a closer look at the argument that runs as follows:

1. My ticket has lost.
2. If it has lost, it is worthless.

3. If it is worthless, it is best for me to sell it, even for a penny.
4. It is best for me to sell my ticket, even for a penny.

It may be thought that this argument is bad, and that it is bad simply because one does not know its first premise. After all, only what one knows can properly be used as a premise in such practical reasoning. So that's why the argument is bad. Its first premise cannot properly be used for good enough reasoning in line with that argument.

We are supposed thereby to have a reason to reject that a lottery proposition such as 1 can be known. However, consider the practical syllogism that continues the argument as follows:

5. If it is best for me to sell my ticket for a penny, then I shall so sell my ticket.
6. I shall sell my ticket for a penny.

And suppose the further conclusion of this practical syllogism is my selling of my ticket for a penny.

This argument might now be put in question through the sorts of considerations adduced above. Whether it is appropriate for one to reason in accord with the practical syllogism, and even to act accordingly, would seem to depend on what other information is at one's disposal, including the relevant objective chance that selling the ticket for a penny might have disastrous consequences. So, one can reject the full practical reasoning involved without questioning whether premise 1 is known. That premise might or might not be knowable. This argument would seem to leave that question unaffected.

9

Epistemic Agency

This chapter will take up epistemic agency, its varieties, and its relations to normativity, freedom, reasons, competence, and skepticism.

A. Two Varieties of Agency and Epistemic Normativity

1. Our lives contain states or events of three sorts: (a) sufferings—pains or itches, for example—or mere doings, such as reflex actions; and performances of two sorts: (b) functionings (functionally assessable states); and (c) endeavors (with a freely determined aim). This trichotomy has a practical, ethical side; and a theoretical, epistemological side. Here we focus on the latter.

Endeavors populate a region of freedom.[1] Endeavors can and often do derive from freely determined choices and judgments. The freedom that defines our region of endeavors might be sharp, libertarian, and fundamental or it might be a matter of degree, compatibilist, and derived. Here we leave open that whole set of metaphysical issues.

The region at the opposite extreme contains sufferings and mere doings, where the doer is relevantly passive. If pushed off a cliff, you fall passively despite how fast you may be moving, and you kill a rabbit passively if you

---

[1] One might alternatively opt for a broader notion of "endeavor" according to which any aiming, any teleology even if merely functional, would involve "endeavoring" to attain that aim, as does the heart when it beats regularly, aiming to circulate the blood. Our "endeavors" here, by contrast, are *intentional*, and along with functionings make up a broader class of aimings. This chapter also restricts its focus to endeavors that are not only (constitutively) intentional but also free, while leaving it open that some intentional endeavors might be unfree, as when the addict reaches for his fix.

squash it at the end of your fall. A doctor's mallet can make a patient kick a nurse if the nurse is in the way of the reflex kick. So, the patient does something (by kicking the nurse) even if it is not (in a relevant sense) a doing of his, one attributable to him as his own doing. He exercises no real agency by kicking the nurse, or by kicking at all on that occasion. The passivity that is relevant to our project is epistemic passivity. The nature of this passivity will soon emerge.

2. How does "justification" relate to those three divisions? And how might the deontic framework pertain? I mean the framework concerning what one ought to believe, what one may believe, and even what is obligatory or permissible in the way of belief.

The region of freedom is where the deontic epistemic framework is most clearly applicable, the region of passivity where it is most clearly inapplicable. There is, however, an intermediate region, which admits a kind of agency, even if performances in that region are not freely determined endeavors, which constitute or derive from choices or judgments. Performances can be rationally determined even when they are not freely determined.

Here is an example. After measurement reveals a given line to be an inch long, let a second line be unveiled so as to form the familiar Müller-Lyer pattern. This induces the illusion, and also the derived seeming that the second line is over an inch long. No pondering or decision is required; the process is quite involuntary. One seeming, one attraction to assent, derives rationally from others, by a sort of rational basing. One seeming is based rationally on other seemings, even if none is constitutive of, or derivative from, any free judgment or choice.

Even if the deontic framework does not strictly apply in that intermediate region, it does apply loosely. We may thus distinguish between two frameworks. There is, first, the strict deontic framework, which presupposes free, intentional determination, such as that involving free choices and free judgments. But there is, secondly, a more loosely deontic *functional* framework containing no freely and intentionally determined endeavors.

Within that second, functional, normative epistemic framework we instead assess proper functioning, be it servo-mechanic, biological, etc. We there distinguish performances that do from those that do not satisfy at least minimal standards for proper epistemic operation. For functional performances we feel no gratitude, resentment, or any such reactive emotion.

We can of course have attitudes of approval or disapproval, but these do not find expression in the praise that is correlated with blame. Yes, there is a broader "praise" that requires only favorable evaluation, and aligns as much with admiration as with the assessment of agency. We can distinguish the praise or blame that applies strictly only to the free agent from broader correlates applicable also to the functional agent. Agents who merely function are subject to flaws or faults, rather than to sins or infractions or other violations that presuppose freedom and intention.

However, we need not commit to any linguistic theses about "praise" or "blame" or their proper or strict application. It is enough to distinguish the strict deontic attitudes from more broadly assessing attitudes, however these may find expression in strict English.[2]

The looser deontic framework still requires functionings, assessable as proper or not. Rational functionings, in particular, involve rational motivation of a sort. Here one functions in a certain way based on motivating reasons, reasons *for which* one functions as one does.[3] When the line in our example seems to me longer than an inch, I function a certain way, just as much as when I kick the nurse because of the doctor's mallet. True, it is a passive sort of functioning. I am helplessly attracted to assessing the line as over an inch

---

2. I have distinguished between the reactive attitudes that apply in the region of freedom, and our approval and disapproval in the region of functionings. Granted, "praise" can march in step with admiration, which would not presuppose free agency. And we do extend talk even of "blame" *far* beyond the region of freedom, as when we "blame" a weak strut for the collapse of a bridge. And there is also the bearing of fully blameworthy negligence. Take an agent who gives free rein to his unreflective attitudes although he should have been more "thoughtful." We do blame this agent, but we do not necessarily blame him simply for having acted in line with his unreflective animal-level beliefs and desires. We blame him more fully because of the negligence of which he is "guilty." Moreover, when he *properly* does not reflect, when he acts instinctively or automatically on his unreflective animal-level beliefs and desires, we do not necessarily praise him simply for having acted in line with those unreflective attitudes. We praise him more fully because he was implicitly sensitive to when reflection is required, and had the good sense to omit reflection *without negligence*. Arguably (but not here), such sensitivity and negligence reside in the region of freedom.

3. Again, even if we do not really need them, the following linguistic points seem plausible enough. Plausibly, we do not strictly "praise" good epistemic functioning on automatic pilot: the acquisition of trivial beliefs that guide everyday conduct. Nor do we strictly "blame" someone who malfunctions, whether practically or theoretically. The malfunction might be due to drink or drugs or lack of sleep, or might simply show lack of relevant skill. We deplore it, but tend not to blame the agent if he was just functioning automatically and was not deciding or judging freely. Of course, fine distinctions are needed here, particularly on a compatibilist metaphysics of freedom. (But metaphysics is off our already full agenda.) Even in a case where we may not, strictly speaking, *blame* someone for drink-induced malfunction (as when their vision turns blurry, or their balance unsteady), we might *still* blame him for being drunk, and especially for *getting* drunk, when it was important that he not malfunction, as when he is a driver.

long. I function well by doing so on a certain broadly rational basis: on the combined basis of that line's seeming longer than the nearby line that I clearly remember to measure one inch. I have reasons that in combination motivate me in a broadly rational way to take the line to be longer than an inch.

3. In a given context, three verbal formulas can function with normative equivalence: (a) I am attracted (to some degree) to think that p, (b) it seems to me (to some extent) that p, (c) I give some (positive) weight to the claim that p. The first of these connotes passivity, the last connotes activity, and the intermediate one connotes neither; it seems agentially neutral. From a normative point of view the three can differ at most trivially, so that these passivity/activity differences become normatively negligible. This is suggested already by how little an agent may really "own" something that is nevertheless something he "does," paradoxical as this may seem. Consider how passive we can be in kicking the nurse of our example, even though we verbally "do" something in that case. Despite the fact that we do it, it is not our "own" doing.

Compare the "doing" involved in giving some weight to the claim about one of the lines, that it is over an inch long. This too adds no significant agency to the "attraction" we are subject to when attracted to assent accordingly. Either way, there is a kind of agency, but it is the unfree agency of proper functioning, as when the leg goes up in response to the mallet. We function properly precisely by being passively attracted to the right extent, just as a magnetized device can function properly by being attracted to a nearby magnet. The distinction between the passive and the active is here negligible by comparison with the distinction between states that are and those that are not functionally assessable. There are passive doings that are not thus assessable (such as one's squashing a rabbit at the end of one's fall), unlike other passive doings (such as our perceptual functioning when we are attracted to a claim about the color or shape of a perceived item). Finally, the epistemic functionings in our middle region are assessable in a specific epistemic respect, by relation to truth.

B. The Agrippan Trilemma

Reflective assessment cannot regress infinitely, nor can it circle endlessly. Nor can it rely ultimately on some arbitrary stance. We must still face this Agrippan trilemma if we are to understand epistemic justification.

Judgments that endeavor after truth are subject to the Agrippan trilemma. Neither infinite regress nor circularity is acceptable. Only rationally appropriate foundational judgments could ground other judgments and beliefs, however, so as to render them rationally appropriate in turn. Arbitrary, freely determined judgments are rationally repugnant. But how could a judgment avoid arbitrariness except through a proper rational basis? Yet, a truly foundational judgment's proper rational status cannot derive wholly from some rationally supportive basis. After all, if it did derive its status that way, then its status would be, not foundational, but (broadly) inferential. We are thus driven back to the circle or the regress.

We are now interested in epistemic assessment, in assessment of judgments and other cognitive states in respect of the sort of normative status that is constitutive of knowledge. This is a certain sort of status that a true belief needs in order to constitute knowledge, whether at the animal or at the reflective level.[4] How can we stop the regress of justification for rational judgments while avoiding arbitrariness?

We next try regress stoppers that are not endeavors but are still performances with obvious epistemic relevance, such as rational functionings that derive from no free choice or judgment by the agent. Now we move to the region intermediate between freedom and passivity. Freely determined epistemic judgments (which are endeavors) can be based on degrees of confidence (credences, credential states that are functionings), functionally rational performances. Thus might we hope to escape, in that foundational way, the Agrippan trilemma for endeavors.

The trilemma applies once more, however, now in a new form. Consider performances generally, even those that are not free endeavors. How might such a performance attain the epistemically normative status required for knowledge; how is this to be explained quite generally, when we include both functionings and endeavors among our performances? Again we need foundational regress stoppers, but now regress-stopping foundations would not do the job simply by residing outside the region of freedom. Now we need states beyond the region of freedom, but also beyond the middle region, the region of functioning. Our search for regress stoppers must turn next to the region of non-functional passivity.

---

4. Some have looked for such a status among our practical attitudes. In their search for a regress-stopping status they have turned to pragmatic attitudes. I am not myself persuaded that this can give us the justification of distinctive interest in epistemology: namely, epistemic justification, the kind appropriately tied to truth. So I look elsewhere.

Our project being epistemological, such regress stoppers must be non-functionally passive in epistemic respects. An itch might be functionally assessable as appropriate by calling for scratching, which might serve some biological purpose. But the itch is not assessable epistemically if it does not serve any epistemic purpose. So it is not the sort of thing that could have epistemic status, not even epistemic functional status, much less epistemic free-agential status. Compatibly with all of that, however, it might still serve as a regress-stopping basis for a proper epistemic functioning, if the subject immediately gains propositional awareness of his itch based rationally on nothing other than the itch itself. What makes him properly aware of the itch is the self-presenting itch itself.

As with endeavors, so with functionings. It is no more plausible that there could be a whole set of functionings each epistemically justified entirely through rational support by other members of the set. Foundational *endeavors* would be deprived of rational motivating bases to explain their status as rational. Such endeavors would hence seem *arbitrary* and thus irrational. Foundational *functionings* do not share that same problematic status. Involving no choice at all, they involve no arbitrary choice. Consider, however, a set of credences of various degrees of confidence, functional states not chosen freely by the subject. It is most implausible that such a set could attain the full epistemically normative status pertinent to knowledge simply in virtue of the rational interrelations of its members, in isolation from the external world that determines their status as true or as false.

Given, self-presenting states have long had a prominent role in epistemology. No doubt we can know directly when we suffer an itch or a pain. We need not obtain this knowledge merely through inference from other things we know. This is foundational knowledge. How are we to understand its special status? How can it have this status without the support of reasons?

C. Reasons and Foundations

1. Reasons come in at least two sorts: the factive and the stative. Consider a fuel gauge. How does a reading become someone's reason for a belief (or, alternatively, for a positive credence: for a positive degree of confidence) about the amount of fuel remaining? The subject needs to be aware of the reading, and this awareness can then serve as a stative rational basis for a

belief (credence). What form might this awareness take? It often takes the form of a belief (or credence), and this belief (credence) can then combine with other beliefs (credences) or with pro-attitudes so as to ground further beliefs or pro-attitudes. This is the form guidance can take through inferential reasoning, practical or theoretical.

The fact that one is in pain is of course a factive reason for belief (or credence, or confidence) that one is in pain. Generally if a fact is to ground a belief, one needs some awareness of it. But awareness that amounts to belief that one is in pain would be useless in the present instance, since you would need to have been guided already in the formation of the relevant belief. This is why such facts or their truth-makers must be self-presenting if they are to do their foundational work. It cannot be that they would provide guidance the way factive reasons normally do so, namely through prior cognitive awareness of them (via which they are presented), through some prior belief or credence. So the question remains as to the kind of awareness of them that will serve for the required guidance.

A distinction between constitutive awareness and noticing awareness may help. When you jump a jump, or kick a kick, or smile a smile, this should not be viewed on an act-object model, where the doing has a separable object. Rather, the jump is just the jumping in a certain way, the kick is the kicking in a certain way, and likewise for the smile, etc. Similarly, when you experience an experience—say, an experience of pain, when you feel a pain—this does not plausibly have an act-object analysis. Rather, experiencing such an experience is experiencing in a certain way.[5] And, since experience is a form of awareness (not a noticing sort of awareness, but a form of awareness nonetheless), therefore you cannot avoid being aware of your experiences, since you must experience them.

Accordingly, one cannot experience a pain without being "aware" of it. And such awareness can then plausibly guide the formation of a corresponding belief or credence. You might then believe or be inclined to believe that you are in pain, and the rational basis for your belief, or your

---

5. This is not to subscribe to a radical adverbial theory, since the "way" in which you experience when you experience a visual experience may require the hosting of a propositional content. This propositional content may be false, however, so that there is no truth-maker to function as the object of one's experience. The propositional content is not the "object" either. We don't sensorily experience propositional contents. Rather, the propositional content gives the content, not the object, of the experience. Hosting the propositional content is essential to the way of experiencing involved in the having of that sensory experience, which need have no object whatsoever.

inclination to believe, would be your awareness of your pain. This awareness might play a proper role in your cognitive dynamics by giving rise to a corresponding credence or belief.

2. That provides a way beyond the Agrippan trilemma pertaining to the middle epistemic range populated by involuntary credences that form a rational structure since some have their proper status by being based rationally on others. Pure experiences (such as experienced pains) in the region of passivity can function as regress-stopping states that are not even performances, and are hence unmotivated by reasons for which they are hosted.[6] Even your awareness of such a state is not a performance. This is true at least of the constitutive awareness of a pain, the awareness of it that you have simply in virtue of suffering it. The pain is thus self-presenting since your constitutive awareness of it comes necessarily with the pain itself. And the pain is not motivated by any reason. (Here we focus on physical pain, which occurs for a reason—a cut or a bruise, etc.—but is not motivated by reasons for which you suffer it. Emotional pains seem importantly different, but we put those aside.)

Pains admit not only constitutive awareness, however, but also noticing awareness. We apply concepts to our pains. We think of them as pains, and indeed as pains of various sorts. Think now of a hypochondriac who takes his imagined pains to be real, or confuses with pain what is at most discomfort and not pain. Suppose he is near the region where pain shades off into discomfort, a region where he is often mistaken. Does he know that he is really in pain simply because this time it is in fact a pain that is making it seem to him that he is in pain? Not plausibly.[7]

D. What Sort of State Can Constitute a Rational Basis?

1. Let us pause and step back. We have posited various mental states as cognitively relevant and taken note of the cognitive mind–world relations that

---

6. Here I am thinking of a normal case, not that of self-inflicted pains, which introduces irrelevant complications.
7. Our hypochondriac problem is akin to the speckled hen problem for givenist internalism. A problem of this sort applies both to experience-based belief or credence about the scene before you, and also to introspective belief or credence about the states of consciousness within you.

they enable. At one end are passive doings and other self-presenting mental states. These attract the subject to assent willy-nilly. They could properly give rise to such attraction in either of two ways. What one is attracted to believe is perhaps that one is in such a state, as when a headache attracts one to believe *that one suffers a headache*. One thus seems to suffer a headache and it is precisely the suffering of the headache that properly gives rise to the seeming.

Does one have a reason for that seeming, a reason for which one is then attracted to accept that one suffers a headache? Surely one does, yet one's being attracted for that reason does not require a separate awareness that one aches—a belief, perhaps, that one aches—based on which through *modus ponens* one could come to believe that one does ache, or at least to be attracted to believe accordingly. This is out of the question, since it would require that one have already formed the belief that one aches. Rather, the rational basing must involve as a basis the headache itself, which must provide the motivating basis for the seeming, for the attraction to assent. This attraction must then vie with whatever else might bear motivationally on what to think about whether one is in pain (as opposed to discomfort). Out of the clash of such vectors a resultant will emerge (including as a limiting case the null vector). That resultant vector will correspond to a resultant seeming or attraction. Concerning the headache, the resultant vector will be a credence of a certain magnitude, perhaps a positive credence with high magnitude.

That is one way in which one might properly derive a credence with high magnitude. But one might do so in a quite different way, where the mental state that attracts one to assent has itself a propositional content. It might for example be a visual experience as if one sees a white and square surface. Now one may be attracted to accept not just that one has such a visual experience, but also that one does see such a surface. And again we need to allow that the visual experience can be self-presenting, so that its sheer presence can provide a rational basis for the corresponding seeming that one sees such a surface. That is to say, its ability to attract our assent need not be mediated by propositional awareness of it in turn. Seemings that are based thus perceptually or experientially might then vie with other rational forces—rational seemings or attractions to assent. Out of this clash would emerge a resultant seeming, a credence whose magnitude can be high.

2. We have surveyed how you can function short of conscious free choice so as to acquire a credence of high magnitude to the effect that p. Suppose you then pose the question whether p. Might you explicitly take note of

your high degree of confidence—of your credence of high magnitude—and apply a policy that calls for affirming that p based on such a credence? Might you apply your policy through a practical syllogism?

No, that is a blind alley. As we have seen already, all three of the Agrippan options are precluded if we restrict ourselves to the region of endeavors. Free judgments cannot gain epistemic status arbitrarily, with no rational basis for the gain. Nor can there be a set of free judgments each of which derives its epistemic propriety entirely through rational basing upon other members of the set. It does not really matter whether the set is finite (the case of circularity) or infinite (the case of infinite regress). In neither case is it plausible that such a set could attain, in that purely set-internal way, epistemic propriety for its member beliefs. In neither case could those member beliefs attain thus the required epistemic justification, a specific sort of normative status required in a belief if it is to constitute knowledge. That is to say, in neither case would such a status be attained—through such mere mutual interrelation—for the set's member beliefs. It is particularly implausible that such status could be earned in that set-internal way for beliefs about an external world beyond the subject's mind, despite the isolation of the whole set from that surrounding world. And the relevant "isolation" is the rational-basis isolation that would deprive our free judgments of any epistemic reliability.

But why should that spoil the practical syllogism for explaining how judgments can be formed freely and foundationally?

Here is why. We saw earlier why rationally supportive states are needed beyond freely determined judgments. We need such reasons, so as to escape foundational arbitrariness. But once we see why we need such regress stoppers, it is clear why we must restrict how a free judgment can be "properly based" on such a reason. This basing cannot be of the sort that involves judgmental awareness of the basis, along with belief that such a basis brings with it the truth of the belief to be based on it. This would involve *modus ponens* reasoning, with freely judged premises and a freely judged covering belief. And that would not escape the region of freedom in the way required. We would still need to consider the epistemic status of the freely judged premises (and perhaps also that of the freely judged covering generalization).

So that cannot be right. Instead, we appeal to the functional state itself as a rational basis. We span the divide between the region of freedom and the region of functionings. We invoke a relation of rational basing that allows a basis within the region of functionings for a free judgment in the region of freedom.

That is why we appeal to transregional rational basing. Such basing spans the border between two epistemic regions of mental states: the region of functioning and the region of freedom; and similar reasoning reveals how useful it is also at the border between the region of passivity and the region of functioning.

E. The Importance of Competence

1. So much for the crucial place of transregional rational basing in the human cognitive economy. However, our reasoning also highlights the importance of competence for the epistemic justification that is constitutive of knowledge. Sometimes the rational propriety of a credence does not plausibly derive entirely if at all from rational basing. Pertinent here are the beliefs of super-blindsighters, as well as our simplest arithmetic, geometric, and logical beliefs, and other simple beliefs that require no rational basis. What matters for the epistemic propriety of these various beliefs is in good part simply that they derive from proper epistemic competence, which in these cases need not be reason based. Although human belief is very often competent through rational basing, it might also be competent through subpersonal means. It is presumably through subpersonal means that the blindsighters know. Also indirect is the knowledge that over two seconds have elapsed since one awoke, as one lies in bed about to get up.[8]

Our reasoning pertains not just to the functional justification of rational performances within the region of proper functioning. It pertains also to the deontic justification of rational performances within the region of

---

8. What seems here subpersonal is the process whereby one is attracted to assent to the relevant propositional content. The attraction itself of course need not be subpersonal. Still lacking in this case is any *experiential* state analogous to one's visual experience as of a fire, say, or a hand, etc. Very plausibly one might insist that no *belief* can be justified groundlessly, which would seem particularly plausible when applied to *judgmental* (as opposed to functional) belief. There would always be a prior *intellectual seeming* or attraction to assent, one detachable from the full-fledged belief, since collateral reasoning might have blocked full belief, as with the solution to a paradox, like the Liar or the Sorites. Although I take this to be the right view of the matter, I suppress it here for a simpler exposition, one modifiable in due course into the more sophisticated variant that will give intellectual seemings their proper rational role.

responsible free judgment. True enough, the competences pertinent to the latter, to free endeavors, crucially involve the will, as Descartes saw so clearly in recognizing a volitional faculty of free judgment, along with his functional faculty of divinely determined understanding.

However, mere correspondence between a credence or belief and a given, self-presenting state—mere coincidence of content—will not suffice for the epistemic justification that knowledge requires. Take the correspondence between my subjective visual field with ten speckles and my direct belief that there are ten speckles in that visual field. That correspondence fact does not suffice to ensure that my belief is epistemically justified. In addition, relevant competence is also required. My ability to subitize must extend to the case of ten items, which it is far from doing.

The phenomena of blindsight and time perception make it doubtful, moreover, that foundationalism must rely essentially on pre-belief psychological states based on which one can believe rationally. Although the competence relevant to knowledge can operate based on such states—states of pain, for example, or of basic visual experience—it need not do so. Again, it can also operate by means of subpersonal mechanisms that yield belief or credence directly through causal inputs via light, open eyes, and a brain and nervous system that enable responsive and discriminative belief.

The like seems true in addition about "introspective" knowledge. What could preclude direct, reliable knowledge of one's own mental dispositions? Even mental self-knowledge might be secured thus through direct competence, with no prior guiding awareness.

2. Recall why circularity and regress seem vicious regardless of whether we restrict ourselves to free judgments or include also rational functionings. It seems out of the question that a whole set of judgments or beliefs or credences could all be epistemically justified or competent simply in virtue of their rational basing interrelations. Again, this is made implausible by the following two considerations: first, that epistemic justification could not be wholly isolated from truth; second, that such a set with its rational interrelations could be relevantly isolated from truth, which would deprive its members of full justification, no matter how well they may interrelate. Even intricate, rational interrelations within such a set can still be out of touch with how probably true the members may be. An intricate story held in the mind of a great novelist could host much rational interrelation with no vestige of relevant truth. A novelist deranged enough to start believing

his story would not thereby attain a status required for knowledge, that of competently justified belief. And this cannot be remedied simply through the addition of members, of further beliefs, not even unto infinity.

The remedy favored by many requires relations to given, self-presenting states in the region of epistemic passivity. We do seem to stop the regress of justification through such foundations, since these given, self-presenting states are not of a sort to be justified, nor do they need to be justified in order to provide justification for further credences or beliefs based upon them. We might moreover thereby obtain the required relation to the world beyond beliefs and credences, since such self-presenting states are themselves part of that world beyond, and since they might in addition provide a reliable channel to the world altogether external to the subject's mind.

3. Even if that all seems right, what does not seem right is that only through the postulation of such foundationally basing, self-presenting mental states could we secure the relevant relations of truth reliability to the world beyond our minds. Might there not be subpersonal mechanisms that equally reliably relate our beliefs to that external world? Cases of blindsight and of time perception show this to be more than just a conceptual possibility.[9]

Moreover, we now have reason to reconsider the status of contentful sensory experiences. We had placed these in the region of epistemically non-functional passivity, where the subject is in no way an epistemic agent. That region supposedly lies beyond the region of epistemic functionings, some rationally motivated by others, even if no mere functioning is freely determined. But now we have found reason to countenance such functionings—of the blindsighted, for example, and of our time perceivers—that have no basis in the region of passivity, since they are based on no proper mental states at all. Thus, the credences of the blindsighted require no mental basis at all. They derive rather from subpersonal states involving transmission of energy from the environment through the subject's receptors and his brain and nervous system, where this all happens subpersonally yet in some way that is epistemically competent and truth reliable.

---

9. Moreover, our simplest beliefs of logic, arithmetic, and geometry provide further examples where foundational beliefs attain epistemic justification with no help from pre-belief self-presenting, given mental states. Mere understanding plausibly gives us the access we need to the relevant set of simple truths, provided we are reliable enough in such understanding-based beliefs.

Such subpersonally competent credences can thus gain proper epistemic status, and can provide an epistemic basis for further credences, and eventually even for free judgments. Contentful sensory experiences are hence not properly consigned to the region of pure epistemic passivity; they deserve a place in the region of functionings. For they too derive from subpersonal inputs through the subject's brain and nervous system, and they too can be more or less truth competent. There is hence no rational obstacle to locating them in the region of functionings, along with credences and seemings, even if these latter distinctively involve concepts. Credences (and seemings), it is true, distinctively involve some stricter application of concepts. They might hence still deserve to be distinguished from sensory experiences, in that their contents are immediately available to serve as premises for conscious reasoning. Experiences by contrast may not be immediately available for such competent reasoning, not even through the use of demonstratives.[10] This is a lesson of the speckled hen problem. Nevertheless, experiences can still be competently veridical, manifesting thus a kind of perceptual competence on the part of the perceiver. This distinguishes, for example, those with good, sharp vision from those not so well endowed.

F. The Self-Presenting

We earlier found a stopping place for the regress of justification with passive states, physical pains among them. "Pains do have propositional content," comes the reply, "and can hence be assessed epistemically at least to the same extent as perceptual experiences." This controversial issue we can avoid, if we make some further distinctions.

1. We have already recognized that perceptual experiences are inherently epistemic. Some are representational and can hence be assessed as veridical or as illusory. But it is less plausible that pains, and especially itches,

---

10. Take a pattern that to me has religious significance, so that I can recognize it, and store beliefs with concepts that correspond to that visual pattern. To you that pattern might be just a squiggle. In this case my beliefs can feature that pattern itself in their content in a way that is not available to you. As you look away from the squiggle your prior belief is accessible through "the squiggle I just ostended" or the like. By contrast, I can forget how I acquired my belief with no detriment to its full content that I can now retain in storage. I might for example retain an important religious belief to the effect that instances of that pattern are worthy of veneration. The former sort of squiggle belief, with its purely demonstrative/indexical content, would insufficiently nourish our body of beliefs.

are plausibly enough interpreted as having such content. So, we might prefer to suspend judgment on pain representationalism. For example, one may well doubt that a headache or even a foot ache has any distinctive content such as "damage" of any sort. True, the footache does come with an inherent representation of an ostensible body part, which does seem a representational foot in the door.

2. The fallback, fuller answer is one that can apply to all three items: to clearly representational sensory experiences, itches, and pains, as well as to other bodily sensations, and even to mental phenomena generally, whether representational or not. We need a notion of a mental state that, whether active or passive, whether representational or not, can serve as an epistemic basis for belief, without so serving only dependently on its own prior epistemic status. Such states are thus "passive" in the sense that it is not their successful and/or competent epistemic activity—if there is any such—that suits them for serving as a proper basis for further epistemic performance. Any mental state or act that can thus serve as a basis would be relevantly passive. That is to say, even if it is active, it is not its status as successful or competent that bears on its qualifying as a proper basis for epistemic performance. A *false, unjustified* belief can still serve as a perfectly fine basis for the believer's justified belief that he holds that belief.

3. Of course, once we realize this, it will be plausible enough that even free acts of judgment or choice might play a relevantly "passive" role. They too can serve as bases for epistemic performance without their suitability for so serving depending on their own epistemic success or even competence.

4. As that suggests, the epistemic categorization relevant to the Pyrrhonian problematic is hence not so much ontological as epistemically functional. In particular, there can be regress stoppers at each of the three regions distinguished ontologically: (a) that of passivity, (b) that of functionings, and (c) that of free endeavors. What is distinctive of the occupants of (a) is that there is no possible confusion of a sort that remains possible for the other two regions. Since occupants of (a) are not relevantly agential, there is no temptation to think that the regress has not stopped with them for the reason that we need to assess their own performance epistemically. Either (i) they are not even thus assessable, as in the case of phenomenally accessible mental states that are not even representational, such as itches perhaps, or else (ii) even if representational, their ability to function properly as epistemic bases for further beliefs

is not dependent on their own epistemic status, which can be lowly with no detriment to their serving as bases for further beliefs.

5. Maybe pains and itches are ontologically active in epistemic respects, maybe not. In any case there are phenomena more fully passive through lack of representational content. How about being conscious, where this spans wakeful and dream states? Does the state of being thus conscious have representational content?

6. However we settle those questions, it now seems dialectically less important whether there are many, or even any, occupants of the region of passivity. Here is what now seems the crucial point for our project: For epistemological purposes we can suspend judgment on whether the region of passivity is empty or not. Actually, this had already seemed a relatively unimportant question, since even blindsighters can stop the regress while devoid of any relevant passive states on which they can epistemically base their beliefs. It is competence that really matters fundamentally, by stopping the regress when the competence is foundational and does not involve rational basing.

G. Choice, Judgment, and Freedom

1. Our distinction between two sorts of epistemic agency, the free versus the unfree, bears on the Agrippan trilemma wielded by Pyrrhonian skeptics, which we took up as follows. First we distinguished choices and judgments that are from those that are not free. On some ostensible options the agent is not plausibly free to choose. I do not take myself to be free to choose to take my pen right now and stick it deep into my right eye. I am perhaps free to do so *if I so choose*. My arm is free, my grip good, my pen available, my aim fine, and so on. But I do not believe I can now make that choice. Nor do I find it plausible that, given my actual present situation, I could in the next minute choose to divorce my wife. Of course, had I been differently situated, or in bad enough psychological shape, then I might well have been able to do so. But given my present shape and situation, in my judgment I am not able to so choose now, not really. On closer inspection the scope of free choice seems narrower than might have appeared on a casual first look. But this is far from showing that we have no freedom of choice whatever. We do seem free to choose when we are rationally required to choose between two options neither of which is

preferable to the other. From the time we choose which shoe to put on first as we arise in the morning, to the time we choose which to remove first as we retire, we face such choices at many turns. On many options faced in an ordinary day, moreover, even when there are good reasons in favor of choosing a certain way (unlike the case of the shoes), there will often be countervailing reasons, and it will be up to us just how to strike a balance.

The case of judgment is different from that of choice in that there is no such thing as proper arbitrary judgment. When the weight of the evidence favors neither the affirmative nor the negative, one cannot judge arbitrarily, not properly. One must rather suspend. When the balance of reasons favors neither choosing to put the right shoe on first nor choosing not to do so, however, one can properly choose either way, arbitrarily.

That is one reason why it might seem initially that the scope for free choice far exceeds the scope for free judgment. It might seem that there is no scope for proper arbitrary judgment whereas there is plenty of scope for proper arbitrary choice. Since we are bound to be rational except when special forces drive us to irrationality, we are thus apparently forced to judge as we do whenever we do judge. Either we are subject to the force of reason, or we are subject to some irrational force, to some bias, perhaps, or to some culturally derived superstition. Choice and judgment differ in that regard. Choice can be very broadly arbitrary without being irrational, so it can be freely made with no need of force whether rational or irrational.

That does reveal a vast difference between choice and judgment in respect of freedom. Nevertheless, we enjoy broad freedom both for choice and for judgment. We need only recall how often we freely conclude deliberation or pondering. We then decide whether to accept that the balance of reasons sufficiently favors either side over the other. Very often, on issues both weighty and trivial, it is up to the agent which way to turn.

2. An animal/reflective distinction may be helpful at this juncture. Plenty of general animal beliefs are acquired through childhood as our brain develops and our cultural identity is formed. Other beliefs are acquired later and remain in storage even after we forget how they were acquired. Both early and late, animal beliefs can guide our conduct subconsciously, whether the conduct be physical or intellectual. Biases, for example, can guide even someone who would reject them when brought to consciousness. Such guiding implicit beliefs are often beyond the control of our conscious free agency. They are at least not under the direct control of a single free choice. We cannot change them that way. This is true both

of the deep general beliefs acquired through normal child development and of our constant flow of perceptual beliefs.

Our distinction has animal, action-guiding beliefs on one side, and reflective judgments on the other. This distinction is akin to one between deep biases and conscious, sincere suspension of judgment. Pyrrhonists who avowedly suspend judgment need not be disavowing animal beliefs beyond their control. They may only be forbearing from endorsing them consciously and freely. The distinctions are similar even if the bigot disavows his bias whereas the skeptic need not disavow his animal belief; he need only forbear from endorsing it through conscious judgment.

That is not to say that free judgment always diverges from animal belief. Suppose we add a long column in our heads as we view it on a piece of paper. We may do so flawlessly, and yet distrust our computation and refuse to endorse the result. We consider whether to trust it and decide against doing so. Suppose we next use pencil and paper. Now we may consider anew whether to trust our result. And here again it is up to us. In this way we can control our beliefs. If we freely adopt and store the result of our computation, that can guide our conduct in the future, even after we have forgotten the source of our belief.

That is a case where we seem freely responsible for the relevant belief. But there are plenty of cases where present conscious reasoning is unable to affect entrenched beliefs acquired through past childhood or present perception. Recall the case of deeply entrenched bias that is sincerely disavowed at the surface of consciousness. This suggests that conscious endorsement need not be driven by a corresponding animal belief. Note furthermore what would otherwise follow, implausibly, about the Pyrrhonian skeptic: that he must be either a liar or self-deceived when he professes to suspend judgment on commonsense beliefs.

Our reasoning suggests a distinction between such animal belief and reflective, judgmental belief. Animal belief can be constituted by a stored state that guides conduct subconsciously. Reflective, judgmental belief, by contrast, is a disposition to judge affirmatively in answer to a question, in the endeavor to answer correctly, with truth, reliably enough or even aptly. And this "judgment" that one is disposed to render is a distinctive conscious act or consciously sustained state. It is this act or state that is within our free control about as often and as plausibly as are the choices we make ordinarily and the conscious intentions that we sustain.

Note finally the peculiar way in which we freely control such beliefs. Suppose the relevant belief is constitutively a disposition to assent freely upon consideration if one endeavors to answer correctly and aptly. Let us now distinguish dispositions based on the will from those that are passive. A disposition can be passive because its host is no agent at all, as with the solubility of a sugar cube. A disposition can also be passive even when the host is an agent, but still passive with regard to that disposition, as when you are disposed to kick your leg under the doctor's mallet. By contrast, a disposition seated in the will can amount to a freely chosen or sustained policy. Take the policy of signaling your turns as you drive. This can lead to a choice, conscious or subconscious, to signal on a certain occasion as you approach a turn. The particular free choice then implements the policy, the freely chosen general commitment to signal your turns. You are disposed to signal as you approach your turns, and your particular chosen signalings are guided by that policy, and manifest that freely sustained disposition.

That same idea is applicable to the sorts of beliefs now in our focus. These are supposedly dispositions to affirm freely, and such a disposition can itself reside in the will; it can itself amount to a freely adopted evidential policy. These beliefs thus stand in contrast to animal beliefs acquired through the unfree "automatic" proper functioning of our cognitive mechanisms. The commitments now in our focus are intentions acquired differently. They are instead chosen freely, so that the "mechanism" is itself voluntary. Our freely chosen commitments govern our free judgments when we consciously weigh a question in the light of all the reasons synchronically in view. Some inquirers are more careful, more conservative, than others. Their will to believe is on a tighter leash, even when driven disinterestedly by the search for truth.

In addition to such will-involving commitments, however, *involuntary* competences of reasoning can also bear on our judgments. These involuntary competences involve proper functioning built into our brains as we mature intellectually. Of course these would not themselves be freely chosen. By contrast, our voluntary dispositional beliefs are freely acquired and sustained, as when one acquires and sustains the belief that Steve Jobs was brilliant but morally flawed. This involves a free choice to judge affirmatively upon bringing that question to mind, pending further relevant evidence, provided we are aiming to get it aptly right. This policy can be changed, again freely and rationally, if new evidence does come to light. One will need to weigh the new evidence along with whatever other relevant reasons may be in view, and decide whether to change one's belief: that is to say, whether to change one's "policy" to answer in the affirmative, to oneself, and to others when sincere.

H. Is There No Safe Retreat from the Determined Skeptic?

Are we now landed once again in a similar predicament? The skeptic could after all replicate his doubts on the second order. He could put in question our trust in our own second-order competence while touting the quality of his corresponding self-trust. Once again it would seem stubbornly irrational to just take our side with no supporting reasons. Rationality would seem to require reasons synchronically available to us, if we are to sustain our self-trust properly against the doubt of our opponent.

Is it irrational to ignore such an opponent? That depends on the context. What else requires our attention at the time? Suppose we put aside practical considerations. Even so, what other intellectual or epistemic concerns require our attention at the time? There may surely come a time when we do best intellectually to insist on our side of a controversy based simply on self-trust. And our judgment on the lower order may also be well-enough rendered, as is required if that judgment is to constitute knowledge. A knowledge-constitutive judgment need only avoid relevant epistemic flaws, even if it could still be enhanced through further scrutiny and reasoning.

Take two opponents who proceed alike with equally plausible justification. Suppose them to be on a par as concerns any conscious reasoning they employ or might easily employ. Each considers himself reliable on the question dividing them. Each has better things to do than to resolve their disagreement, moreover, even considering just intellectual or epistemic concerns. To this extent, accordingly, the two are equally rational in agreeing to disagree, in carrying on with their intellectual lives. However, this does not entail that they are on a par epistemically in doing so, nor that their beliefs, and their corresponding judgments on the first order, are equally well justified epistemically, if what we pick out by such "justification" is the normative status requisite for knowledge.[11] One of the disagreeing beliefs may be much better justified epistemically than the other.

Those opponents are strikingly similar in the ways detailed. Despite that, one of them may trust himself on a far better diachronic basis than

---

11. That is the status "picked out" by "epistemic justification," which does not mean that this expression is to be defined as "the status required for propositional knowledge." All things considered, I myself prefer a terminology of "competence" for that status.

does the other. We cannot ascend infinite ladders of synchronic endorsement. At some point our defense must rest, and it will then matter how well founded our relevant dispositions may be. At some point we will have reached the end of the synchronic line. Only diachronic factors might then bear epistemically on the self-trust resident on that level, and those factors must be given their due. If you reason no more and no less well than a given opponent, at a certain level of reflection, but the two of you still differ epistemically in the quality of your relevant diachronic dispositions, this must be allowed its proper bearing in assessing your relevant judgments and beliefs. You might now be well advised to stiffen your spine and move on.

As we have seen, we rise above the animal level through endorsement based on reasons within our synchronic purview. This does not mean that we deplorably fall short as reflective humans if unable to reach infinite levels of reflection available at most to the infinitely omniscient. First of all, ought implies can no less for epistemic than for moral agency.[12] Besides, suppose we could ascend to a higher level yet, under the prompting of disagreement on a given level. And suppose our relevant beliefs would be epistemically enhanced by success in this further endeavor. Even so, the better is not necessarily the obligatory. Our belief might be improvable epistemically through such ascent without being so much as *flawed* even if we decline to ascend, and even if we do not so much as consider ascending. We might just have better things to do epistemically than to defend our belief on that higher plane.[13]

---

12. "No less," I say, leaving room for important and subtle issues on the way in which and the extent to which the dictum does apply even in the moral realm.
13. This concluding stance gains plausibility when we distinguish between (a) positive suspension of belief and (b) simply not seriously considering a question, even with that question before our minds. The latter is a refusal to go further into the matter of what attitude to take to that question, even the attitude of suspending.

   Moreover, it might just be that proper human cognitive practice requires no such defense. Given all the tradeoffs involved in human flourishing (including the cognitive components of such flourishing), perhaps our cognitive practice requires no such further ascent, despite the cognitive enhancement that would supervene upon it. This raises questions, some clearly non-trivial. What is cognitive practice? What is a cognitive practice? Is there a single human such practice part of a "human form of life"? Or are there (also?) culturally specific practices that bear (as well) on a kind of epistemic justification available to members of the relevant culture? Do all such practices have proper normative bearing, or is there room for illusion in them, and even for superstition, at least in the culturally specific ones? This general approach might reveal varieties of epistemic justification specific to species or even cultures, even if they all share important structural similarities and a common aim at reliable attainment of truth. Armchair intuitions might then reflect our commitments to such practices, whether these are inevitable through normal child development or imbibed with the culture. Given that illusion and superstition are also acquired in those ways, however, these practices would require evaluation. And the epistemic evaluation of epistemic practices must of course involve truth reliability.

PART IV

Main Historical Antecedents

10
Pyrrhonian Skepticism and Human Agency

1. More than just an epistemology, Pyrrhonism is a way of life. What more devastating an objection could there be to it, therefore, than that it could not possibly be lived? And that is just the charge brought by David Hume as follows.

> A Stoic or Epicurean displays principles, which may not only be durable, but which have an effect on conduct and behaviour. But a Pyrrhonian cannot expect that his philosophy will have any constant influence on the mind: or if it had, that its influence would be beneficial to society. On the contrary, he must acknowledge, if he will acknowledge anything, that all human life must perish, were his principles universally and steadily to prevail. All discourse, all action, would immediately cease, and men remain in a total lethargy, till the necessities of nature, unsatisfied, put an end to their miserable existence. It is true; so fatal an event is very little to be dreaded. Nature is always too strong for principle. And though a Pyrrhonian may throw himself or others into a momentary amazement and confusion by his profound reasonings; the first and most trivial event in life will put to flight all his doubts and scruples and leave him the same, in every point of action and speculation, with the philosophers of every other sect, or with those who never concerned themselves in any philosophical researches. When he awakes from his dream, he will be the first to join in the laugh against himself, and to confess, that all his objections are mere amusement, and can have no other tendency than to show the whimsical condition of mankind, who must act and reason and believe; though they are not able, by their most diligent enquiry, to satisfy themselves concerning the foundation of these operations, or to remove the objections, which may be raised against them.[1]

So far the charge is that the Pyrrhonian's way of life is an option that human nature disallows. The constraints of human nature preclude our living that

---

1. David Hume, *An Enquiry Concerning Human Understanding* (1748), section XII.

way. More recently, Myles Burnyeat has argued that, far from being just *psychologically* impossible for us to live that way, it is somehow intrinsically incoherent. The reasons why such a life cannot be lived go deeper than mere psychology.

2. In order properly to consider these charges, we must first try to understand the proposed way of life. What is Pyrrhonian Skepticism? What are its components, and how are they combined?

   a. First come the modes. These are argument forms, especially the ten of Anesidemus, and the five of Agrippa, and others besides. They are the resources that the skeptic uses to balance the reasons pro and con with regard to any given propositional claim or question. The aim is to bring about *isosthenia* or equipollence with respect to any such proposition <p>, for any given subject S and time t. As a result, the subject will be rationally justified neither in believing nor in disbelieving that p.

   b. *Isosthenia* leads to *epoché*: i.e., equipollence leads to suspension of judgment and belief, to conscious suspension on the question whether p.

   c. *Epoché* in turn leads to *ataraxia*, to tranquility. This is a freedom from disturbance, a blissful calm.

   d. *Ataraxia*, finally, is tantamount to, or an essential component or source of:

   e. *Eudaemonia*, of flourishing, or true happiness, or faring well.

Those then are the five main components in order: modes, *isosthenia, epoché, ataraxia, eudaemonia*.

3. Hume finds such a way of life psychologically impossible. One defense against that charge begins by distinguishing, with Jonathan Barnes, between two types of Pyrrhonism:

> The first type I shall call, following Galen, *rustic Pyrrhonism*. The rustic Pyrrhonist has no beliefs whatsoever: he directs *epoche* towards every issue that may arise. The second type of Scepticism I shall call *urbane Pyrrhonism*. The urbane Pyrrhonist is happy to believe most of the things that ordinary people assent to in the ordinary course of events: he directs *epoche* towards a specific target—roughly speaking, towards philosophical and scientific matters.[2]

---

2. Jonathan Barnes, "The Beliefs of a Pyrrhonist," in E. J. Kenny and M. M. MacKenzie, eds, *Proceedings of the Cambridge Philological Society* (Cambridge: Cambridge University Press, 1982), 2–29; pp. 2–3.

The terminology is complicated through a distinction drawn by Burnyeat between "belief" and "assent," one he claims to find in the Pyrrhonists themselves. Where assent is the genus, belief is just the species of assent that concerns objective matters, matters beyond the subjectivity of the assenting subject, beyond that subject's conscious states at the time, or, perhaps, beyond his mental states more generally.

That yields three levels of assent:

First, *subjective assent*, about one's own concurrent subjective states.

Second, *commonsense assent*, about ordinary matters of everyday concern, issues that we take to be decidable through straightforward commonsense beliefs and procedures.

Third, *theoretical assent*, on more general, abstract matters of scientific or philosophical concern.

There is also a distinction, explicitly drawn by Sextus Empiricus, between the evident and the non-evident, where the latter encompasses matters demanding inquiry—and thus reasoning, inference—for their determination. Thus, according to Sextus: "We must . . . remember that we do not employ them [the modes] universally about all things, but about those which are non-evident and are objects of dogmatic inquiry" (*PH* I: 208). However, the distinction between matters that require inference and those that do not cuts across all three levels of assent recently distinguished. Even about our concurrent mental states, even the conscious ones, for example, there seem clearly to be questions that we cannot answer without the special sort of inferential processes that are involved in counting, where we arrive at an answer not just through simple inspection but only as a result of a rational procedure that takes time and reasoning, one subject to mistakes.

4. Strong support for the urbane interpretation apparently resides in the fact that the skeptic's way of life includes a fourfold commitment as follows:

> Adhering, then, to appearances we live in accordance with the normal rules of life, undogmatically, seeing that we cannot remain wholly inactive. And it would seem that this regulation of life is fourfold, and that one part of it lies in the guidance of Nature, another in the constraint of the passions, another in the tradition of laws and customs, another in the instruction of the arts. (*PH* I: 23)

This seems prima facie to require one to form opinions on what the laws and customs require, for example, and on facts that one must know in order to master any given trade or craft, any practical art in which one is to be instructed. And the urbane Pyrrhonist has no objection to such beliefs, since he restricts his modes, *isosthenia*, and *epoché*, to general, abstract questions of philosophy or science.

5. Before we yield to what seems prima facie so plausible, however, we need a better understanding of three other elements crucial to Pyrrhonism: first, an account of the "appearances" to which they constantly appeal; second, an account of *ataraxia*, of what is involved in that state so central to the Pyrrhonian way of life; and, finally, an account of how *epoché* leads to *ataraxia* (and thence to *eudaemonia*).

a. Appearances seem for the Pyrrhonist importantly different from beliefs. And that is quite a plausible distinction when we focus on sensory appearances, as when (a) the oar still looks bent though we know it to be straight, or when (b) the Müller-Lyer lines still seem visually incongruent even once measurement reveals them to be congruent. But, as is abundantly clear in the texts, Pyrrhonist appearances are not restricted to sensory appearances. Instead they include also intellectual seemings that survive even when one believes the contradictory or a contrary. For a convincing case in point, consider a powerful paradox, such as the Liar, or the Sorites. Even when one's solution requires rejecting a proposition constitutive of the paradox, that proposition might retain considerable intellectual attraction nevertheless, a lingering appearance of being true.

b. *Ataraxia* is a matter of tranquility or calm, of the absence of frustration, anxiety, tension, disturbance. (Compare Stoicism.) One sort of frustration is constituted or yielded by a combination of a belief of <p> with a favoring of the opposite: <not-p>. However, the absence of such frustration is compatible with the anxiety produced or constituted by a different combination: namely, the combination of a favoring of <p> with the *absence* of belief that p. So, the removal of belief seemingly entailed by Pyrrhonism would seem to leave standing an important sort of unease, namely the anxiety produced or constituted by one's wanting a certain outcome while uncertain that it has or will come about. The level of such unease would be proportional to the degree of one's desire, and could rise to very disturbing levels.

6. How then might *epoché* lead to tranquil *ataraxia*? Can it really do so? Here are some answers in the literature.

a. First, Myles Burnyeat argues that the Pyrrhonian cannot coherently carry out his program, since at a crucial juncture it requires a belief that he is committed to doing without.

> [If] . . . tranquility is to be achieved, at some stage the skeptic's questing thoughts must come to a state of rest or equilibrium. There need be no finality to this achievement; the skeptic may hold himself ready to be persuaded that there are after all answers to be had. He is not a negative dogmatist furnished with a priori objections that rule out the possibility of answers as a matter of general principle once and for all (cf. PH I: 1–3). But *ataraxia* is hardly to be attained if he is not in some sense satisfied—so far—that no answers are forthcoming, that contrary claims are indeed equal. And my question is: How can Sextus then deny that this is something he believes?[3]

b. Bredo Johnsen tries to rescue the Pyrrhonian from such incoherence, however, through the following alternative account of how *epoché* gives rise to *ataraxia*.

> [The settled Skeptic] . . . suspends belief not out of anxiety or frustration, but as a result of having brought to bear on the question at hand one or more of the vast battery of arguments of his tradition, with the result that it appears to him that no answer to the question is forthcoming. Burnyeat's question is how *that* process could bring about *ataraxia* except on the assumption that the arguments have led the thinker to believe that no answer is forthcoming.

> The answer, I submit, is [this:] . . . We should take it that it appears to Sextus that: Either the truth can be determined or it can not; if it can, then since he remains open-minded he may yet succeed in determining it; if it can not, then by suspending judgment he has at least avoided the danger of mistakenly thinking that he has determined it, as well as the anxiety associated with being aware of the possibility that he has succumbed to that danger.

> It is perhaps worth underscoring the diametrical opposition between Burnyeat's and my proposals: whereas he locates the genesis of *ataraxia* in belief, I, with Sextus, locate it (in part) in the absence of belief. In my view, the belief he attributes to Sextus—that contrary claims are equally balanced—would have been a source not of *ataraxia* but of anxiety; the fact that such propositions—versions of the Skeptic slogans—were as threatening as any other nonevident propositions in this respect helps to explain Sextus's emphatic insistence on their self-applicability and his consequent suspension of belief concerning them (PH I: 187–209).[4]

---

3. Myles Burnyeat, "Can the Skeptic Live His Skepticism?," in M. F. Burnyeat, ed., *The Skeptical Tradition* (Berkeley: University of California Press, 1983), 117–48; pp. 139–40.
4. Bredo Johnsen, "On the Coherence of Pyrrhonian Skepticism," *The Philosophical Review*, 110 (2001): 521–61; pp. 544–5.

Burnyeat and Johnsen thus disagree on what for Pyrrhonism is in fact the source of *ataraxia*. For the former it is a belief that contrary claims are equally balanced, permanently so. For the latter it is rather a suspension of belief along with a certain complex appearance, and an ongoing open-mindedness.

c. However, given what we have found to be the nature of ataraxia, it is not immediately evident how either of these answers can be correct. How could either of the sets of factors identified by our two authors secure *ataraxia*, i.e., freedom from disturbance? How does either of these sets of factors serve to remove or avoid either frustration or anxiety?

If disturbing frustration is a matter of believing something to be so when you oppose its being so (or disbelieving something when you favor it, which amounts to the same), then in order to preclude such frustration by way of suspending belief, what you would apparently need to do most directly is to suspend belief in things you oppose. So now we face some questions for Burnyeat and Johnsen: How could the belief identified by Burnyeat be essentially involved in precluding such disturbing frustration? After all, to remove frustration by way of your doxastic attitudes you would need to reject belief rather than embrace it; at least you would need to reject *certain* beliefs, those in propositions to which you are opposed (or those in the contradictories of propositions that you favor).

It may be replied that the *ataraxia*-securing belief does its work indirectly: that is, once one is convinced that the conflicting answers on any "whether"-question are fated to remain in equipollence, one will be led to suspend belief on any such question that one might face, including the questions on issues of concern, where one favors one side and opposes the other.

Although that has some plausibility, it does leave a puzzling question: Why are the Pyrrhonists interested in *general* skepticism, in general *isosthenia* and *epoché*? After all, what matters for *ataraxia* is quite restricted to beliefs on matters of concern to the subject. For these are the only matters on which belief can combine with emotion so as to produce disturbing frustration.

d. Johnsen's account of how *epoché* leads to *ataraxia* is also open to a similar question. Why all the extra content beyond relevant suspension of belief? Why require also the open-mindedness, or even the appearance that "either the truth can be determined or it cannot . . .," etc.?

In any case, as we have seen already, there is a much more serious question for these two accounts, a question that strikes at the heart of Pyrrhonism itself. The question arises because frustration is just one variety of disturbance. Is not *anxiety* also disturbing in its own way, where to be anxious is to favor something intensely (or to oppose or disfavor something, but this is just a special case) while consciously *unsure* of the outcome. This now makes it unclear just how the epistemic practice of Pyrrhonism is supposed to fit with its whole way of life. Recall that through the use of the Modes, the Pyrrhonist puts reasons pro in balance with reasons con, regarding any given question, which leads to *suspension of belief.* But suspension of belief is an essential component in disturbing anxiety. So now it appears that far from protecting us from disturbance and helping us attain *ataraxia*, the Pyrrhonian practice has the potential rather to bring about disturbing anxiety.

7. If there is a way around this, it is likely to be via the other component of disturbance, namely the emotional component, the favoring or opposing. Could it be that *epoché* helps us remove or moderate emotion with a corresponding improvement in our level of *ataraxia*, of tranquility. And note that we have begun to recognize that *ataraxia* is not just a black/white, on/off matter. It is obvious rather that tranquility comes in degrees, as does of course disturbance, which comes in degrees of frustration or anxiety. One can be more or less frustrated, more or less anxious. Pyrrhonism can *help* even if it does not yield absolute *ataraxia*, so long as it helps us attain more of it.

a. Pyrrhonism may perhaps be seen to enable such results once we recognize that in a rational being emotion will be attuned with evaluative belief. It will not do to care about something if you are convinced that it is not worth caring about. Indeed you still fall short of proper rational coherence if you care about something while unable to tell whether it is worth caring about. Accordingly, you are more rational to the extent that you bring your emotions in line with your evaluative beliefs. The degree to which you are rational in a certain combination of such attitudes re <p> depends presumably on such things as how much it matters that p, how sure you are that it does matter that much, how much you care about <p> and in what way, whether by favoring it or by disfavoring it.

Therefore, by promoting general *epoché* one thereby promotes *evaluative epoché*, that is to say suspension of belief on what matters and how much. Suspending such beliefs will then comport in a rational being with removal of the corresponding emotions, or at least will do so to the extent that the being is guided by reason.

That does seem to give a more satisfying explanation of how for the Pyrrhonian *epoché* is supposed to further *ataraxia*. Unlike the earlier proposals, this provides a satisfying account of how the constitution of the two phenomena guarantees a necessary connection between them via which the one may be seen to lead to the other.

As with the earlier proposals, however, a puzzling question remains: Why the general skepticism? All that one now apparently needs for *ataraxia* is *evaluative* skepticism. Why go beyond that?

Our question suggests that Pyrrhonism is not just a way to attain *ataraxia*. That is a by-product, of course, as with the sponge thrown in frustration that unexpectedly produces the desired effect on a painting. But Pyrrhonism is also just a matter of ongoing, open-minded inquiry, which in fact leads through the argumentative modes to *epoché* over a range of questions far beyond the merely evaluative.[5]

b. There is moreover a second way in which, according to Burnyeat, the Pyrrhonian is mired in incoherence. For the Pyrrhonian is supposed to use the modes in order to bring about *epoché*. But the modes are argument forms and to use them is to reason in accordance with the relevant argumentative patterns. But how could one possibly reason thus sans belief of any sort?

It may be replied that the reasoning is like the ladder thrown away once used, or like the laxative expelled as it does its work. But the Pyrrhonian does not stop living, does not put his life on hold, with the attainment of *epoché* on any given question. He continues to inquire, which is part of what it means to remain open-minded. And how could one possibly continue to lead the life of a skeptic, if rational inquiry, the use of argumentative modes, must rely on beliefs aplenty?

It seems accordingly desirable for Pyrrhonists to find some way to understand how the modes can be used in their reasoning without necessarily involving beliefs. Let us next consider this question.

Pyrrhonists claim that their lives are guided not by belief but by appearance. So this is a very natural substitute to replace belief within their mode-patterned reasoning, if it can be made to do the proper work. Let us have a look at how Johnsen implements this idea.

---

5. That is in addition to the fact that many factual questions will bear on evaluative questions when these are a matter of extrinsic, e.g., instrumental, evaluation.

c. Consider, to begin, the sort of reasoning that might be found in a logic class. Such reasoning seems to require no belief or assent. Suppose you reason on the blackboard in accordance with the following pattern:

  i. p
  ii. p ⊃ q
Therefore,
  iii. q.

In doing so, you *suppose* that i and that ii, and you *conclude* that iii, and here we can see no obvious dependence on any belief or assent. But wait, comes the protest, surely you must at least believe or assent to the corresponding conditional of the inference, namely: (i & ii ⊃ iii); perhaps you must even assent to something stronger yet, to a modal claim as follows: *Necessarily*, (i & ii ⊃ iii).

Johnsen demurs. In his view reasoning can fall under our *modus ponens* pattern even if we assent to nothing but *appearances*. Let us consider his full proposal more closely. Here are two relevant passages:

> The upshot is this. Initially, at least, we should see the Pyrrhonist as simply *offering*, or *putting forward*, straightforward arguments such as the following, while *claiming nothing* for them other than that they *appear* to be sound, that is, that each premise appears to be true and each inference valid:
>
> (i′) It appears to S that p
> (ii′) It appears to T that not-p.
> (iii′) All appearances are equally authoritative.
> (iv′) There are no other relevant considerations
>
> Therefore,
>
> (v′) The considerations in favor of p and not-p, respectively, are equally balanced.
> (vi′) If the considerations in favor of p and not-p, respectively, are equally balanced, then one should suspend judgment concerning p.
>
> Therefore,
>
> (vii′) One should suspend judgment concerning p.[6]

This also fits with Burnyeat's understanding of Pyrrhonism as restricting its *epoché* to "beliefs" in his restricted sense, i.e., to objective assentings, to assentings about what is the case beyond the subjectivity of the

---

6. Johnsen, "On the Coherence of Pyrrhonian Skepticism," 537.

thinker at the time. For this leaves the thinker free to assent to propositions about how things appear to him, propositions about his current states of consciousness, and not about objective matters of fact.

d. In considering this line of interpretation, we do well to focus more closely on the nature of appearance. Here first is Johnsen:

> [It] seems that many philosophical, or theoretical, cases share the characteristic that Burnyeat takes to be distinctive of perceptual ones. Consider, for example, the use of paradoxical arguments to bring out the theoretical disasters awaiting those who inadvertently employ illicit self-reference, or attempt division by zero. Such arguments can *appear* to be sound even though it is obvious that they are not. More directly relevant, perhaps, are cases in which philosophers and other theoreticians struggle to detect flaws in arguments that appear to them to be sound, but that militate against their own convictions. In such cases the appearance, or impression, of soundness is clearly not tantamount to assent. In short, whatever the role of *phantasia* in perceptual cases, there seems to be something that corresponds to it in philosophical or theoretical cases.[7]

Burnyeat is more assertive and generalizes more broadly and explicitly:

> I suggest, therefore, that the skeptic contrast between appearance and real existence is a purely formal one, entirely independent of subject matter. The skeptic ... divides questions into questions about how something appears and questions about how it really and truly is, and both types of question may be asked about anything whatever.[8]

Consider the following three attitudes to a proposition <p>, relative to a given subject S and time t: (a) S's judging that p, or assenting to <p>, (b) S's believing that p, and (c) it's appearing to S that p. To each of these there corresponds an operator whose prefixing to a declarative sentence yields a further declarative sentence, as when 'S believes that . . .' is prefixed to 'Snow is white'. Bearing in mind Burnyeat's quite general distinction, we may now take note of the distinction between either of JAp and BAp, on one hand, and AAp on the other. Take the last of these: It can intellectually appear to me that it appears to me that p. Indeed the appearance can be quite strong, much stronger than the lower-level simple appearance that p.

---

7. Burnyeat, "Can the Skeptic Live His Skepticism?," 547.
8. Burnyeat, "Can the Skeptic Live His Skepticism?," 128; and see also the preceding three paragraphs.

And now we really need to see how wide is the scope of the Pyrrhonian modes, particularly the five of Agrippa. If they are *quite* general, that will crucially affect the proposals before us as to how the Pyrrhonian could keep on reasoning. In fact neither proposal, neither Burnyeat's nor Johnsen's, could then be feasible. For both proposals entail that the skeptic keeps reasoning by assenting only to subjective propositions as to how various things appear to him. But if the Agrippan modes lead to general suspension of assent, then the skeptic would not assent to any propositions, *not even to any proposition about how things appear to him*, even though assent to some such propositions would seen required if he is to be able to reason.

Suppose we override the Agrippan modes, and urbanely restrict the scope of Pyrrhonian skepticism to theoretical propositions, excluding humdrum commonsense truths. Or suppose we restrict the skeptic's scope to objective matters beyond the subject's states of consciousness, or to non-evident questions that must be settled through inferential reasoning. Once we allow proper assent to the foundationally justified, however, how widely will this plausibly extend? If there is a kind of foundational justification safe from Agrippan objections, it will not be plausibly restricted simply to the subject's current states of consciousness. Surely the simplest truths of logic, arithmetic, and geometry will also be plausible candidates. And so will the most obvious evaluative truths, like the fact *that it is better for one to be happy than unhappy*. For the properly ordered rational subject, moreover, these will bring corresponding emotions in their train. Thus, one would surely favor one's happiness over one's unhappiness. And now there is room for disturbing anxiety, and by falling thus short of *ataraxia* one will to that extent fall short of *eudaimonia*.

What *ataraxia* seems more plausibly to require, then, is a more general suspension of assent and belief, indeed a quite general suspension. Without such a radical suspension, it is hard to see how to connect the elements of Pyrrhonism properly. In particular, how then could *isosthenia* and *epoché* be seen to lead to *ataraxia* and *eudaimonia*?

That blocks the account of our reasoning proposed by Johnsen as one open to the Pyrrhonian compatibly with giving their *epoché* its required scope. For, that account required us to assent to things appearing to us in various ways as the reasoning unfolds through the skeptic's inquiry. And we have now seen how the Pyrrhonian is precluded from assenting to any such things. He is precluded from assenting not only to the premises and to the validity of the inference, but even to its *appearing* to him that either the premises are true or the inference valid. Is there any recourse for the Pyrrhonian, or is Burnyeat vindicated in thinking that the position is just incoherent and cannot be lived?

e. We need now to distinguish between two things that one can do with regard to one's own propositional attitudes:

i. One can either *express* them, or *voice* them.
ii. One can *self-attribute* them.

Consider how this applies to the full gamut of attitudes: to beliefs, desires, hopes, fears, etc. And note that the voicing need not be a declarative affirmation. For example, it can take the form of an optative: Would that such and such! It can take the form of an expression of intention: I *am to* do this or that, I *shall* do it. Or perhaps: Let me, or let us, do this or that.

When one expresses, voices, one's imaginings, one does not really *affirm* them. It may only be *make believe*. Thus, in recounting an imagined story, one is making no affirmative claims; one is only telling the story.

In each case, voicing the attitude is of course quite different from self-attributing it. That goes for the full gamut: for imagining, believing, intending, wishing, or any other attitude. The storyteller is expressing his imagining when he says "Jack and Jill went up the hill." In order to self-attribute his imagining, he must rather say: "*I imagine* (two kids) Jack and Jill going up the hill," or the like of that.

Moreover, one can self-attribute an attitude either publicly or privately, *in foro interno*. By contrast, "voicing" an appearing, giving expression to its appearing to one that such and such, i.e., *expressing* it, would seem in the normal sense to require a public performance. Is there, nevertheless, a private analogue of voicing, so that within the privacy of one's own mind we can still distinguish between self-attributing an attitude and a kind of *silent* voicing or expressing? Why not just distinguish implicit or stored or subconscious attitudes from their fully conscious correlates? *Consciously* hoping or desiring might then on occasion take the form of a private analogue of the public expression of a hope or desire through voicing an optative. On other occasions, a private hope might take the form of a sustained conscious attitude. Private *attributing* of the hope or desire, by contrast, would involve *assent in foro interno* to the proposition that one *has* the hope or desire.

Next, we must recognize that hopes, desires, favorings, intendings, decisions, and pro-attitudes generally, can figure in reasoning. Conscious hopes and favorings, in particular, can do so. Moreover, they figure in reasoning not only through being self-attributed. It is not just their *attribution* that can be shaped through reasoning. They themselves can result from reasoning, and can serve as inputs to reasoning, even without being self-attributed, as when unselfconscious awareness of what is required for something one wants, leads to a new desire, one based on the input desire through a *sort* of reasoning.

So there may be a way for the skeptic to pursue his inquiries through a sort of reasoning without requiring any assent, so long as appearings can figure in reasonings without being self-attributed by the reasoner. A question remains as to whether reasoning can properly take place without something very much like belief: that is, without one's believing the corresponding conditionals for the steps of reasoning. But it does seem prima facie that even these corresponding conditionals could figure simply as contents of appearances, and might thereby function in cognitive dynamics that look very much like reasoning, where one explains the formation of certain appearings through a kind of reasoning that requires only further appearings, among which are appearings whose contents are the corresponding conditionals of the steps of immediate inference involved in the reasoning.

8. Finally, the skeptic, we are told, is guided by appearances. How are we to understand this? How do, how *can* appearances guide action, physical or intellectual?

Again, it is important to recall what kind of appearances are involved: namely, intellectual seemings generally, not just those of a sensory sort or derivation. So, are we to say that in øing we are guided by the appearance that it is right for one then to ø, or that it is best to ø, or that one should ø, or some such?

Pyrrhonists take themselves to be guided by a fourfold scheme that involves, first, the guidance of nature more generally; second, the promptings of our physical drives and appetites; third, the laws and customs of one's culture and society; and, fourth, the practices of a craft. Does this mean that they are guided by appearances that correspond to these four elements? This would presumably include the intellectual appearance, whether sensorily derived or not, that it is right or best for us to proceed in keeping with the given element: that it is right to drink (when thirsty) or to stop at the red traffic light, or to apply the paint with a roller rather than a brush. And so on. Is this the way in which appearance replaces belief in the guidance of our lives?

It is hard to see how appearances could possibly serve thus as a guide to life if, as is commonly assumed, Pyrrhonian dialectic and reflection always leave appearances perfectly counterbalanced. And this would seem to include the questions governed by the fourfold scheme as nothing more than a special case. After all, on *these* questions we are to follow appearances precisely because we are rendered unable to believe, given the workings of the modes, *isosthenia*, and *epoché*. So, once the skeptic has done his job properly, these questions will be no exceptions: here too our fate is *isosthenia*, and this derives from the conflict of equally balanced intellectual appearances. And now we have a puzzling question: How can appearance ever guide when it must speak with equal eloquence on both sides of every issue?

There are two ways for the Pyrrhonian to answer that question, as emerges when we consider the following two principles.

> First the Pyrrhonian Principle (P): *If on a question, whether p, neither positive confidence (above 0.5) nor negative confidence (below 0.5) is sufficiently great, then one neither believes nor disbelieves; rather, one suspends.*

That formulation is importantly ambiguous. It can be read so as to make P just a descriptive, psychological principle. But it can be read so as to make it a normative principle about the regulation of our epistemic attitudes.

Read descriptively the principle more explicitly says this:

> (PD): *If on a question, whether p, neither positive confidence (above 0.5) nor negative confidence (below 0.5) is sufficiently great, then one in fact neither believes nor disbelieves; rather, one suspends.*

In effect this can be understood as defining three attitudes: belief, disbelief, suspension, based on thresholds over a dimension of confidence covered by the unit interval. On this account there is a threshold of positive confidence, 0.75 as it might be, and a threshold of negative confidence, say 0.25, such that belief is confidence above the positive threshold, above 0.75, disbelief is confidence below the negative threshold, below 0.25, and suspension is confidence between 0.25 and 0.75.

Read normatively, however, the principle says rather this:

> (PN): *If on a question, whether p, positive confidence (above 0.5) is not sufficiently high, nor is negative confidence (below 0.5) sufficiently low, then one must neither believe nor disbelieve; rather, one must suspend.*

We can make sense of the relation between PD and PN if we conceive of relevant belief as *judgment*, as a mental act of affirmation, or the disposition to so affirm. In this case the relevant thresholds are best viewed as the points where we begin to be disposed to affirm (for the positive threshold) or stop being disposed to deny (for the negative threshold). The extent of proper suspension within the unit interval would be the subinterval between the proper affirmation threshold and the proper denial threshold. This could vary from a vanishingly small single point, 0.5, to some positive interval [*d*, *a*] where *a* is the positive threshold and *d* is the negative threshold (whereby we now stipulate that *a* is distinct from *d*).

That opens up two possible ways to supplement the Pyrrhonists' stance, when they say one must suspend on a given question, whether p. On one interpretation, they are saying that the reasons for and the reasons against are always *perfectly* counterbalanced, so that what is rationally required is that one have no more *resultant* confidence in favor of <p> than against <p>. On question after question, as they inquire, they find themselves in that position, in a position where reason requires adopting a credence of 0.5, and hence of course requires a disposition neither to affirm nor to deny on whether p. And they can then conclude, on question after question, that suspension is required, and this will be so *no matter what standard of "sufficiency" is adopted for PN.*[9]

Can Pyrrhonism be a guide of life on this way to understand the Pyrrhonian stance? Or are Hume and other skeptics right to dismiss the Pyrrhonian philosophy of life as unliveable? How might a resultant appearance guide us in the light of our strong understanding of the Pyrrhonian stance? It might do so precisely through its being a vector of magnitude zero, i.e, through the perfect balance of reasons for and reasons against, which (properly) leads one to a credence of magnitude 0.5. Somewhat surprisingly, in a way this *does* provide guidance! The guidance is that we are free to choose as we will. We are perfectly free.[10] Accordingly, the Pyrrhonists *can* choose, existentially, to live in accordance with their fourfold scheme. This is quite in keeping with a perfectly rational decision procedure. And Hume now seems wrong in supposing that the Pyrrhonian philosophy *would* bring life and society to a standstill. True, the mode-involving reasonings of Pyrrhonism would make it hard or impossible to predict what a rational Pyrrhonian would do. But we can no more predict lethargy and a general

---

9. Presumably these "conclusions" that they would reach need not amount to confident assertoric affirmations; in line with Johnsen we could see them as mere (intellectual) appearances, to which we would be led through the modes.
10. Thus, an authority could provide guidance to its subdits by specifying, not only what is required, but also what is permitted.

lassitude than we can predict hyperactivity, or anything else. Of course, if we include the advocacy of the fourfold scheme, then the Pyrrhonian philosophy would involve an existential stance that would thereafter render their behavior conventionally predictable, at least to us non-Pyrrhonists, on the assumption that the stance is retained.

However, we are still left with a question of coherence for the Pyrrhonists. For beliefs are evaluable not only epistemically but also in other ways; pragmatic ways, for example. The adoption of a belief, insofar as believing is something we relevantly *do*, whether freely, voluntarily, or not, is then something evaluable not just *epistemically*, though it is of course evaluable that way. It is also evaluable more generally as something we do, or at least bring about in rationally controllable fashion. We are assessable for our states of belief, it would seem, no less than for whether we are overweight. But now our states of belief, insofar as we do *form* them, would seem to be states that will take their place in our lives under the proper sway of the fourfold scheme. So why would we be rationally bound to suspend belief? Perhaps we are no more forced through overall rationality to suspend belief than to refrain from acting or from bringing about any of the other states that take their place in a normally conducted life. Of course, we *are* free to suspend belief, but we are equally free to believe, and to disbelieve. Suppose our existential choice is to follow the fourfold scheme, which includes a first component that has us willingly follow the dictates of nature. This would seem to entrain that we will be forming beliefs after all, and forming them, moreover, in just the way in which for Hume we do form them ordinarily, that is to say naturally. The Pyrrhonist will disagree with Hume, however, on one important point. The Pyrrhonist will presumably hold that we are acting quite in accordance with reason in proceeding as we do. This is because our existential adoption of the fourfold scheme is permitted, all things considered, since there is no alternative option to it that is rationally preferable.[11]

9. So there seems a way for the skeptic to pursue his inquiries through a kind of reasoning with no need of assent, so long as appearings can figure in reasonings without being self-attributed by the reasoner. A question remains as to whether reasoning can properly take place without something

---

11. Conceivably the Humean point is that even if movement remains possible in the absence of belief, action requires more than movement, and indeed the action of interest to him, *intentional* action, constitutively *requires* belief. This is an interesting line of interpretation, but the account of intentional action in Chapter 7 rules it out.

very much like belief: that is, without one's believing the corresponding conditionals for the steps of reasoning. But it does seem prima facie that even these corresponding conditionals could possibly figure simply as contents of appearances, and might thereby function in cognitive dynamics that look very much like reasoning, where one explains the formation of certain appearings through a kind of reasoning that requires only further appearings, among which are appearings whose contents are the corresponding conditionals of the steps of reasoning.

However, that requires the guiding appearances to be *resultant* seemings. What are these? Consider the deliberative process of weighing reasons for and against, one that sets out from the initial attractions to assent or dissent. Through some sort of vector addition, we eventually come up with a *resultant* seeming, a credence or inclination, perhaps, or an absolute suspending.

On this view, then, we can be guided through reasoning by appearances. This happens through a two-stage process. First comes the pondering, the theoretical deliberation that eventuates in a resultant appearance. Then this resultant appearance or intellectual seeming, this credence, plays its role in guiding us, and among the acts that it can guide is that of opting among affirmation, denial, and suspension. Such resultant seemings will themselves be based on other seemings, and proper basing here will require that the premise seemings must themselves be proper. So we face the familiar Agrippan trilemma.

The resolution of the trilemma will often require that there be bases for some seemings that are not themselves evaluable in the same way as seemings. Some such foundational judgments or seemings may be based on person-level mental states of the subject's that are not themselves at all evaluable, not even as are cognitive unfree functionings. Rather they provide a basis for competent seemings or judgments in another way, through self-presenting, "given" mental states, such as pains or itches, that can be competently "taken" by the subject through a seeming or judgment, with high enough reliability. There is a rational structure of such given appearances at any given time in the human mind, these being seemings, or attractions to assent, initial or resultant. As we have seen, some appearances are rationally based on others, either foundationally or inferentially.

However, some seemings need not be based on any other person-level mental states. They can be proper instead by manifesting a foundational competence of the subject's, one that need not operate through a basis provided by some such mental state. Rather, such a foundational competence might operate through *subpersonal* mechanisms that render judgments or seemings sufficiently truth reliable.

How could we conceivably be guided to form *beliefs* in the absence of beliefs already (or concurrently) formed? Are beliefs among the attitudes that appearances might guide us to adopt? Beliefs here are dispositions to assent at least *in foro interno*, to judge affirmatively. Such beliefs are thus occurrent *judgments*, or dispositional, judgmental beliefs, dispositions to judge. Suppose the Pyrrhonian allows that appearances *could* conceivably guide us to form such judgments or judgmental beliefs. On this account of Pyrrhonism, it would be *possible* for one to escape the Agrippan trilemma. All it would take is that there be epistemically appropriate resultant appearances or seemings that properly guide one to judge affirmatively, to assent to some proposition. One would thereby escape arbitrariness in assenting to that proposition. One would escape arbitrariness because one *would* have a reason for deciding to assent, even if the reason was not a judgment or belief itself voluntarily adopted. Instead the reason might just be a passive resultant appearance or a combination of such appearances. Moreover, the principle of inference might itself be adopted through a resultant seeming, one that guides the thinker to actually believe, and not just to a further appearance.

Yes, that all could conceivably happen. It's just that the Pyrrhonists never reach a resultant appearance or credence that enables them properly to assent. One could, however, join the Pyrrhonists in their conception of epistemology, without joining them in their universal suspension. I would argue that this is exactly the case of Descartes, whose epistemology is closely correlated with Pyrrhonian epistemology. The framework, and the methodology, are there to be found. Unlike the Pyrrhonists, however, Descartes *can* see his way clear to assenting freely and voluntarily to a rich body of beliefs. Moreover, he finds a way to do so even while taking quite seriously the skeptical arguments and concerns that the ancients found so troubling and indeed paralyzing.

11

Descartes's Pyrrhonian Virtue Epistemology

Descartes is a virtue epistemologist. Not only does he distinguish centrally between animal and reflective knowledge: in his terms, between *cognitio* and *scientia*. In addition he conceives of *cognitio* as apt grasp of the truth: i.e., grasp whose correctness manifests sufficient epistemic competence.[1] First-order knowledge is such *cognitio* or apt belief, which can then be upgraded to the level of *scientia* through competent reflective endorsement. So Descartes both (a) advocates aptness as an account of simple knowledge, and (b) highlights a higher knowledge that requires endorsement from a second-order perspective. This includes both main components of a sort of "virtue epistemology" found in contemporary philosophy.

In what follows I will argue that we can make sense of Descartes's epistemological project only as a second-order project that fits with the view of his epistemology just sketched. Along the way supportive detail will reveal more fully his commitment to this project.

---

1. "The fact that an atheist can be 'clearly aware that the three angles of a triangle are equal to two right angles' is something I do not dispute. But I maintain that this awareness of his [*cognitio*] is not true knowledge [*scientia*], since no act of awareness that can be rendered doubtful seems fit to be called knowledge [*scientia*]. Now since we are supposing that this individual is an atheist, he cannot be certain that he is not being deceived on matters which seem to him to be very evident (as I fully explained). And although this doubt may not occur to him, it can still crop up if someone else raises the point or if he looks into the matter himself. So he will never be free of this doubt until he acknowledges that God exists." (From the Second Set of Replies as it appears in *The Philosophical Writings of Descartes*, ed. J. Cottingham, R. Stoothoff, and D. Murdoch (Cambridge: Cambridge University Press, 1991), Vol. II, p. 101. This collection will be cited henceforth as "CSM.")

A. The Method of Doubt and Its Objectives

What is Descartes up to in the *Meditations* and in his other relevant writings? On one level at least, he is *not* engaged in a project of determining what he should believe, what it would be reasonable for him to believe. Consider, for example, the following two passages.

> [When] it is a question of organizing our life, it would, of course, be foolish not to trust the senses, and the skeptics who neglected human affairs to the point where friends had to stop them falling off precipices deserved to be laughed at. *Hence I pointed out in one passage that no sane person ever seriously doubts such things.* But when our inquiry concerns what can be known with complete certainty by the human intellect, it is quite unreasonable to refuse to reject these things in all seriousness as doubtful and even as false; the purpose here is to come to recognize that certain other things which cannot be rejected in this way are thereby more certain and in reality better known to us. (Fifth Replies, CSM II: 243; emphasis added)

> My habitual opinions keep coming back, and, despite my wishes, they capture my belief, which is as it were bound over to them as a result of long occupation and the law of custom. *I shall never get out of the habit of confidently assenting to these opinions, so long as I suppose them to be what in fact they are, namely highly probable opinions—opinions which, despite the fact that they are in a sense doubtful, as has just been shown, it is still much more reasonable to believe than to deny.* In view of this, I think it will be a good plan to turn my will in completely the opposite direction and deceive myself, by pretending for a time that these former opinions are utterly false and imaginary. (Meditation I, CSM II: 15; emphasis added)

If we take him at his word, then, no one sane *ever* seriously doubts his habitual opinions, which are *much* more reasonably believed than denied.

What else might be involved in the Cartesian method of radical doubt, beyond *pretending* our customary opinions to be doubtful and even false? Let us examine the method more closely. Here first is a crucial passage:

> [Those] who have never philosophized correctly have various opinions in their minds which they have begun to store up since childhood, and which they therefore have reason to believe may in many cases be false. They then attempt to separate the false beliefs from the others, so as to prevent their contaminating the rest and making the whole lot uncertain. Now the best way they can accomplish this is to reject all their beliefs together in one go, as if they were all uncertain and false. They can then go over each belief in turn and re-adopt only those which they recognize to be true and indubitable. Thus I was right to begin by rejecting all my beliefs. (Seventh Replies, CSM II: 324)

Near this passage Descartes invokes the famous apple-basket metaphor. Upon discovering some rot in one's basket, what is one to do? His answer: dump out all the apples and readmit only those that pass inspection. Only thus can we be sure that no rot will continue to spread undetected.

The apples are beliefs or opinions, among them old familiar ones, stored since childhood. Once the beliefs in our basket are found to contain the rot of error, we are to dump them *all*. But how do we understand this metaphor? What is it to "remove" a belief from the basket? What is it to *reject* a belief?

On a familiar view, to reject a belief is to give it up, to withhold, or suspend judgment, on its content. The ground by the empty basket would then be free of *believings*, since on the present view to dump a believing is to destroy it. Strewn there would be found *believables*, contents earlier believed. Concerning all of those contents, the subject would now be withholding or suspending. That is the view.

Several reasons make that view highly problematic. For one thing, rejecting all our beliefs that way would entail believing nothing, replacing belief universally with unbelief. What would that require? Could one bring up each content separately, replacing acceptance of it with suspension? Surely not. The contents would need to be handled in manageable clusters, for collective suspension in one fell swoop.

Suppose accordingly that we identify the beliefs in question indirectly, as for example "beliefs I hold" or "old and customary opinions learned since childhood." If we pick them out only so generally, however, no mental operation available to us would seem to result in the desired universal suspension. It is doubtful that we can suspend judgment *de re* on *each* content thus picked out—just as, say, "long-held opinions"—simply by taking it *de dicto* that they are all doubtful, or supposing that they are all false.

And there is a further reason why Descartes's "rejection" cannot plausibly amount to suspension or withholding. Recall how the process is supposed to go. The beliefs dumped out of the basket must undergo inspection. Only those that pass will be readmitted. But the relevant inspection will have to involve some process of reasoning. It is through such reasoning that we would determine whether a certain condition is satisfied, which will earn readmission. And how could we possibly perform any such reasoning while deprived of beliefs? Note well: the reasoning in question cannot be just conditional. The desired conclusion is that the belief under examination passes inspection. Thus would we obtain the assertoric basis for a practical syllogism that warrants readmission. An assertoric conclusion requires assertoric premises, however, explicit or implicit. That is to say, we can attain epistemic status for a conclusion through a bit of reasoning only if our reasoning has premises with assertoric status of their own.

We have found three weighty reasons why Descartes has no intention of "rejecting" his beliefs by abandoning them all, replacing the attitude of belief with that of suspension. First, we have seen his outright statement that "no one sane would *ever* do such a thing." Second, doing so *de re*, for each belief in turn, lies beyond our psychological capabilities. Third, if he *were* to accomplish such universal suspension, he would necessarily block his own project! His project requires inspecting the "rejected" beliefs, so as to determine whether they deserve readmission. And this inspection, this determination, must be done through reasoning, which in turn would seem to require beliefs. Given how problematic it is to understand rejection as abandonment, let us set aside that view of rejection, and explore an alternative.

Descartes's project is, I submit, on the second order, at least in important part. Taking a belief out of the basket is declining to endorse it epistemically in a certain way. (This is how he "rejects" a belief, while "pretending" that it is false. This pretense is itself on the second order; it picks out clusters of beliefs under a certain description, and under that description pretends, about them generally, that they are false.) Whether one had earlier endorsed them or not, one now declines to do so. But just *how* does Descartes decline to endorse his "rejected" beliefs? Recall the special importance of the status of *certainty*, whereby one is in no doubt whatever that one's belief is true. *Here* is perhaps the key to how we should understand endorsement. Proper Cartesian endorsement of a belief requires one to have no reason, not the slightest, for any doubt about its truth. This is then the proper endorsement of a belief as *doubtless* true.[2]

Cartesian rejection would involve forbearing from such endorsement: i.e., from endorsement of a belief as doubtless true, not just as true. To dump a belief from one's basket of beliefs is to forbear from thus endorsing it. One may or may not have previously endorsed it. One may have failed to so much as *consider* whether to endorse it. In any case the belief is dumped when one now positively forbears to endorse it. And now the dumping of a belief, its relevant "rejection," seems compatible with undiminished confidence in its content. So we would surmount two of the three key problems encountered earlier. If our account is correct, Descartes need not reduce his confidence in order to engage in his project of Cartesian doubt. Nor would

---

2. Textual evidence is adduced in Appendix 2 of this chapter.

he be deprived of beliefs in terms of which to conduct the inspection. On our account, Descartes retains undiminished confidence on the first order, so that his first-order beliefs can all remain even when on the second order they are not endorsed. By retaining his first-order action-guiding animal confidence he can sanely go on about his everyday business, adroitly avoiding deadly jumps off high cliffs, and his first-order reasoning can still be nourished by those retained beliefs.

However, we do still face the third of our problems. How can Descartes access his beliefs individually *de re*, so as to reject them, or, eventually, so as to endorse them? The answer is that his project requires no such distributed access to his beliefs, separately one by one. He explicitly notes how hopeless that would be.[3] The relevant *rejection* and the correlative *endorsement* must be *under a description, de dicto*. We must be able to pick out beliefs in clusters so as to reject them or endorse them as those that satisfy a certain condition. Thus, for example, if we find that doubt inevitably clouds any belief based (directly or indirectly) on perception, then we may be able to dump all "beliefs based essentially on perception" by forbearing to endorse them under that description. That is perhaps how the project is supposed to go. But we must next consider a further twist.

B. Credence versus Judgment

Recall Descartes's insistence that no one *ever* seriously doubts the deliverances of the senses, and that his habitual opinions are highly probable opinions that it is much more reasonable to affirm than to deny. That raised this question: How then could he ever "reject" such opinions as doubtful, or false, even when engaged in the project of determining the extent of possible human certainty?

Well, there *is* something he clearly *can* do. He can "pretend" anything he likes, while still harboring his old and customary opinions with undiminished assurance. In the second passage considered above (from Meditation I) *pretending* is what he explicitly proposes to do (Latin *fingem*, French *feignant*). Moreover, he can still employ in his reasoning his belief that not-p even while pretending that p. Thus, at the movie theater I can appropriately forbear shouting a warning even when I pretend that I see someone about to

---

3. See the second paragraph of Meditation I (CSM II: 15).

be brained from behind with a hatchet. Here I seem to rely through implicit reasoning on an assumption that no one within earshot really needs any such warning. And this action-guiding reasoning can be perfectly appropriate despite my concurrent pretense to the contrary. Make-belief is one thing, real belief quite another.

That does however bring up a further question. Why should Descartes have thought that pretending that not-p would help him resist the temptation to continue to believe that p while entertaining no relevant doubt? It helps here to draw a distinction between two attitudes that might be called "belief." One is an implicit confidence that suffices to guide our action, including action on practical options, such as whether to shout a warning. The other is an act of judgment made freely and voluntarily, or a disposition to so judge upon considering the relevant question. In his philosophical meditation, Descartes is clearly concerned with the second of these. He emphatically distinguishes two faculties. There is *first* a faculty of understanding, whose deliverances, received passively, are "perceptions" with some degree of clarity and distinctness. And there is *second* a faculty of judgment, based on the subject's free will.

A possible explanation thus opens up for why Descartes may have thought that by pretending that p one might be helped to avoid believing that not-p. At the theater we might pretend (through visual imagination) that someone is about to be hit with a hatchet. Surely one would *not* then also freely judge that no one is about to be hit. In particular, one is unlikely to judge consciously that the scene before one is unreal. The "suspension of disbelief" involved in such imagination tends to block one's consciously disbelieving by affirming the opposite of what one imagines (the two of which may even fail to cohere).

Note, however, that this can leave one's underlying subconscious credence still in place with undiminished confidence. One certainly does not lose one's confidence that one is sitting in a darkened theater viewing a screen (and not seeing a gory murder instead). Despite making it harder to *judge* that not-p, moreover, pretense that p does not constitute an *insurmountable* obstacle. That might thus be just how Descartes thought pretense would help in his project. It would counteract our normal automatic tendency to judge in line with our stored credences, but it would not make it *impossible* for us to so judge. However, we would now be more free to judge in line with true reason and not just custom.

Accordingly, we can also see how our everyday guiding attitudes, such as the appearances of the Pyrrhonists, can remain in place below the surface of consciousness, and do their guiding, even if one forbears endorsing them, while suspending conscious assent. One can sustain highly confident credence that p, despite suspending any conscious endorsement of that attitude, and withholding any correlated conscious judgment that p.

Consider the Cartesian "perceptions" that can have various degrees of clarity and distinctness. These are not just *sensory* perceptions. Indeed, among the most clear and distinct of them would lie a priori intuitions involving rational rather than sensory awareness. These are rather *seemings*: not only sensory seemings but also a priori seemings. Moreover, we should focus not just on *initial* seemings that might enter into conflicts to be resolved through pondering or deliberation. We should focus rather on *resultant* seemings, *credences* involving some degree of confidence, representable through the unit interval.

Those seemings will then qualify as having some degree of clarity and distinctness, but the degree that they may *seem* to have is not necessarily the degree that they really have. In order to qualify as *really* sufficiently clear and distinct, such seemings must satisfy epistemic requirements, and we might incorrectly take a seeming to be thus clear and distinct even when it falls short.

As did the Pyrrhonian skeptics long before him, Descartes believes that we can guide our lives practically through such confident-enough seemings or appearances, ordinary opinions that it would be laughable to put in serious doubt as one navigates an ordinary day. Such beliefs are *never* put in serious doubt. Some gain the status of sufficient clarity and distinctness, moreover, *not* through direct, unaided intuition, but only indirectly, through deductive reasoning. It would appear, then, that we reason through such "perceptions," through such resultant seemings, through such Pyrrhonian "appearances." Just as did the Pyrrhonists, Descartes could continue to inquire, and to guide his daily life, through the use of such credences (perceptions) even once they have been put in doubt. To put them in doubt is *not* to disable them from functioning in the guidance of action, nor even in the reasoning required for inquiry. Compatibly with a belief's retention of its animal/*cognitio* status and its ability to provide the guidance expected of such beliefs, the believer might refuse to endorse his belief when it is brought to consciousness for rational inspection.[4]

---

4. The guiding "beliefs" that are retained alike by Descartes and the Pyrrhonists are on this view just *credences*, or resultant seemings confident enough to provide such guidance. Descartes thinks he can go on to properly acquire and sustain *judgmental* beliefs are well, but here the Pyrrhonists demur as they continue their *skepsis* without endorsement.

C. The Project of the Meditations

Consider how it goes in the early Meditations, leading up to the *cogito* passages. Descartes argues that *cogito* propositions at long last give us what we *can* believe with proper endorsement. These offer absolute safety from deception. In arguing for this, he must of course make use of certain premises. These are the premises in the reasoning that shows *cogito* beliefs to pass Cartesian inspection. Among these premises is the assumption <If I think that I am, then I am>. Take a skeptic who puts in doubt simple truths of arithmetic and geometry. Take one who doubts even that there really are any shapes at all. No such skeptic is likely to grant us without question knowledge of the following: *that if I think that I am, then I am*. The reasoning by which Descartes means to underwrite his certainty of the *cogito* can thus be seen to have a certain limitation: namely, that of relying on a premise that seems also subject to skeptical doubt.

Descartes aims to establish that our beliefs with certain contents or with certain sorts of contents would be *bound* to be correct (and to do so without blatant bootstrapping or other vicious circularity). However, his reasoning turns out to be *open to skeptical challenge*. *Provided* I know <If I think that I am, then I am> I can thereby underwrite that I could not possibly go wrong in affirming that I exist, which protects my affirmation from radical deception. But the radical skeptic of Meditation I has put in doubt even the simplest a priori truths of arithmetic and geometry. No such skeptic will allow Descartes to just help himself to the premise that if he thinks he exists then he does exist.

Accordingly, Descartes will need to consider whether *such assumptions*, the ones he needs for his underwriting even of *cogito* thoughts, can themselves be upgraded in the sort of way he tries to upgrade *cogito* thoughts (with the limited success we have observed). Taking his cue from Meditation II, he needs some way to legitimate such assumptions, to endorse them properly. This, I submit, is what sets up the project in the rest of the *Meditations*. Descartes goes in search of reasoning that will satisfy certain specifications:

(a) that it raise key beliefs to the required superlative level, even those that are now in some slight, metaphysical doubt,
(b) that it do so while avoiding blatant bootstrapping, and
(c) that the beliefs so raised include the ones that enable him to endorse *cogito* propositions.

This project he pursues through the rational theology prominent in the later Meditations. It is through such reasoning that he thinks he can upgrade his relevant beliefs. He can show them to have the required status because he can reach through proper reasoning the conclusion that his clear and distinct perceptions will reliably enough provide deliverances that he can therefore properly trust. And this reasoning will avoid blatant bootstrapping such as that involved in assuming as a premise the very conclusion to be argued for.

Let us back up a bit. What has put Descartes's beliefs in such slight doubt? Recall the skeptical scenarios of Meditation I: the dream scenario, for example, and the evil demon. In some of these we retain a normal set of beliefs about the world around us, based on perceptual evidence, as is the normal way of such beliefs. Although in such scenarios we are radically deceived, it is hard to see how we can possibly rule them out. If we cannot do so, however, then we can hardly be *certain* in our beliefs. Those are scenarios wherein our beliefs would be false and hence *not* known to be true. Unless we can rule out that we are now so deceived, therefore, we can't be sure we really know that our present beliefs are true.

That is one way of constructing a dream scenario, but there is also a second way to which Descartes would have attributed similar skeptical import. According to the first way, in the dream scenario we dream that p *while it is false that p.* According to the second way, we dream that p *whether it is true or false that p.* That this second case has for Descartes similar skeptical import is suggested by his fourth skeptical scenario. In that scenario there is no God to create us or sustain us; we emerge through "fate or chance or a continuous chain of events, or by some other means [other than Divine agency]" (Meditation I, CSM II: 14). Under that supposition there is no metaphysical grounding for our assured competence. With respect to any question we take up, we might or might not be well enough constituted and well enough situated that we would not go wrong while properly using our faculties (our epistemic competences or abilities).

Note the strength of what Descartes requires, as suggested by the status he gives to that scenario: In order to attain *true certainty* on a question whether p, we *must* be so constituted that we *could* not go wrong (given adequate care and attention). Absent a powerful and benevolent enough creator and sustainer, however, we would *not* necessarily be so constituted. Descartes accordingly requires, not just the aptness of one's belief, but its *superlative* aptness, which includes also its "security." A belief is thus secure only if the competence manifest in its truth is so safely in place that it could not possibly have been missing.[5]

D. A Deeper Problem

Our proposal meets the three objections to the naive view of the way Descartes addresses his epistemological problematic: (a) that he emphatically affirms that no one sane would *ever* put ordinary beliefs in serious doubt so as to reject them; (b) that it is hard to see how he could manage to put his vast corpus of ordinary beliefs in serious doubt, so as to reject them individually and seriatim; and (c) that if the rejection involved is withholding of belief (and disbelief), then he deprives himself of the wherewithal required for the inspection to which rejected beliefs must be subjected before they can be properly readmitted into his corpus of beliefs.

Our proposal distinguishes between animal beliefs that can continue to guide us subconsciously in the everyday, and the consciously reflective beliefs that are not needed for such animal guidance. What would be insane is the abandonment of the beliefs needed for guidance. The judgments involved in conscious reflection can be suspended, however, with no need to abandon the corresponding animal beliefs. These judgments do require the rational endorsement that is made problematic by the skeptic. So much for objection (a).

As for (b), it helps again to distinguish the vast storehouse of implicit animal beliefs from the conscious reflective beliefs that constitutively involve judgment. These are *judgments*, as when we say of someone asleep that in his judgment we ought to pursue a certain course of action. We are not saying that he is at that moment, while asleep, performing a certain act of judgment. Rather we are saying that he is disposed to so judge occurrently if he considers the question and endeavors to answer it correctly, that he is disposed to affirm accordingly at least to himself, *in foro interno*. Suppose these judgments are largely ones over which we exercise voluntary, free control,

---

5. Of course Descartes does allow us a measure of freedom that makes it possible for us to go wrong even if thus endowed. Where we cannot possibly go wrong is in our understanding, in our having the ability to perceive with sufficient clarity and distinctness what is thus perceivable (so long as we avoid inattention, passion, and other such disablers). It is this ability that is *securely* our God-given endowment.

as Descartes emphatically believed. In that case, the dispositional judgments in question would be in effect freely upheld policies to answer corresponding questions affirmatively. And it is not at all implausible that *these* beliefs, these judgments, these policies of response upheld by the will, could be modified with a general act of will. The act of will involved would be quite like the act by which we could resolve to abandon our policy to signal our turns as we drive. In one fell swoop, we would affect the policy as it concerns each of the corners where we turn as we drive home every evening. Through a general dispensation we change each of those policies, by changing the overall governing policy. Similarly, we could try to change our general disposition to respond affirmatively to a great variety of questions as we took them up. Skeptical reasoning could surely affect our beliefs that way. As a result of the conscious reasoning we might try to give up our policies to respond affirmatively to "Is there such a thing as snow?" "Is it white?" "Is there such a thing as the sky?" "Is it blue?" And so on, and so forth. So, once we focus on the sorts of beliefs that held primary interest for Descartes, as for the Pyrrhonists, we can much more plausibly consider a universal abandonment of our beliefs, i.e., of our judgments, i.e., of our dispositions to respond affirmatively, freely and voluntarily.

What of objection (c)? Despite rejecting judgments, we had noted, we could still retain credences, i.e., confidence in various degrees, and even animal beliefs that guide our actions and performances generally. Among the performances so guided might be inferences, surely; so, despite having abandoned judgments, we might perhaps still retain the ability to subject our beliefs generally to the sort of inspection required for readmission into our set of judgments.

How plausible is it, however, that we *could* conduct the sort of reasoning required, that we could perform the inferences that constitute such reasoning. There is reason for concern here. After all, the reasoning that Descartes needs is *meditation*, i.e., consciously reflective thought that will involve conscious reasoning. And it is not at all clear that he will have what is required for *this* sort of reasoning once he abandons judgments generally. How could one engage in conscious reasoning, how could one rehearse and perform conscious arguments in the absence of the judgments that would seem to be required for the affirmation of the premises?

That is indeed a serious problem if Descartes rejects *all* judgments when he turns over his basket of such judgmental beliefs, and if in order for a belief to pass the inspection that a potential judgment must pass for readmission into the subject's set of judgments, we need to gain conscious awareness that the judgment in question satisfies the conditions required. If the only way to do this is through discursive conscious reasoning, we still have a problem, once we have rejected all judgments. Discursive conscious reasoning will require premises, and these will need to be consciously affirmed, and the affirmation of the premises would seem to require proper prior epistemic standing so that reasoning from them validly can endow the conclusion with its own proper standing in turn. But one had abandoned *all* judgments, *all* conscious affirmation, as deprived of proper standing. One is now attempting to admit a judgment back into the set of proper judgments, but one is trying to do so based on no judgment whatsoever. This is what now would seem to lie beyond our capabilities, for lack of judgments with prior proper standing of their own.

The solution is to reject the assumption that only through conscious reasoning from prior judgment could one attain status for a rejected judgment. Recall first that the global rejection of judgments was accomplished through a cluster rejection *de dicto* of judgments under a certain description, perhaps simply as "beliefs that I have stored in the normal human way over the course of my childhood, through perceptual interaction with my environment." The global rejection is for Descartes an act of will, analogous to the act of will by which we might reject a policy of obeying the traffic laws without question, and the policy of signaling our turns in particular. Such a global act of will might very, very largely attain the objective that from then on we do act in accordance with our global decision. However, it might fail to attain *universal* success. Not only that, but arguably one might fail to act in accordance with it, *and the exception might be quite epistemically appropriate*. This, I will now argue, is an option available to Descartes, and one that he in fact takes.

For Descartes there are certain questions that one cannot answer except with assent. The answer assented to is therefore indubitable. One is unable either to deny or even to suspend on such a proposition, once one has it in mental focus. There is no alternative to assenting consciously. Now, this could happen in either of two ways. One might be totally brainwashed so that one's mind is improperly but tightly closed on the matter. Alternatively, it might be the sort of question on which the proper operation of our intellect itself leaves no alternative. We *must* assent because that is what a properly constituted mind must do unless it is subjected to unfortunate distorting forces. But if that is how it is for certain cases of simple logic and mathematics, and other elementary a priori truths, then *are we not unfree* with regard to these after all, so that our judgments here do not after all derive freely from the will? Not for a compatibilist like Descartes, according to whom in effect we are never so free as when we are wholly compelled by reason in the absence of distorting forces.

Here then is the solution to problem (c) that now opens up. What again is that problem? Descartes decides to reject his judgments generally as he meditates. And he will now readmit only those beliefs that pass the inspection imposed by the method of doubt. But this inspection will of course be rational inspection, and this would seem to require reasoning. And this reasoning would seem in turn to require judgmental premises already in place with prior standing! However, entirely deprived as we are of such prior judgments, there's no way to ever properly readmit a judgment. So, Descartes's epistemological project must abort.

That is how it seems, but only on a questionable assumption. Although Descartes has "rejected" all his judgments globally as ones he has acquired in the past, that is only a general, *de dicto* rejection under that description. He signs on to the policy that he will never assent to any such proposition upon consideration. However, if he tries to implement that policy systematically, he will encounter cases where he cannot do so once the proposition is before the mind *in propria persona*. He will not after all be able to withhold his assent to some propositions, therefore, and so his global commitment will actually fail in many particular cases. These will be the cases of propositions that are *de re* indubitable for him. And this set of propositions will include those that he accepts through rational intuition either in answer to an isolated question then before his mind, or else in the course of some train of deductive reasoning, when he makes an immediate inference. And so he still can after all retain plenty of conscious, intuitive judgments in terms of which he can conduct the inspection required in order to readmit a rejected judgment.

E. Four Key Concepts of Cartesian Epistemology

We have touched already on *certainty, doubt,* and *endorsement,* but we have yet to consider Cartesian *error*. What we uncover about this crucial concept will bear also on the other three.

Error. Ordinarily we take error to consist in falsity. An erroneous belief or opinion is just a false one. How far this is from Descartes's own view may be seen in the following two passages.

> But there was something . . . which I used to assert, and which through habitual belief I thought I perceived clearly, although I did not in fact do so. This was that there were things outside me which were the sources of my ideas and which resembled them in all respects. Here was my mistake; *or at any rate, if my judgment was true, it was not thanks to the strength of my perception.*[6] (Meditation III, CSM II: 25; emphasis added)

> If . . . I simply refrain from making a judgment in cases where I do not perceive the truth with sufficient clarity and distinctness, then it is clear that I am behaving correctly and avoiding error. But if in such cases I either affirm or deny, then I am not using my free will correctly. If I go for the alternative which is false, then obviously I shall be in error; if I take the other side, then *it is by pure chance that I arrive at the truth*, and I shall still be at fault since it is clear by the natural light that the perception of the intellect should always precede the determination of the will. In this incorrect use of free will may be found the privation which constitutes the essence of error. (Meditation IV, CSM II: 41; emphasis added)

Falsity is *sufficient* for error, but not *necessary*. One can still be in error with a true belief, so long as its truth is not attributable to one's *perception*—to one's clear and distinct enough perception. One's belief is then true by accident:

> It is also certain that when we assent to some piece of reasoning when our perception of it is lacking, then either we go wrong, or, if we do stumble on the truth, *it is merely by accident*, so that we cannot be sure that we are not in error. (CSM I: 207; emphasis added)

In the crucial second paragraph of Meditation III we find a further clue. By that point we have finally reached a true certainty, *sum res cogitans*. Having wondered aloud as to what could possibly yield such certainty, Descartes answers his own question. "*As far as I can see, certainty here derives from clear and distinct enough perception.*"[7] Perception of such clarity and distinctness is said to yield certainty, however, only if nothing could ever be so clearly and distinctly perceived and yet be false. It is such clarity and distinctness,

---

6. In the Latin: "Atque hoc erat, in quo vel fallebar, vel certe, si verum judicabam, id non ex vi meae perceptionis contingebat." In the French: "Et c'était en cela que je me trompais; ou, si peut-être je jugeais selon la vérité, ce n'était aucune connaissance que j'eusse, qui fût cause de la vérité de mon jugement."
7. As he notes in the third paragraph of Meditation III; see CSM II: 24.

then, that will properly account for the correctness of one's perception, with no chance of falsity, so that it will perfectly explain why the corresponding judgment must be true. It must be true because it corresponds to a perception by that subject so clear and distinct that it could not possibly be false.

The *essence* of error is said to reside in a judgment that does *not* manifest the sort of competence required: namely, the sort of competence whose manifestations would leave little enough to chance. (See the Meditation IV passage above.) So, even when we judge with truth, as Descartes emphasizes, we can be in error, if our judgment fails to be true "thanks to our perception," with its required level of clarity and distinctness. When our hitting the mark of truth is *not* thus explained by a competence that leaves nothing to chance, our judgment is still in error despite being true.

A judgment might be not only true but indeed *necessarily* true, while still in error. Suppose one believes that the square of 2 squared is 2 to the fourth power. One hence multiplies four 2s, concluding thereby that the square of 2 squared is 16. Suppose one arrives at how many 2s to multiply, however, by *adding* the exponents. Only because adding these two exponents (2 + 2) yields the same as multiplying them (2 × 2) does one here get the right result. If the exponents had been in any way different, one would have arrived at the wrong result. It is no thanks to competence that one hits the mark of truth. Yet one's judgment could not possibly be false, since the square of 2 squared could not possibly be anything other than 16.

Certainty. To attain absolute certainty, then, is to hit the mark of truth in one's judgment or belief thanks entirely to (the quality of) one's perception, which could not possibly lead one astray. To attain such certainty is thus superlatively to avoid error. One hits the mark of truth, true enough, and moreover does so thanks to (the quality) of one's perception. But one does even more than that, since one's perception is of such high epistemic quality that it leaves no room for error (for failure of aptness).

Doubt. To doubt a certain content is to forbear endorsing belief of it, and in Descartes's quest for certainty one is to forbear unless one can endorse one's belief as certainly apt. No matter the intensity of one's credence, one still entertains some doubt, concerning that belief, so long as one forbears endorsing it as certainly apt. A reason for doubt is, accordingly, a reason to forbear endorsing.

There is more than one way to adopt such a meta-attitude to a credence that you hold. You might adopt it under a description, where you pick out the credence as one that satisfies a certain condition: "credence whose source is perception," as it might be. Alternatively, your meta-attitude might instead target a belief whose content is on display at the focus of your attention, *in propria persona*. If this is how you forbear from endorsing your belief that p as certain, your forbearing will bring with it your suspending on the question whether p: you will judge on that question neither affirmatively nor negatively, you will neither affirm nor deny.

Endorsement. And so we come to this important concept. In keeping with the foregoing thoughts, to endorse a belief is to regard it as correct, and in Descartes's project that requires one's endorsing it as *certainly* apt, as one that hits the mark of truth thanks entirely to the subject's clear and distinct perception, where this in turn amounts to an infallible competence. If one endorses the belief while aware of its content *in propria persona*, one will also judge affirmatively on the question whether p. For Descartes this requires certainty, moreover, so that the belief must manifest infallible competence.

Note again how indirectly one might grasp that belief while thus endorsing it. For example, it is easy enough to endorse all certain beliefs as certain, if one does so *de dicto* through assent to the proposition <All certain beliefs are certain>. This is not sufficient for purposes of the Cartesian project. For one thing, it is compatible with proper doubt on a particular belief that is nevertheless quite certain. Take, for example, a belief picked out as, say, "the first belief I acquired from guidebook G, although I now believe G to be unreliable." (That belief might in fact happen to be a certain truth well confirmed through experience, or even through proof, since the time when one first acquired it from that guidebook, although one is not now conscious of this fact.)

On the other hand, the project would be clearly unachievable if it required the *de re* endorsement separately and individually, of each belief that one hosts.

Here then is the Meditator's predicament. The project is supposed to yield a high epistemic status for the beliefs that pass inspection. To pass inspection a belief must withstand the search for reasons to doubt it. One must be able to rationally dispel all doubt, however metaphysical or slight. One must counter every reason to consider that belief less than superlatively apt, to regard it as a belief that, even if true, would be true excessively due to chance. However, in order to pass inspection a belief need not be present to the Meditator *in propria persona*, with its content in full display. It can be picked out rather by description, as a "belief owed essentially to perception," or the like. If beliefs can pass inspection when picked out so indirectly, however, then might we just pick out all relevant beliefs under the following description?

> Beliefs that are superlatively apt, i.e., true thanks sufficiently to the believer's perception, and its degree of clarity and distinctness

So, the way such beliefs would then allegedly pass inspection is through our belief that *all superlatively apt beliefs are true*. But this is silly, and of little use. Endorsing such beliefs under *this* description will do little to upgrade them above their pre-endorsement level.

What is needed is a more helpful conception of how we acquire and sustain beliefs. Once we can pick out a set of our beliefs as ones dependent on a certain way of acquiring and sustaining them, the reliability of their source may be pertinent to their epistemic status. Plausibly, the epistemic status of a belief will be dependent on its fullest relevant source, on the fullest disposition that the subject manifests in receiving that deliverance. Suppose the subject then exercises his epistemic agency, his faculty of judgment, by assenting *only* when the understanding's deliverance is so clear and distinct that none such would ever be false. Only then will the judgment be certain. But it is crucial that we be able to pick out the specific source, and the correlated way of acquiring beliefs: i.e., by trusting the deliverances of that specific source as such.

Suppose our sifting critique to uncover about a disposition—an epistemic source—that it does not meet that standard. The deliverances of that source are then under a cloud, as are the corresponding judgments.

So long as we can easily enough attribute to a credence a source that is clearly enough sufficiently reliable, we can then make the corresponding judgment with epistemic justification. The Cartesian method of doubt downgrades our credences when it leads us to conclude that our characterization of them is *not* like that. We run into serious skeptical difficulties to the extent that we are unable to trace our credences to sources that by our lights are sufficiently reliable, and for the Cartesian project, of course, *sufficiently* reliable means *infallible*.

F. The Cartesian Project

The Cartesian epistemological project is at a minimum one of examining human epistemic competence, our actual modes of acquiring and sustaining beliefs. Descartes considers how defensible our actual modes are, and also what are the best ways available to us.

One way in which a first-order credence—whether continuing or newly acquired—might benefit from such a project is by the subject's picking it out specifically, with its content in full display, and by the subject's endorsing it while thus picked out. Such endorsement, if fully proper, would require the subject to know the competence involved to be sufficiently reliable and to be manifest in his holding of that first-order credence.

A normal human could not upgrade many of his credences up to that level, at least not *through conscious reflection*, at any given time. There is a limit to the scope of our concurrent attention.

If we moderate our ambition we can widen the reach of certainty, however, by allowing the second-order endorsement to be implicit and to remain implicitly stored in memory. We require that the judgment be made or be sustained competently enough, through the sufficient competence of the faculty that prompts it. We may even require further that the subject have an appropriate second-order account of why that faculty is so reliable. However, we must *not* require, for this more realistic level of upgrade, and for the corresponding endorsement, that the specific belief be picked out separately and consciously, in propria persona. It suffices that (a) the subject have some implicit awareness of it as belief of an epistemically relevant sort, as belief that manifests the competence in question; and that (b) his sustaining of that belief be positively influenced by that awareness.

G. Concluding Remarks

In the view I've defended, Descartes uses his principle of clarity and distinctness in order to raise his first-order judgments, up to the *scientia* level. He must assure himself that judgments rationally based on clear and distinct perceptions avoid error. *Error* is what one must avoid, not just falsity. So, he seeks not just truth but *aptness*. And aptness requires a good enough competence, one that is reliable enough. You are to assure yourself that you attain such aptness, which is required for confidence that you avoid error, and attain certainty. But this assurance is forthcoming only with assurance that the operative source of your judgment is indeed a reliable-enough competence. Since that includes all of your judgments—past, present, and future—it raises an issue of circularity, since it is hard to see how you could really assure yourself of how reliable your competence is in the absence of any first-order premises. We seem doomed to vicious circularity, and face the notorious Cartesian Circle. This circle also affects contemporary virtue epistemology, moreover, when it postulates a level of reflective knowledge above that of animal knowledge. This is no surprise, given the parallel between the two epistemological distinctions: that between the animal and the reflective on the contemporary scene, and that between *cognitio* and *scientia* in Cartesian epistemology. Virtue epistemology, whether Cartesian or contemporary, must address this allegedly vicious circle, and in my view it can do so with success.[8]

Already for his contemporaries it was hard to make sense of Descartes's epistemological project, with its distinctive quest for certainty. This comes out most famously and clearly in the *Objections and Replies*. I myself see no way to do so except by (a) ascending to the second order in the sort of way we have done, (b) distinguishing credence from judgment, (c) highlighting the fact that some propositions are indubitable, since even when considered consciously and reflectively they demand our assent, and (d) addressing the problem of the Circle through the distinction between *cognitio* and *scientia*. But proceeding in this fourfold way raises the difficult interpretive and philosophical questions that we have taken up.

In all important structural respects, Cartesian virtue epistemology is the same view as a virtue epistemology defended on the contemporary scene, virtue perspectivism.[9] The structure of the view does not require the theological content that Descartes gives to his own version. The role of theology can be played instead by science, by common sense, or by the two combined. Although I have argued in this chapter that the two versions of virtue epistemology are closely akin, the full extent of the kinship remains to be detailed, and should become increasingly clear as the contemporary view is developed to include more explicitly the epistemic agency that played so central a role in Cartesian epistemology. This is a development of the contemporary view that is now under way.[10]

---

8. Epistemically vicious circularity is the theme of my *Reflective Knowledge* (Oxford: Oxford University Press, 2009).
9. This is the view that I myself defend in other writings.
10. In this very book, *Judgment and Agency*, which concludes with the present chapter.

Appendix 1

A passage from the Replies deserves comment:

> First of all, as soon as we think that we correctly perceive something, we are spontaneously convinced that it is true. Now if this conviction is so firm that it is impossible for us ever to have any reason for doubting what we are convinced of, then there are no further questions for us to ask: we have everything that we could reasonably want. What is it to us that someone may make out that the perception whose truth we are so firmly convinced of may appear false to God or an angel, so that it is, absolutely speaking, false? Why should this alleged "absolute falsity" bother us, since we neither believe in it nor have even the smallest suspicion of it? For the supposition which we are making here is of a conviction so firm that it is quite incapable of being destroyed; and such a conviction is clearly the same as the most perfect certainty. (Second Set of Replies, CSM II: 103)

What Descartes here calls "the most perfect certainty" may well be viewed as rather unlike superlative aptness, and he even seems to grant that such certainty is consistent with the falsity of the certainly held conviction.

That all does seem troubling initially. But there is a way to read the passage so as to accommodate it:

a. Note first the antecedent of the conditional in the first paragraph. The persuasion has to be so "firm" that *we could never have any reason for doubting what we are thus persuaded of.* So, the assumption is not just that we are fully, perhaps stubbornly, psychologically sure. There is rather an apparent normative component: we *could never* have *any reason* for doubting.

b. Note that the hypothetical case is not one where a thing we are certain of does appear false to God and is hence absolutely false. No, all that is imagined is rather this: that someone *imagines* all of that. So, what we do not care about is not outright falsity. No, "this alleged 'absolute falsity' " that we do not believe in or in the least suspect, is just an *imagined* absolute falsity, a case where someone imagines that the thing we are certain of is in fact false.

c. But when we suppose that we enjoy "a conviction so firm that it is quite incapable of being [rationally] destroyed, . . . equivalent to the most perfect certainty," surely we will then properly, rationally withhold probative force from any *imagining* to the contrary.

This further question does remain: "Why is this perfect certainty equivalent to superlative aptness?" And that does require some further explanation. Here is a sketch of how the explanation might go.

> Suppose first that the belief in question is not superlatively apt. Then it falls under the fourth skeptical scenario. If so, Descartes is then committed to the view that this provides a reason for doubt. So, it is not then "perfectly certain."

Secondly, what if the belief in question were not "perfectly certain." In that case it *could* be rationally removed. This means that there could be a good reason against it. A false reason is not a good reason. Plausibly, such a good reason would have to amount to a truth to the effect that we were less than perfectly guaranteed to be right (even though we had proceeded in a situation appropriately normal for the use of our faculties). And this means that the belief would not be superlatively apt; it would not be one whose correctness could be *fully* explained just by appeal to the perfect competence of the believer.

Appendix 2

Here I adduce textual evidence for the suggestion that Descartes's radical doubt is *not* a matter of *reduced confidence*, not primarily anyhow (and I think not at all), but rather just a matter of *withdrawal of or forbearance from endorsement of a belief that one does not see to be certain.*

a. From Meditation I:

> [Regarding my old and customary beliefs,] I shall never get out of the habit of confidently assenting to these opinions, so long as I suppose them to be what in fact they are, namely highly probable opinions—opinions which, despite the fact that they are in a sense doubtful, as has just been shown, it is still much more reasonable to believe than to deny. In view of this, I think it will be a good plan to turn my will in completely the opposite direction and deceive myself, by pretending for a time that these former opinions are utterly false and imaginary. I shall do this until the weight of preconceived opinion is counter balanced and the distorting influence of habit no longer prevents my judgment from perceiving things correctly. (Meditation I, CSM II: 15)

Note the distinction between opinions and judgment, and also the insistence that his ordinary opinions are "in truth" highly probable and much more reasonable to believe than to deny. Also, he will *suppose* a certain thing for a time, which of course does not require him to reduce his confidence.

b. Compare in that light this, from near the end of Meditation I:

> So in future I must withhold my assent from these former beliefs just as carefully as I would from obvious falsehoods, if I want to discover any certainty. (Meditation I, CSM II: 15)

Since, no one of sound mind ever seriously doubts such opinions as that there really is a world, he does not thereby seriously put their contents in doubt.

All he does is perhaps to forbear endorsing them, given that he cannot see them to be certain. True, there is the passage cited earlier where he claims that it would be unreasonable as part of his project not to consider his ordinary beliefs to be *false*. But we have seen how this is understandable given that those beliefs are to be thus rejected *under an indirect description, general or specific, and not in propria persona, with the content fully in view*. Thus his ordinary perceptual beliefs could be rejected as false, simply as "ordinary perceptual beliefs of mine," or "beliefs I acquired through the senses," or the like. Of course, if *all* such empirical, ordinary beliefs are to be rejected, then even these beliefs in the falsehood of ordinary perceptual beliefs are themselves to be rejected. But there seems no special problem in "rejecting" even these *under some description* while continuing to hold them individually nonetheless.

c. From the Synopsis of Meditation VI:

> [T]here is a survey of all the errors which commonly come from the senses, and an explanation of how they may be avoided; and, lastly, there is a presentation of all the arguments which enable the existence of materials things to be inferred. The great benefit of these arguments is not, in my view, that they prove what they establish—namely, that there really is a world, and that human beings have bodies and so on—*since no sane person has ever seriously doubted these things*. The point is that in considering these arguments we come to realize that they are not as solid or as transparent as the arguments which lead us to knowledge of our own minds and of God, *so that the latter are the most certain and evident of all possible objects of knowledge for the human intellect. Indeed, this is the one thing that I set myself to prove in these Meditations*. And for that reason I will not now go over the various other issues in the book which are dealt with as they come up. (Synopsis of the Following Six Meditations, CSM II: 11; emphasis added)

Note what no sane person *ever* seriously doubts. And note also his objective: *to establish the certainty of such and such* (not the truth of it, but the certainty).

Index

AAA structure of normative assessment 19, 25 n. 28, 59, 67 n. 5, 94–5, 124
ability 37, 69, 90, 95, 98, 141 n. 10, 143–7, 171–4; *see also* competence; knowledge-how
acceptance 200, 235, 245
achievement 46 n. 18, 72, 103, 142
action
  basic 98 n. 6, 136–8, 143, 148, 159, 163–6
  complex 136
  first-order/second-order 126, 177
  means-end 136–7, 140, 142, 146–7, 154, 167
  reflex 47, 192–3
  virtuous 134, 138 *see also* aimings; deeds; doings; endeavorings; intentional action; performance
actional sufficiency 159, 164
affirmation
  apt 55, 66, 77, 79–84, 86–7, 90–5, 111–17, 124–6, 129, 149–53, 165–6, 176, 180–1, 184
  competent 55, 80, 82, 90–1, 149–50
  conscious/subconscious 51–2, 66 n. 3, 244
  and credence 90–2, 151, 186, 201, 229
  declarative/optative 226
  and endeavorings 52–6, 66, 77, 80–3, 87, 90–3, 149–51, 165–6, 177–8, 184
  first-order/second-order 75–6, 80–3, 86, 112, 114–15, 150–2

free affirmation 167, 210
fully apt affirmation 69 n. 6, 80–1, 93, 112, 116–17, 125–6, 129, 165–6
functional/intentional 51–2, 93, 116, 124,
and imaginings 226, 238
and judgment 52–3, 58, 77, 80, 82, 124–5, 151, 166, 171, 180, 232
in philosophical contexts 56–8, 60, 215
perceptual 149–50, 152–3
public/private 52 n. 26, 54–7, 66–8, 74, 89, 93, 124, 177, 180–2, 184, 187
qualified/flat-out 54 n. 29, 56, 58–60, 66 n. 4
and safety 79–80, 112, 152
and social factors 51, 55–6, 60, 66, 181
subcredal 91
synchronic 186
withholding 55–6, 82 *see also* assent; disposition, to assent; guessing, and affirmation; suspension, and affirmation; volition, and affirmation
aim 140, 164
  action with more than one aim 77, 93–4, 124, 136, 161, 181
  animal/reflective aim 71
  basic 71, 73, 85–6, 115, 124
  of belief 12, 24, 51, 53, 171, 178 n. 11, 181–2
  constitutive 14 n. 11, 24, 80 n. 21, 126, 165, 178 n. 11

aim (cont.)
   first-order aim 71, 141
   freely determined aim 192
   hierarchically ordered 160–1
   intentional 10, 25, 136, 163
   relative to domain 104–5, 169
   teleological/functional 20, 24–5, 51, 67 n. 5, 192 n. 1 *see also* endeavorings; intention
aimings 19, 24, 124
   and AAA structure 19, 124
   functional/intentional 19, 124, 178 n. 11 *see also* action; deeds; doings; endeavorings; intentional action
alethic/praxical distinction 67–8
   about affirmation 52–3, 60, 66, 68, 77, 151, 166, 180–1
   and beliefs 53, 230
   and judgment 55–6, 93
analysis (linguistic, conceptual, metaphysical) 7–9, 16–17, 19, 32–3, 128–9, 154, 194
Anti-luck Virtue Epistemology 117–19
appearances, *see* Pyrrhonism
aptness
   of action 141, 146, 154–5, 159
   of attempts 124, 126
   of awareness 81, 86–7
   of belief 9–10, 12–13, 15, 18, 43, 45, 59, 95, 111–12, 116, 121, 125, 146–52, 171, 174–6, 178–9, 233, 241, 247
   of choice 88
   and competence 18, 24, 43, 68, 80, 101, 107, 110, 117, 146
   in degrees 155, 157–9, 175
   of epistemic performance 82, 128, 178
   first-order (animal)/reflective aptness 69–70, 72, 76, 81 n. 22, 85, 87, 107, 117, 148
   of guessing 155, 177–8
   of intention 19, 156
   of intentional action 155, 159, 165–6
   of judgment 77, 79–80, 93, 114, 116–17, 125, 151–2, 165–6, 178, 210
   by luck 86
   meta-aptness 72, 77, 168–9, 174
   and norms 171
   of performance 12–13, 18–19, 65, 77, 85–7, 110, 115, 117, 123–4, 141–2, 174–5, 178
   of representation 22, 94, 148
   and safety 79–80, 115, 146
   and selection 168–9
   of shots 13, 49, 68–72, 86, 147–53, 168–9, 180
   of success 14, 25, 72, 80, 85, 101, 151–3, 158–9, 165, 210
   superlative aptness 241, 248–9, 252–3
   and supposition 114, 148, 155 *see also* affirmation, apt; Descartes, René, and aptness; full aptness
archery/hunting example 13–14, 24, 73
   and domain-internal standards 168–9, 173–4, 188
   with guardian angel 102–3
   hopeful/superstitious hunter 142–5, 160 n. 4
   and objectives 168–9
   and reliability 170
   and Sextus Empiricus 65 n.1
   and shot selection 68–9, 96–7, 108
Aristotle
   and action 139–42, 167
   Aristotelian view of persons 8–9
   and flourishing 133–5, 140–4, 156, 167
   and goods 134, 137
   and the soul 134, 137–9, 156
   and virtue 34, 133–4, 136–7 *see also* flourishing

INDEX

assent
  attractions to assent 108, 193, 195, 200, 202 n. 8, 231
  conscious 239, 244, 251
  and Descartes 58–60, 234, 243–6, 248–9, 251
  in foro interno 181, 226, 232, 242
  proper 52, 232
  and Pyrrhonism 216–17, 223–7
  withholding of 239, 254 *see also* disposition, to assent; volition, and assent
attainment
  of aim 19, 124, 150, 155–6, 164–5
  of aptness 152, 165
  of competences 60
  epistemic attainment 46 n. 18
  individual/collective attainment 164
  of knowledge 42, 49–50
  of success 157–8
attempts 13, 23 n. 24, 69, 72, 96–7, 157
  evaluating 108–10
  full attempt 124–5
  nested 126
  structure of attempts 110, 124, 129
attractions
  to accept 200
  to affirm 167
  to assent 108, 193, 195, 200, 202 n. 8, 231
  to believe 200
  to choose 139, 167
  intellectual attraction 218
  to represent 93
  to think 195 *see also* confidence; seemings
awareness
  apt 81, 85–7
  conscious 79 n. 20, 81, 244
  constitutive/noticing 198–9
  first-order/second-order 68, 72, 79–81, 84–7
  of headache/itch 197–200
  implicit 250
  judgmental awareness 201
  of limits 69–70, 72
  sensory 239
  unselfconscious 227

Baehr, Jason 34–41, 45–7, 49
  account of intellectual virtues 39–40
Barnes, Jonathan 216
bases
  for action 183–4, 187
  for belief 117, 123, 183–6, 196–8, 204, 206–7
  for credences 204–5
  for deliverances 116
  forgotten bases 89–90, 172, 179, 182–3, 185–6, 205 n. 10
  for judgment 108, 196–7, 201, 231
  motivating 197, 199
  rational basing 199–202
  for seemings 149, 193, 200, 231 *see also* reasons
belief
  animal/reflective 194 n. 2, 208–10, 239, 242
  belief-forming mechanisms 27, 37, 203–4, 210, 232
  and competence/virtue 10, 12–13, 24, 40–3, 45, 118–19, 145–7, 172
  and confidence 90–2, 171, 180, 185–6, 201, 228, 238
  conscious/unconscious 51, 67, 109, 167, 208, 226
  de re/de dicto 235, 237, 244–5, 248, 254
  as disposition to affirm/assert/judge 182, 187, 228–9, 232
  dispositional 66 n. 4, 210, 232
  and dreams 112
  first-order/second-order (compare animal/reflective) 109, 125, 149–51, 185–6, 194, 212, 237

belief (*cont.*)
  foundational 204 n. 9
  full 202 n. 8
  functional/intentional 51–4, 56, 67–8, 91–2, 146, 178 n. 11
  guiding conduct 69, 84, 186, 194 n. 3, 208–9, 222, 227, 239, 242
  implicit 50, 53, 208, 226, 232, 242
  judgmental belief 25, 52–7, 66–7, 79, 90 n. 1, 92, 140, 151, 180, 184, 209, 232, 238, 242–3
  make-belief; mock belief 52–3, 66, 226–7, 236–8
  storage 89–90, 179–80, 182–7, 208–9, 250 *see also* aim, of belief; aptness, of belief; justification, and belief; luck, and belief; means-end, belief; perception, perceptual belief; suspension; volition, and belief
bias 208–9
Bonjour, Laurence 129
Burnyeat, Myles 216–17, 219–20, 223–6
by-relation 162–4, 166

causation
  and aptness 25
  and competence 23–5, 41
  deviant 10–14, 23–4, 28 n. 29, 31
  "in the right way" 11–13, 18, 22–5, 30–1
chance, *see* luck
choice 137–40, 207–8, 210, 229
  arbitrary 97, 155, 197, 208
  competently made 140
  conscious choice 167, 200
  free to choose 137, 167, 200, 207, 210, 229
  fully apt choice 88
  and judgment 67, 192–3

rational 134
reckless choice 123, 125 *see also* competence, and selection; volition
circularity 195–6, 201, 203, 240, 251
  see also skepticism, Agrippan
closure principle 121
cogito, *see* Descartes, René
coincidence 13–14, 24, 40; *see also* luck
common factor view (traditional view) 13–18
communication 102, 181, 186–9
  see also testimony
competence
  agential 23, 38, 48, 54–5
  basic 29, 143, 145
  "blind" competence 107
  broader; two-ply competence 90
  competent seemings 88, 231
  complete 26–7, 43 n. 17, 61, 71–2, 80, 95–8, 110, 114, 117, 148, 154
  complex 42, 115, 135
  conceptual 149
  core epistemic competence 171
  in degrees 96, 72, 90, 157–8
  as disposition to succeed 24, 43, 95–7, 98–100, 143–6, 163
  distal/proximal 30 n. 30, 101
  domain-specific 28–9, 86, 157–8, 163, 169, 173–4
  epistemic propriety of 201–2
  executive 44, 136
  first-order/second-order 68, 72, 81 n. 22, 83–5, 107, 117, 148–50, 152, 165, 211
  foundational 231–2
  full 27, 43, 71, 145, 147, 155
  inner 26–7, 95–7
  innermost 26–8, 83, 61, 95–7, 100, 103
  involuntary competence 210
  and intention 163

and knowledge 145, 147, 174
outstanding 157
overall 157
perceptual 21–3, 31 n. 32, 42, 136, 149, 152, 205
and phobias 97
quasi-competence 97 n. 5
range of shapes and situations 97–101, 104–6, 144
rational competence 88
of reasoning 210
reflective 68–9, 76, 84, 233
relative to shapes and situations 100–1, 104, 146, 157–8, 160
and selection 68, 98–9, 108, 123, 127
and social conventions 28–9, 101, 104–6, 115–16, 125–8, 170–3
socially seated competences 115–17
sorting competence 31 n. 32, 38
and subpersonal mechanisms 35, 202–3, 205, 232
threshold of 85–6
unreliable 173–6
and vagueness 71 n. 8
without motivation 49–50 *see also* aptness, and competence; disposition; manifestation, of competence; SSS structure, SeShSi; virtues
Competence Virtue Epistemology, *see* Virtue Reliabilism
confidence 54 n. 29, 66 n.4, 68, 76, 109, 171, 200–1
and awareness 198
functional 92, 196–7
and judgment 108, 180, 184, 251
proper 77, 200, 205
quasi-judgmental credences 66 n. 4
and rational structure 199
and reliability connection 89–91, 182, 185–6

resultant seemings 54, 68, 91–3, 109, 200, 229, 231–2, 239
and self-presenting states 203
and subpersonal mechanisms 203
and thresholds 171, 180–2
and the unit interval 91–2, 109, 239
see also belief, and confidence; suspension
conjunctive analysis, *see* common factor view
context 56, 58–60, 183, 186–7
and competence 98–101, 105, 127–8
and knowledge 114, 121–2, 178–9, 187
and norms 60
and risk 73, 183–4
shifts in 60 *see also* aim, relative to domain; affirmation, in philosophical contexts; competence, domain-specific; pragmatic encroachment
conventions, *see* social conventions
credence, *see* confidence; seemings, resultant
credit
and affirmation 149
and Anti-Luck Virtue Epistemology 118
causal/consequential 160 n. 5
and competence 28–9, 69–72, 86, 97, 103, 142–4, 153
full credit 71, 86, 147, 156
and groups 115–16
and intentional action 153
and luck 24, 69, 72, 83, 127, 136, 142 3, 152, 155, 160 n. 4
and manifestation 29
for performance 94, 98, 103, 127, 175
and representation 94
without intervention 47

Davidson, Donald 10–11, 14–15, 18, 21–3, 25, 158
deeds 124, 162–4, 166; *see also* action; aimings; doings; endeavorings; intentional action; performance
defeaters, *see* reasons
deliberation 39, 110, 138–9, 180, 182, 208, 231
   collective 51–2, 55–8, 66, 167
deontic framework 193–4, 202
   epistemic obligation 212
Descartes, René
   and aptness 59, 233, 241, 247–50
   and basket metaphor 234–6, 243
   beliefs *de re/de dicto* 235, 237, 244–5, 248, 254
   Cartesian Circle 251
   and certainty 235, 246–8, 253–4
   and clarity and distinctness 238–9, 241, 246–50
   cogito 59, 83–4, 240
   cognitio 233, 239
   and confidence 236–7, 249, 253
   and doubt 112 n. 3, 247, 254
   and endorsement 55–6, 59, 248–50
   and error 246–7, 250
   and freedom 203, 232, 238, 242 n. 5, 245–6,
   and inspecting beliefs 235–6, 240, 248–9
   and language 58
   and meditation 243
   and method of doubt 234–6, 245, 249, 253
   and movie theater analogy 237–8
   and pretense 236–8
   and reflection 36, 51, 53–4, 74, 243
   scientia 233, 250–1
   and suspension 232, 235–6, 248, 254
   and suspension of disbelief 238
   and virtue epistemology 59, 99 n. 7, 113, 233, 251 *see also* assent, and Descartes
DeRose, Keith 120 n. 11
disagreement 211–12
Disjunctivism 15–17
disposition
   to act 68
   to affirm 51–2, 69 n. 6, 92, 180–1, 186–7, 209, 228–9
   to assent 209, 232
   to believe correctly 43, 105
   conditional analysis of 104
   diachronic/synchronic 212
   dispositional concepts 28
   distal/proximal 101
   finks 96 n. 3
   fragility 27–31, 100–1, 145
   to judge 51–3, 55–6, 66, 68, 92, 113, 209, 232, 238, 243
   masks 96 n. 3
   mimicking 29
   passive 210
   seated in the will 210
   social categorization of 28–9, 30 n. 30, 101–5
   SSS structure of 26–30, 95–6, 99 n. 7, 100, 104–5
   triggers 28–30, 101, 104
   trumping 29
   well-founded 212 *see also* competence; manifestation; SSS structure, SeShSi
doings
   attributable doing 124, 193
   and belief 67 n. 5
   and choice 137
   and intention 15, 18, 22–3, 25, 125, 135–6, 138 n. 5, 161–4
   and knowledge 142, 145–6
   mere doings 162, 192–3

INDEX

and passivity 162, 195, 200 *see also* action; aimings; deeds; endeavorings; intentional action; performance
doxastic voluntarism, *see* volition

endeavorings
  and Agrippan trilemma 196–7, 201
  foundational 197
  and freedom 192–3, 203, 206
  full 135
  rational 197
  simple 140, 184
  and supposition 177
  teleological/functional 192 n. 1 *see also* affirmation, and endeavorings; volition, and endeavorings
etiquette 26, 101–2
evidence 14 n. 11, 43–4, 51–2, 81 n. 23, 109, 147, 190, 208, 210, 241
evolution 20, 29, 93, 126–8
examples, analogies, and illustrations in text
  assassin 49
  bad Apple 119, 123
  baseball 155–7, 174, 175 n. 8
  basketball 69–73, 79, 85–7, 114–15, 126, 174–6, 180
  blindsighter 75, 78, 81, 89, 115, 202–4, 207
  chess 126, 161, 188
  chicken sexer 37, 75, 78, 81, 89, 115
  cliff rabbit 192, 195
  cup/subitizing example 112
  doctor's mallet 162–3, 193–5, 210
  driving 26–7, 61, 95–6, 100
  escaping prisoner 158
  eye-exam 74–6, 80–1, 91, 114, 151, 154, 155 n. 2, 177–8

  fuel gauge 197
  game show contestant 55, 82, 151
  Gauguin 60–1
  golfer 158–60, 163
  headache 200
  hypochondriac 199
  Macbeth 21–2
  Norman the Clairvoyant 75 n. 15, 78–81, 107–8, 115, 129
  saxophonist 123, 128
  Sears Tower 118
  shattering (zapping) dumbbell/pewter mug 23, 29–30, 100, 145
  shattering (zapping) wine glass 23, 29–31
  sheep/wolf 135–8, 140–1
  Simone 78–9, 146–53
  skateboarder 125, 128
  soccer goalie 97
  speckled hen 199 n. 7, 203, 205
  swimming at sea 155–8
  tennis 94, 98, 127, 157–8, 169–70, 173–4
  Truetemp 75 n. 15, 78–81, 115, 129
  waiter 10, 18, 23, 158
  woozy partygoer 113–15 *see also* archery/hunting example; Gettier cases; lottery case
experience
  apt 18, 20–2, 149–50
  of pain/itch 198–9, 203, 205–7, 231
  and propositional content 20, 198 n. 5, 205
  sensory 11–12, 31, 198, 204–6
  visual experience 12, 22, 31, 42, 149–50, 198 n. 5, 200–3
  see also perception; seemings; self-presenting states

experience machine 189–90
expertise 29, 37, 41–2, 49–50, 59–60, 101, 105–6, 128

faculties, *see* virtues
first-order/second-order
  action 126, 177
  affirmation 75–6, 80–3, 86, 112, 114–15, 150–2
  aim 71, 141
  aptness 69–70, 72, 76, 81 n. 22, 85, 87, 107, 117, 148
  assumption 116
  awareness 68, 72, 79–81, 84–7
  belief 109, 125, 149–51, 185–6, 194, 212, 237
  competence 68, 72, 81 n. 22, 83–5, 107, 117, 148–50, 152, 165, 211
  defeaters 83
  doubts 211
  endorsement 55, 250
  grasp 148, 151
  intention 82, 110, 126
  judgment 54, 81 n. 22, 83–5, 211, 250
  knowledge 84–5, 149, 233
  performance 71–2, 85–6, 108–9
  perspective 185, 233
  reasons/reasoning 183, 237, 251
  representation 148, 152
  safety 72, 79, 115
  SSS conditions 81 n. 23
  success 72, 108, 128
  threshold 115
flourishing 29, 105, 127, 212 n. 13, 216
  and action 167
  and Aristotle 133–5, 140–4, 156, 167
  of groups and societies 29, 116, 167, 176, 188–9
  and knowledge 44, 48, 188–9,
  and luck 142, 156

freedom, *see* volition
full aptness 69–70, 72–4, 76–7, 93–4, 107–8, 110–13, 123–6, 128–9
  fully apt affirmation 69 n. 6, 80–1, 93, 112, 116–17, 125–6, 129, 165–6
  belief 69, 107, 116
  performance 65, 69, 73, 85–7, 99 n. 7, 136
  virtue epistemology 129 *see also* aptness; first-order/second-order, aptness; knowledge, full well
functioning, proper 91–2, 128, 193–5, 197, 202, 210
functionings 192, 194
  credal states 196, 205
  epistemic 195–7, 204–5
  foundational 197
  and freedom 201–2, 204, 206, 231
  malfunction 194 n. 3
  and passivity 194, 204, 206
  rational 194, 196, 202–3
  and seemings 205

Gettier cases
  and aptness 12–13, 24
  fake barn cases 31 n. 32, 78–80, 87, 111, 115, 118
  Gettier tradition 75, 77, 129
  Havit/Nogot case 77
  and intuitions 28 n. 29, 31 n. 32, 78 n. 18
  and knowledge full well 85, 87
  and means-end belief 140–1
given, the, *see* self-presenting states
goal, *see* aim
Goldman, Alvin 16 n. 8
Greco, John 39
Grice, Paul 10–13, 15, 18–22, 25, 31
guessing 80, 85–6, 91, 107, 114, 155
  and affirmation 55, 74–6, 82, 90–1, 151
  apt 155, 177–8

and apt action 154
and norms 179 *see also* examples, game show contestant; examples, eye-exam

hallucination 17 n. 14, 21
  veridical 22
Hume, David 57–8, 215–16, 229–30

illusion 21–2, 149, 189–90, 205
  Müller-Lyer 55, 193–5, 218 *see also* hallucination
induction 121
infallibility
  and the cogito 83
  and competence 156, 158, 171–2, 186, 248–9
inference
  conscious reasoning 205
  inferential reasoning 198, 223, 225–7, 245
  practical syllogism 201
  practical/theoretical 198 *see also* reasoning
intellectual virtue, *see* virtue
intention
  change of 68
  and choice 139
  and competence 163
  conscious/unconscious 51, 163, 209
  higher-order intention 82, 110, 126
  implementation of 135–6, 139–40
  intentional agency 39, 46–9, 55
  intentional (double-)omission 82, 109–10, 180
  intentional representations 66 n. 3
  intentional success 155–6, 159–60
  intentionally correct affirmation 66, 166
  master intention 161–2

motivating 49 *see also* aim; intentional action; plan
intentional action
  and AAA structure 124
  as apt intention 19, 156, 158–9, 165–6
  and belief 44, 51, 230 n. 11
  and competence 30
  Davidson's account of 10–11, 15, 18–19, 22–5
  and judgment 165–6
  and knowledge 155
  metaphysics of 162–6
  and performance 20, 72, 125, 159
  and SSS structure 30 *see also* action; intention
intuition, faculty of rational 245
intuitions
  a priori 107–8, 239
  disagreement about 87, 129
  explaining away 81, 120, 129, 148
  see also Gettier cases; X-Phi
Invariantism/Variantism 179

Johnsen, Bredo 219–25, 229 n. 9
judgment 67–8, 124, 151
  and action 25, 171
  and arbitrariness 196, 201, 208, 232
  and competence 45, 57, 59, 69, 82, 84, 114, 152
  and confidence; credence 108, 251
  conscious/unconscious 44, 51, 53, 66–7, 84, 209, 238–9, 245
  dispositional 243
  first-order/second-order 54, 81 n. 22, 83–5, 211, 250
  foundational 196, 201, 231
  and knowledge 15, 19, 76, 79, 178
  occurrent/dispositional 232
  private 56
  quasi-judgmental credences 66 n. 4
  rational 51, 196

judgment (cont.)
  second-order endorsement 54, 75, 115, 250
  and selection 168–9
  suspension of 82, 91–2, 208–9 see also affirmation, and judgment; aptness, of judgment; bases, for judgment; confidence, and judgment; judgmental belief; knowledge, judgmental
justification
  and belief 50, 77–8, 143–6, 202–6, 211, 216
  epistemic 171, 176, 193, 195, 197, 201–3, 211, 249
  foundational 225
  and knowledge 202–4
  of performance 202
  and regress 196, 205

Kant, Immanuel 21 n. 21
knowledge
  actionable 184–5, 187, 190–1
  and affirmation 56, 91, 149, 171, 180
  animal/reflective 36–9, 42, 53, 55, 59, 74, 76 , 81, 84, 89, 112, 128–9, 148–56, 233, 251
  as apt belief 10, 12, 15, 18, 24, 146
  basic 54, 76
  concept of 9
  credal/subcredal 43, 152–3, 155
  easy 46
  extended 115
  flat-out 180
  for sure 183
  foundational 197
  functional/judgmental 19, 25, 54, 66, 69 n. 6, 76, 90, 128, 178
  introspective 203
  perceptual 46, 54
  propositional 12, 24, 145–7

subcredal animal knowledge 40, 76, 79–80, 151–6 see also knowledge full well; luck, and knowledge; value of knowledge
knowledge-first 15, 17
knowledge full well 69 n. 6, 74, 79–82, 84–7, 111–13, 125, 129, 148
knowledge-how 125, 141 n. 10, 145–8, 157
credal/subcredal 153 see also ability; competence

Lehrer, Keith 77, 129
lottery case 117–23, 190–1
  Vogel-style 121–2
luck
  and belief 10, 13, 24, 40
  and choice 137, 156
  and competence 19, 22, 24, 72, 81, 136, 142, 144, 158, 171
  and flourishing 142, 156
  and knowledge 12–13, 24, 112, 118, 142, 150
  and performance 9, 12–14, 71–2, 86, 98, 136–8, 141–2, 158–60 see also credit, and luck
  and supposition 155–6

manifestation
  of adroitness 68
  of character/virtues 34, 37, 40, 43, 45, 135
  of competence 18–19, 21, 24–6, 28–32, 40, 42, 71–4, 95–8, 117, 123, 135, 147, 156
  of disposition 23, 28–31
  fake/true 29–31
  primitive relation of 31–2
  of skill 103–4 see also competence; dispositions
means-end
  action 136–7, 140, 142, 146–7, 154, 167

belief 137, 140, 145, 147–8
information 156
knowledge 154–5
proposition 137, 154
supposition 155
memory 52 n. 25, 89–92, 94–5, 114, 116–17, 179–80, 182–7, 208–9, 250
Meno problem, *see* value of knowledge
methodology
 bullet biting 33
 and counterexamples 33, 129
 disagreement in philosophy 33
 kinds of analysis 7–9
 prescriptive aims 32–3
 relations between ethics and epistemology 34, 44–5, 48, 61 *see also* analysis; intuitions; X-Phi
mode of presentation 146
Moore, G. E. 14 n. 11, 58, 170 n. 2

negligence
 epistemic 43–4, 47–8, 83, 85, 194 n. 2
 in performance 71, 73, 86, 108, 110–11
norms
 of action 178, 185
 and affirmation 59, 171
 and aptness 171
 of assertion 170–2, 175–6, 179, 181
 of belief 50, 170–2, 179
 determination of 170–5
 domain-internal 172–3
 of judgment 171
 knowledge norm 170–2, 178–9, 181, 184
 of performance 171
 and reliability 179
 social/biological 55, 90, 184
 social epistemic 59–60, 184
 and truth 50

Nozick, Robert 16 n. 8, 120–1; *see also* sensitivity

omission; double-omission 82, 109–10, 180; *see also* suspension
ontology 8–9, 21 n. 19, 67 n. 5, 69 n. 6, 104, 206–7

paradox
 Liar 202 n. 8, 218
 Moorean conjunctions 170 n. 2
 Sorites 202 n. 8, 218
passivity
 epistemic 54–5, 59, 68, 91–2, 195–7, 200, 202, 204–7, 232, 238
 general 47, 162–5, 199–200, 210 *see also* volition
perception 11–12, 18–19, 22, 24, 31, 117
 apt perceptual experience 18–22, 149–50, 152
 causal theory of 11, 15–17, 20, 31
 comparison to reference 23 n. 23
 and manifestation 31–2
 non-visual sense modalitites 20 n. 17, 21 n. 21
 objectual perception 19–21
 perceptual belief 36, 42, 54, 111, 149, 209, 254
 perceptual evidence 241
 perceptual faculties 34, 39
 sensory 35, 46, 239
 of time passing 108, 202–4
 see also affirmation, perceptual; competence, perceptual; knowledge, perceptual
performance 124
 agential 54
 and aims 67 n. 5, 73, 124, 136
 apt performance 12–13, 18–19, 65, 77, 82, 85–7, 110, 115, 117, 123–4, 128, 141–2, 174–5, 178

performance (*cont.*)
  epistemic 49, 60, 82, 206
  first-order/second-order 71–2, 85–6, 108–9
  fully apt performance 65, 69, 73, 85–7, 99 n. 7, 136
  teleological/functional 67 n. 5, 192–3, 196
  intellectual 110, 178
  meta-apt 174
  normativity of performance 129, 170–1, 124
  rational 193, 196, 202
  transcending standards (free performance) 127–8 *see also* credit, for performance; luck, and performance; negligence, in performance; reliability, of performance; risk, and performance; thresholds, of reliability in performance
Peripatetics 137
perspective, I-now 185
plan 137, 139–41, 158–9, 163, 166–7
Plato 40, 87
politeness, *see* etiquette
pragmatic encroachment 60, 168, 179 n. 12, 172, 183–4
praise/blame 28, 102, 110, 125, 194; *see also* credit; reactive attitudes
praxical; practical, *see* alethic/praxical distinction
Price, H. H. 11–13
Pritchard, Duncan 117–19, 123; *see also* safety
pro-attitudes 139, 198, 226
promotion/opposition/neutrality 110; *see also* suspension, and affirmation/denial
Pyrrhonism 53–59, 206–7
  and anxiety/calm 216, 218–21, 225
  and appearances 54, 217–18, 220, 222–5, 227–8, 231–2, 238–9
  and belief/assent 216, 218, 220, 222–5, 232, 243
  and coherence 219, 221–2, 230
  and emotions 221
  and equipollence 216, 220, 228
  and flourishing 216, 218, 225
  and fourfold commitment 217, 227–9, 230
  and guidance 221–2, 227–9, 231–2, 238–9
  and modes 216–18, 221–2, 225, 229
  and open-mindedness 220–2
  and rationality 221
  and reflection 36, 51, 53, 74,
  and suspension 209, 220–3, 225, 228–9, 232
  urbane 216–18, 225
  as way of life 215–17, 221, 229

rationality 211, 230
reactive attitudes 193–4
reasoning 139, 144 n. 11, 186–7, 205, 209, 217, 222–3, 225, 227–31, 235–8
  conscious/unconscious 52 n. 25, 66–8, 109, 167, 182, 205, 211, 243–4
  practical 178, 191, 198,
  steps of reasoning 52, 66 n. 3, 227, 231, 245 *see also* reasons; inference
reasons
  absent defeaters 81 n. 23, 117, 185–6
  and attractions 200
  balance of reasons 208, 216, 219, 221, 223, 229
  and beliefs 107
  counterweighing 83
  defeaters 52 n. 24, 83–5, 116
  diachronic/synchronic 183, 210–12
  factive/stative 197–8
  false reason 253
  first-order 183

and judgment 83, 107
motivating 194–5
responsiveness to 82
undermining 83
weighing of 39, 82, 231 *see also* bases
regress 145–6, 185, 195–7, 199, 201, 203–7, 212; *see also* skepticism, Agrippan
reference, theory of 23 n. 23
reflection
   conscious/unconscious 242–3, 250
   infinite levels of 212
   reflective assessment 195–6 *see also* aptness, reflective; belief, animal/reflective; competence, reflective; Descartes, René, and reflection; knowledge, reflective; Pyrrhonism, and reflection
   reflective judgment 54, 209
   Reid, Thomas 58
relativism about knowledge 105–6; *see also* context; pragmatic encroachment
Reliabilist Virtue Epistemology, *see* Virtue Reliabilism
reliability
   and affirmation 80, 176–7, 181, 187
   and aptness 75, 159–60
   of belief-forming 90, 117, 175, 201
   and competences 70–1, 98, 102, 127–8, 156, 172–6, 180, 250–1
   degrees of 96, 172
   and dispositions 98, 126
   domain-specific 159, 174
   low 154, 160, 173–5
   of performance 70, 108–10, 147
   reliable enough 57, 60, 70–1, 75–6, 86, 90, 96, 98, 117, 123, 126–8, 151, 156, 160, 170–4, 176–80, 250–1

   in social sources of information 116, 175, 186
   for storing beliefs 89–90, 179–80, 183, 185–7, 250
   and thresholds 75, 96, 105–6, 123, 126, 184 *see also* confidence, and reliability connection
representation
   apt/fully apt 148
   first-order/second-order 148, 142
   functional/judgmental 92–4
   hybrid 93–4
   and mental states 206
   and perceptual experience 205
   representational content 207 *see also* aptness, of representation
risk 127–8, 172–3, 175
   and affirmation 82
   assessment of 68–9, 125, 169, 172, 190
   cognitive 110–11
   deliberate 70
   and domain-internal standards 172, 174
   and eye-exam 76
   and judgment 87, 109
   and performance 70, 73, 85–6, 123–5, 127, 168–9, 174
   and practice 99
   and saxophonist 123
   and stakes 183
   and virtue 43–4, 60

safety 111–15, 117–23
   backwards-unsafety 152–3
   and fake barn county 79–80
   first-order/second-order 72, 79, 115
   forwards safety/unsafety 152–3
   and judgment 79–80
   of performance 72–3
   principle of 117
   and Simone case 79, 147–9, 152

Santayana, George 126
seemings 17 n. 14, 108–9, 149–50, 193, 195, 205
  and basing 149, 193, 200, 231
  competent 88, 231
  functional 54, 93
  and headaches 200
  initial/resultant 54, 68, 91–3, 109, 200, 229, 231–2, 239
  intellectual 202 n. 8, 218, 227, 231
  perceptual 54, 149–50, 239
  and Pyrrhonism 54
  and representation 93 see also attractions
self-presenting states 197–200, 203–4, 231
sensitivity 120–2
Sextus Empiricus 65, 86, 217, 219
Situationism 87
skepticism
  Agrippan 195–6, 199, 201, 203, 207, 216, 225, 231–2
  dream 111–12, 241
  evil demon 241
  insanity 111–12
  and second-order doubts 211
  sensitivity-based 120–2 see also Descartes, René; Pyrrhonism
skill 103–4; see also ability; competence; SSS structure, SeShSi
social conventions
  and competence 26, 28–9, 101–5, 126–8
  culturally specific factors 212 n. 13
  and dispositions 28, 30 n. 30, 101–5
  and etiquette 26, 101–2
  ineffable 26, 101–2
  and judgment 57, 66
  and reliability 175, 187
  and thresholds 73, 181–3, 184
  and virtues 104 see also affirmation, and social factors; competence, and social conventions; disposition, social categorization of; norms; testimony
SSS structure, SeShSi
  of complete competences 24, 26–7, 61, 72, 81, 95–104, 110–11, 113–15, 149–50
  of dispositions 26–30, 95–6, 100, 104–5
  first-order SSS conditions 81 n. 23
  shape 83, 90, 97, 99, 157, 207
  situation 90, 97, 99, 146, 157, 207
  skill 83, 99–100, 194 n. 3
stakes 172, 178–80, 182–7
Stoicism 57, 134, 137–8, 218
subitizing 203
  see also examples, speckled hen; examples, cup/subitizing
subjunctive conditionals 120–2; see also safety; sensitivity
suspension 44, 54, 85, 88
  and affirmation/denial 44, 82, 88, 91–2, 109–10, 180–2, 228–9, 231, 248
  double-omission 82, 109–10, 180
  and freedom 230
  functional 91
  of judgment 82, 91–2, 208–9
  and skepticism 216, 230, 232
  and the unit interval 91–2, 109, 180, 228–9 see also Descartes, René; Pyrrhonism; thresholds, for belief/suspension/disbelief

testimony 13 n. 10, 36, 46, 54, 115–18, 179, 181, 184–7; see also norms, of assertion
thresholds
  and basketball example 85–6, 114
  for belief/suspension/disbelief 91–2, 109, 180–2, 228–9
  detecting safety 115

determining thresholds 172, 182, 184
and eye-exam 74
first-order 115
ineffable 171–2
of reliability in performance 70–3, 85–6, 95, 105–6, 123, 126, 147
of safety 115
set by social or biological norms 73, 90–2, 184
and woozy partygoer case 114
trust
in others 54, 115–17, 185–6
in reason 87
self-trust/trust of senses/memory 46–7, 117, 183, 186, 209, 211–12, 241, 249
and stakes 183, 187

unity of action, perception and knowledge 24–5, 32, 129
Utilitarianism, Rule 105

value of knowledge 40, 45–6, 49, 54–6, 61, 66, 87, 142, 155, 168, 188–9
virtue
activity in accordance with virtue 134–7, 140–3, 156
auxiliary/constitutive virtues 22, 36, 41–5, 60–1
complete 134
courage 39, 41–4
deliberative 138
and faculties 34–5, 37–9, 48
intellectual virtues 34–6, 38–46, 48, 61
and motivation 45–50, 61
open-mindedness 39, 41–4, 219–20, 222
perseverance 45

and personal worth 39, 45, 47–9, 61
socially seated virtues 115–16
virtuous actions 134, 138 *see also* competence
Virtue
Perspectivism 251
Reliabilism 9, 34–43, 48–50, 55, 59, 61, 107, 119
Responsibilism 34–41, 45–51, 55, 59
Vogel, Jonathan 121–2
volition
and affirmation 93–4, 167, 210, 243
and assent 59, 209, 232
and belief 209, 230, 232
and confidence 197, 199
and deontic framework 193
and endeavorings 192–3, 203, 206
and faculties 203
free agency 195, 207
free judgments 196, 201–3, 205, 208, 232, 238
free to choose 137, 167, 200, 207, 210, 229
and functioning 202
involuntary competence 210
and reflection 54
and virtue 35, 39, 49
voluntary control 92–5, 162 *see also* choice

will, the 100, 210, 243–5
Williamson, Timothy 15 n. 13, 73 n. 10, 171 n. 4

X-Phi 31 n. 32, 78 n. 18; *see also* intuitions

Zagzebski, Linda 35–6, 45–7